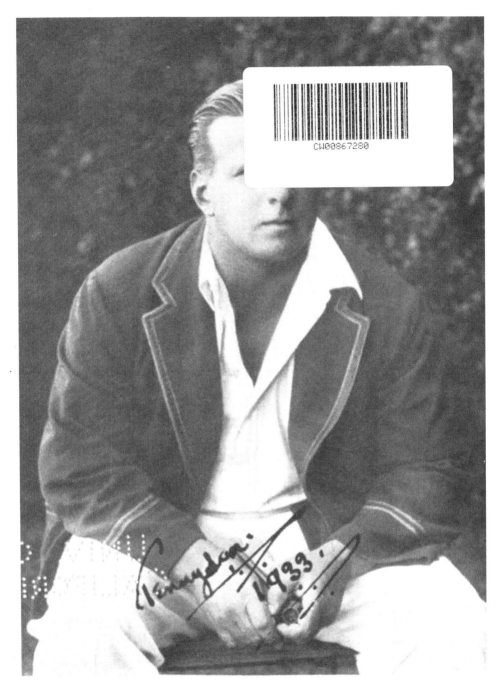

[Image credit:] *Charles Harris*

FROM VERSE TO WORSE

By

LIONEL LORD TENNYSON

[The following text and image (La Belle Sauvage) do not apply to this edition, but are included for documentation.]

WITH EIGHT PLATES

CASSELL AND COMPANY LIMITED

London, Toronto, Melbourne and Sydney

First published 1933

[dcterms:modified 2016-01-20T23:08:33Z]

[character support check: £ ½ æ œ à ç é è ê î ᶜ ć]

[The following text does not apply to this edition, but is included for documentation.]

PRINTED IN GREAT BRITAIN BY THE EDINBURGH PRESS,
EDINBURGH

F20.933

To the Memory of
MY GRANDFATHER
STILL THE GREATEST AUTHOR IN THE FAMILY

CONTENTS

ILLUSTRATIONS

CHAPTER I

IT is with some diffidence that I offer these reminiscences to my readers.

I hope, however, that this, my first book, will prove to be a source of interest and some amusement, seeing that I have had many varied experiences in my life.

I arrived in this world on November 7th, 1889, and during my first three years my grandfather, the great Victorian poet Alfred the first Lord Tennyson, was still alive.

He was at that time past eighty years of age, but as he was fond of children, I assume that he saw me constantly, since my parents and myself lived under the same roof as he did. After leaving Cambridge in 1874 my father acted as the poet's secretary and confidential adviser. That year the health of my grandmother, who had previously acted in this capacity, had broken down. For the rest of her life she was an invalid, and quite incapable, therefore, of dealing with the poet's vast correspondence, and with all the business details arising from the enormous sale of his works and the success of his plays.

When my father married in 1884, the same arrangement was continued, the old poet by that time being too dependent on my father's help to allow of any change being made.

It would perhaps be interesting to other people, as well as gratifying to myself, if I could number amongst my earliest recollections some distinct impressions of my grandfather. But that, I fear, is precisely what I cannot truthfully do. Can I remember him, or can I not? It is beyond my power to say definitely one way or the other. In the first place, I was hardly three years old when he died. In the second place, the walls of Farringford, his house in the Isle of Wight, where I passed my boyhood, were covered with his pictures and portraits by the most famous artists of the day. These reproducing in every room in the house his formidable and majestic appearance, make it impossible for me to remember whether my impression of him is derived from some dim recollection of childhood's days, or whether it is, after all, only second-hand.

And here I might tell a story in connection with a bust of the poet in the dining-room at Farringford. It was of solid marble and stood on a large block of mahogany draped in red baize. We had a cricket party in the House at the time, and on the Sunday after luncheon my father and mother had gone out of the room, leaving us young people alone. Hoping in a boyish fashion (I was about fifteen or sixteen years old) to amuse our guests, who were all schoolfellows of mine, and their youthful female friends and relations, I clapped a hat on the head of my grandfather's bust, and put a cigarette between its lips. Whilst we were all shrieking with laughter, in came my father!!

My poor father! I can see to this day his look of shocked astonishment and indignation. To this day I remember the appalled silence that descended on everyone as in stern tones he bade me remove all traces of the offence and sent me out of the room. No doubt he was rightly indignant with me, on this, as I fear he was on many other occasions. I am recalling this youthful indiscretion principally to give some indication of the atmosphere at Farringford in which we were brought up.

It was an atmosphere of veneration, indeed, that was almost religious, and anything that tended even in the slightest degree to impair it he visited with the severest disfavour. His observations frequently began with the words, "My father said" or "My father thought." In fact, he seemed to refer all questions of importance to that past oracle, so mighty in its own day, and may be said never to have wholly emerged from the Victorian age.

Such devotion, like all things on earth, had its opposite and inconvenient side. My father never realized, I feel sure, that it was impossible for the Farringford tradition to be preserved for ever without change, or that, so far from exercising much restraining influence on myself, it rather tended, by the law of contrariety, to emphasize my natural aversion to a highly solemn view of life.

On this subject, however, enough for the present.

I only wish to explain, to some extent, how and why things have come about in my life as they have done.

My grandfather, however much I may sometimes have suffered on his account, was a great Englishman, and not altogether so solemn, I fancy, as some people believe. Certainly he could crack a bottle, and tell a good story after dinner almost to the last day of his life.

Only one incident of my association with him survives the passage of years, and that one an occasion on which, regrettably enough, I disgraced myself.

At that time the phonograph, an early form of the gramophone, had just been invented by Mr. Edison, the great American who died recently, and he had sent, as a present, one of these instruments to Farringford. On receipt of this gift, and for the interest and edification of posterity, the Laureate was persuaded to make some records by reciting a few of his poems.

One must reconstruct the scene more or less from imagination—the family circle gathered in the room where the experiment was to take place—my father, grave, filial and attentive—my mother, bright, eager, active and anxious to help the old poet in every way, for she was a great favourite of his—my grandmother assisted thither from her invalid couch—and lastly myself, aged about two years. For—and this was the reason of my presence—it was thought only right that I should be there, if only to be able to say in after years, whether indeed the experience stuck in my mind or not, that I had been one of that select audience which heard the great poet declaim for the benefit of future ages.

Everyone in the room (one must suppose) stood hushed to attention, and then after the necessary interval of preparations came the poet's great voice booming and rolling sonorously forth the majestic harmonies of his verse to be recorded for ever on the sensitive wax. But even as the listeners waited entranced, and his organ voice went rolling on, suddenly the whole thing was brought to a disastrous close—by me.

I had emitted some infantile noise that entirely ruined the record.

Though I have not actually heard it myself, I believe this record is now in the British Museum, and that my ill-timed interruption is faithfully reproduced. Owing to some lack of care in preserving the wax-cylinders from damp, however, I am informed that both this and the other records made at the time are lamentably indistinct.

Needless to say, I do not remember this misadventure; the first thing in connection with the poet that I do recollect clearly is the event of his funeral. In fact, it is my first really distinct recollection in life.

For the benefit of my readers who may some of them, very probably, be younger than myself, and therefore not of an age to recall events which occurred so long ago as Wednesday, October 12th, 1892, the date on which the funeral took place, a short description of it will show what a really national event it was.

The evening before, the poet's body had been brought to Westminster Abbey from Aldworth, his house near Haslemere on the border of Sussex and Surrey, where he died. The news of his death had stirred the whole English-speaking world, and every newspaper at home and in the Dominions had given an account, running into pages, of his life and work, homes, haunts and habits.

The result of this universal feeling was that by half-past twelve, the time at which the funeral service was to begin, not a corner of space in the Abbey that would hold a human being was vacant. Vast crowds also, which had gathered together since early in the day and had been unable to gain admittance, occupied every approach to it. Along the nave and transept were lined detachments from the Gordon Boys' Home, which the poet had helped to found, and as a tribute also to the work done by him for the Volunteers, other detachments from the Queen's Westminsters, the London Scottish, and the London Irish paraded alongside the Gordon Boys. Many survivors also, in medals and uniform, of the Charge of the Light Brigade were present to show honour to the man who had commemorated their immortal Charge in immortal verse.

Included in the congregation were the most famous men in every walk of English life.

Their Royal Highnesses the Prince of Wales (afterwards King Edward VII), the Duke of Edinburgh, and the Duke of York (His Majesty, King George V) had sent representatives, as had also the Prime Minister, Mr. Gladstone, and the Prime Ministers of the Dominion Governments.

The pall-bearers were the Marquess of Salisbury, the Duke of Argyll, the Earl of Selborne, the Marquess of Dufferin, the Earl of Rosebery, Mr. White of the U.S.A. Legation, Lord Kelvin, Sir James Paget, Dr. Butler (the Master of Trinity College, Cambridge), Dr. Jowett (Master of Balliol College, Oxford), Mr. W. E. H. Lecky and Mr. J. A. Froude—all of them men renowned in their own day, and the majority of whom are not forgotten even at this distance of time.

Queen Victoria herself had sent two wreaths, with affectionate and admiring tributes in her own handwriting, to be laid with the innumerable others that surrounded the poet's coffin.

But alas! of all this pomp, symbolical of England's greatness at the close of the nineteenth century; of all this vast concourse of enthusiastic admirers anxious to pay their last respects to one who had been its authentic voice, and who for many weeks after the day of the funeral continued to pass by the grave; of all this gathering of the great and good of bygone times; of the music, of the mourning, and the mounds of flowers, I remember nothing (being, as I said, not quite three years old at the time), except walking up the aisle in a little white frock, between my two cousins, Alfred and Charles Tennyson, then schoolboys.

My grandmother, Emily, Lady Tennyson, survived my grandfather three years. She was, as I remember her, a gentle-voiced old lady with exquisite features and a worn face, and spent nearly all her time lying on a couch, having been an invalid for twenty years. In her youth she had been a great beauty, and her talents and accomplishments were many. She set several of my grandfather's poems to music, one of which was sung by the Abbey choir at his funeral. She was also a very clever scholar and linguist.

In spite of her physical frailty, my grandmother had a force of character that made its impression on all, whether men or women, who came in contact with her. I remember the sense of awe I used to feel when taken into her room to see her. She looked so old lying on her invalid couch, almost like a spirit or an inhabitant of some other world, and yet everyone paid her such deference!

The married life of my grandparents lasted forty-two years, and so far as anything in this world can be considered so, may be said to have been perfectly happy. Her thoughts were always of the poet, and her last words were "I have tried to be a good wife."

My grandfather repaid this devotion to himself by writing several poems in her honour.

Of these, the following is my favourite.

13

Rose, on this terrace fifty years ago,
When I was in my June, you in your May,
Two words *"My Rose"* set all your face aglow;
And now that I am white, and you are grey,
That blush of fifty years ago, my dear,
Blooms in the Past, but close to me to-day,
As this red rose which on our terrace here
Glows in the blue of fifty miles away.

CHAPTER II

IT is a peculiar thing, perhaps, that I who have such a passion for London, should have been brought up almost exclusively in the country.

My parents had no London house, though they sometimes took one for a month or two during the season and when Parliament was sitting. They had, however, two country houses, Farringford in the Isle of Wight, and Aldworth near Haslemere in Surrey and just over the border in the neighbouring county of Sussex. As my childhood was, in consequence, spent at one or other of these two homes, and as they are not only beautifully situated and extremely picturesque as well as historic, it will be no doubt interesting to my readers to say something about them. Let me take them, not in the order of my affection—for of the two I am myself far fonder of Aldworth—but in the order in which they came into my family.

Farringford House, as it stands to-day, is a long two-storied house of grey-brown brick situated on a steep knoll that was formerly the site of one of the many Telegraph Stations which were used in the eighteenth century for communication by semaphore. A park, fringed by a belt of firs, sycamores, beeches and many other varieties of trees surrounds the house, and a few hundred yards away is the Home-Farm. The place indeed is famous for its trees—Scotch firs, huge elms, ilexes, and cedars which are favourite subjects still for roving artists in the summer-time. From the front the house, which stands roughly N.E. by S.W., commands a view past Golden Hill Fort over the Solent, dotted in the summer with white sails; from the windows on the other side it looks out on the huge sloping back of Afton Down and the blue cleft between the chalky cliffs of Freshwater Bay, and beyond that again towards St. Catherine's Point and the Channel. Across the lawns, there are shrubberies and a long narrow copse known as the Wilderness, through which one comes face to face with the steep rolling ridge covered with clumps of gorse and known as the High Down that ends in the Needles about three miles farther west. In the spring the park, copses and woods are full of snowdrops, cowslips, daffodils, primroses and other wild flowers.

The poet who, amongst his many other talents, was a skilful landscape gardener, certainly selected a very beautiful place when in 1856 he bought the house and property from an Isle of Wight family by name Rushworth, and greatly increased its naturally picturesque surroundings by judicious planting of trees and woods.

Except, however, during a few weeks in the summer, our end of the Isle of Wight is a very quiet place. Indeed it would be difficult to find a much quieter one throughout England. There, as children, we led a remote existence, with few others of our own age to play with. We were, moreover, seldom at Farringford during the actual visitors' season, because my parents nearly always continued the old poet's custom of migration to Aldworth at that time of the year. He had, in fact, built that house to escape the tourists and visitors to the Isle of Wight who stared at his cloak and sombrero hat, hid in bushes by the roadside and in the garden to observe him, and generally worried his shyness and robbed him of his seclusion.

Such visitors as came to the house, besides near relatives, were generally survivors amongst the poet's friends. My father, who was the kindest of men and intensely loyal to everything connected with the memory of my grandfather, had, after his death, bidden the old gentlemen in question to regard Farringford as "a home from home" in the same manner as they had done during the poet's lifetime.

So, clad in strange garments (as it appeared to me), these singular old gentlemen used to arrive. Highbrows of a former age, weird and wonderful to look at in the eyes of the coming generation, they were a secret source of mingled terror and amusement to me, and occasionally, I regret to say, the amusement got the better of the terror. I well remember getting into disgrace and being sent up to my room on account of a certain well-known personage, a friend of the poet's whom I will call Mr. K. . . . Old Mr. K . . . stammered a good deal, not only during his conversation, which was diffuse and ornate, but also during his meals, with somewhat disastrous results to those in his immediate neighbourhood. On one occasion as he was eating and holding forth at the same time at the family luncheon table, the sight of those near him with reverential but strained faces endeavouring to preserve on their countenances a look of rapt attention, while at the same time they attempted to dodge the copious showers that heralded each crack-jawed polysyllable, was too much for my youthful gravity, which collapsed in a fit of hysterical giggling.

———————

While in the Island our amusements as children were of a rural character. I remember taking a considerable interest in the affairs of the farm. When the sheep-dipping season was on, nothing except main force could keep me away.

My mother was always deeply concerned with the welfare of her poorer neighbours, besides being a leading member of all the local charitable organizations, such as the Societies for the prevention of cruelty to animals or children. So as to play our part, my brother Aubrey and myself took round the "monthly magazine" to the cottages. Our principal ally amongst these was Mrs. Broomfield, the milkman's wife, who used to reward us liberally with bull's-eyes for thus administering to her mental and spiritual needs. When our supply from Mrs. Broomfield ran low, I regret to say we used to supplement them by surreptitious dealings with the footmen, who obtained stores of sweets by looting the dinner-table after parties given by my parents.

I remember very well the annual servants' dance at Farringford which took place between Christmas and New Year's day. Each one of the servants was allowed to ask enough friends to make up a good party, and a small band and supper were provided by my father. The butler was Master of the Ceremonies, and with eagle eye saw to it that in no instance were the bounds of discretion or decorum overstepped.

Somehow or other strains of dance music have always excited me more perhaps than they do the ordinary run of men. Even in those early days I used to feel the call, and my excitement grew to fever-heat as the day of the Servants' Ball drew near. My anticipations indeed were so great and my behaviour became in consequence so uncontrollable and uproarious, that three years running I was, previously to the dance, spanked by my father.

At Farringford I started to ride on a Shetland Pony called "Dumps." He was about twenty years old then, and the most infernal little brute, and got me off just as he liked. As, however, it was good falling-ground on the Downs, I do not remember ever hurting myself. Our old coachman, William Knight, used to go out riding with me perched up on one of the carriage horses.

"William" was really a most singular character—one remarkable for oddity even five and thirty years ago, and utterly impossible now. He had come to my grandfather not long after his purchase of Farringford and had remained with the family ever since. Of other human beings he was scornful and contemptuous, but he considered all Tennysons the noblest and wisest people on earth. Apart from them, the only other living creatures he took any interest in were his horses. These looked splendid, were never sick or sorry, and always ready for work. Woe betide anyone making suggestions about them! William would then either touch his forelock with an inscrutable expression and just resume his duties; or straightening himself to his full height, which was only a few inches over five feet, deliver a harangue on the inadvisability of persons who knew nothing about horses interfering with coachmen who did. He was extremely ceremonious in his manners, however, towards friends and members of the family. At such times, the grave expression on his comical face with the bright blue eyes, scrubby moustache, and muttonchop whiskers as he bowed and touched his hat, made a combination not easily surpassed.

William hardly ever arrived at our front door or anyone else's except at a hand gallop, his whip raised aloft in his right hand and his cheerful voice encouraging his horses. His pride in the family required from him this display of dash and style. From this habit, and from a reputation he possessed of having been, in youth, a particularly daring horseman, the other coachmen in the neighbourhood called him "Hell-Fire Jack."

Under his guidance my brother and I started hunting with the Leconfield Hounds from Petworth, in the Sussex Weald, about ten miles from Aldworth; and on my seventh birthday, by his advice and to my great delight, I was allowed to go without a leading-rein.

Old William was a literary character himself and a bit of a poet. He had also a very caustic wit. Perhaps like those of many other wits, his retorts were better in the making than in the repetition, especially as they were always accompanied by a look of mock humility, and the affectation of consummate ignorance; at any rate I can only, at this distance of time, recall one of them.

On this occasion William, in his scorn of his fellow-servants, especially of the feminine ones, had chosen to avoid the servants' hall and take his meals, cooked by himself and of a weird nature, in the harness room. When my father remonstrated with him, and asked him to go back to the servants' hall, William replied: "Thank you, my Lord. I prefer my own company, poor as it is, to that of the *Donkey-Drawing-Room*."

William died in the County Infirmary in the Isle of Wight a year or two after the war. He was well past eighty years of age, and had for many years suffered from an illness which eventually brought his life to an end. Previously to this he had been pensioned off in a cottage on the Farringford Estate, where he lived on hard boiled eggs cooked fifty at a time, and on dried goats' flesh.

As I have made a certain reputation as a cricketer, it may interest my readers to know that I started cricket on the lawn in front of Aldworth. Friends older than myself tell me that even at six years old I hit the ball very hard for my age.

About this time—that is to say, the beginning of my cricketing career—I was guilty of a rather sublime piece of impertinence. Canon the Hon. Edward Lyttelton, the Eton and Cambridge cricketer, who was best man at my father's wedding, was staying at Aldworth and very kindly offered to play cricket with me. By some chance, or more probably because he wished to encourage me, I bowled him out, and promptly exclaimed in a tone of contempt: "Why! You are no cricketer!!"

As I began this chapter with a few words about Farringford, it may end with a short description of Aldworth. I love it better than any place on earth, and, if able, would buy it back again tomorrow. I write this because just after the war my father, owing to increase of taxation, had to sell it, and it now belongs to His Highness the Gaekwar of Baroda.

Aldworth was named after the old home of the Sellwoods (my grandmother's family)—Aldworth Manor in Berkshire. It was built in 1868 by Sir James Knowles, the founder of *The Nineteenth Century* magazine, an architect by profession, after the original designs by the poet and his wife. The house stands 1000 feet up on a ledge on Blackdown called Blackhorse Copse, and selected as a site by my grandfather. Seven counties are visible from it on a clear day.

It is a stone house, high-chimneyed and high-roofed with mullioned windows and a lofty portico. A wide terraced lawn, along the length of which runs a stone balustrade, where tall Italian cypresses and hollyhocks shoot up against the blue of the horizon, leads down by other terraces and rose gardens to the woods and copses below, the orchards, the kitchen garden and the picturesque old gardener's cottage. All round the house and lawns are magnificent trees—cypresses, firs, beeches, oaks and mountain ash which the poet, a great lover of trees, planted. Sheltered as they are under the lee of Blackdown Hill some of them have now grown to giant size. There was very good shooting at Aldworth, and one got some splendid high pheasants driven from the slopes of Blackdown out over the meadows at the foot of it.

I have been to Aldworth several times in the course of the last few years just to look at it again for old times' sake. His Highness is kind enough to allow any visitors who wish to see the house and gardens to go over them. Each time I have been there, I have left full of regret that it was not mine. It certainly is one of the most beautiful places in England.

CHAPTER III

SOUTH AUSTRALIA

IN 1898 my father happened to sit next to Mr. Joseph Chamberlain, M.P., then Colonial Secretary, at a dinner party. Mr. Chamberlain was at that time contemplating his scheme for the economic and political Federation of the British Empire.

At the dinner party in question, he found an eager and attentive listener in my father, as great, if not as famous, an advocate of Imperial development as Mr. Chamberlain himself.

As my father wrote with perfect truth and sincerity in his farewell address to the Australian people at the conclusion of his term of office as Governor-General:

> "It was my fortune to inherit a strong and passionate desire to endeavour to the utmost to share in helping the British Empire to realize her mighty and manifest destiny. My belief is that this destiny will find its accomplishment through a closer union, which, while preserving, strengthening and developing every individual part, will so bind the whole together with a common loyalty and common patriotism, that we shall be able fearlessly to lead the nations in the path of truth and justice, righteousness and freedom, peace and progress."

This allusion on my father's part to his lifelong interest in the British nations overseas, and to his desire for their closer union with the mother-country, was, indeed, no idle figure of speech. At a time when even Conservative statesmen in England spoke of the Colonies as an encumbrance, and regarded any money spent on them as waste, my grandfather the poet had been one of the few to protest against such a short-sighted and degrading attitude. My father, then, had been brought up in the very atmosphere which Mr. Chamberlain was endeavouring to create generally throughout the country; and the two men being in such exact agreement on such a vital subject, felt an immediate trust in one another.

The upshot of this conversation was that when, a few months afterwards, the governorship of South Australia fell vacant, Mr. Chamberlain suggested to my father that he should take the post; which he did.

This decision on his part not a little surprised his friends. He was getting on for fifty at the time, and had hitherto led a secluded life, though of course his position as the poet's invariable companion had brought him into contact with many of the most notable and intellectual people of the age.

That he so far altered all his former habits as to become a Colonial Governor in such a distant state as South Australia, was due to no personal ambition, I feel sure, but exactly to the reasons stated so eloquently by him.

Early in 1899, therefore, our family party (my father and mother, my brothers Aubrey and Harold and myself) set out in the S.S. *Ophir*, of the Orient Line, for Australia *via* Marseilles. With us went a relation of my mother's, Captain Lascelles, as my father's A.D.C., and his wife, son and daughter.

The *Ophir* was the same ship in which His present Majesty, King George V (then Duke of York) went out to Australia to open the first Federal Parliament. In those times she was considered a fine vessel, but nowadays would be thought very small in comparison with the Leviathans afloat. Nevertheless she carried us safely and comfortably enough on our long journey. My memories of that journey are remarkably distinct considering I was only nine years old at the time, and one effect that it certainly had upon me was to leave me with a permanent and abiding love of the sea.

On this, my first voyage, one of the sights that struck my boyish fancy most were the long lines of black figures ascending and descending the plank gangways, each with a small basket of coal on the head—for this was the primitive way the ship coaled at Port Said. I have a hazy recollection that those who refused to work properly were tied up to a mast and flogged. There are two other memories of mine connected with Suez and Port Said, and these are of passing the Spanish Transports full of troops going out to fight in the Philippines, and of riding in a donkey-race with some of the other passengers, which I won. My mount was called Ta-ra-ra-boom-de-ay. I recall also that night after night as we sailed through the Red Sea and the Indian Ocean we had the most marvellous sunsets. They were (for some reason which at this distance of time I do not remember), particularly vivid at that season, and it was a wonderful spectacle to see the limitless expanse of the heavens dyed with sheets of saffron, purple and scarlet, and every colour of the rainbow, as the sun shot down

22

beneath the ocean-horizon. Amidst these glorious scenes of nature, we had a strange contrast in observing one of the most cruel practices of mankind. In the midst of the grilling heat of the Red Sea, we passed close to two ships taking cargoes of slaves from the interior of Africa to the opposite shore. They were all manacled together and looked a piteous spectacle. I was much affected by this sight, and had I been older, might have retired to my cabin and composed an "Ode to Liberty."

The chief excitement and tragedy of the voyage was the loss of a man overboard. We were in the saloon at lunch, and knew nothing of the sad occurrence at the time, I remember, and were therefore much surprised when the ship began swinging round in a vast circle to reach the place where the passenger had disappeared from the deck. Boats were lowered, and a search of an hour was made, but nothing was found except the man's cap. Probably the sharks ate all the rest of him and his belongings. One of my father's footmen had caught him by the leg as he was falling, but was not strong enough to hold him.

My father succeeded Sir T. Fowell Buxton, Bart., as Governor of South Australia.

Now Sir Fowell had been born and bred, and grown to middle-age, with strong Evangelical principles. These principles, though in other respects he was, I believe, a capable and popular enough Governor, did not permit him to approve of either dancing or horse-racing. In fact he considered both these amusements distinctly immoral, which was unfortunate, to say the least of it, as they are the amusements of which all Australians are passionately fond. In his official capacity (on the first day of a big State Meeting, for instance) Sir Fowell was obliged, despite the protests of his conscience, to attend the Races. Gossip said that a Very High Authority had insisted on this, and also with Its invariable common sense pointed out the inconvenience of an Evangelical conscience when dealing with Imperial matters. Gossip, however, also related (a little maliciously this time) that on such occasions His Excellency's conscience took an ample revenge for all the indignities it had suffered. Just as the runners were nearing the winning post; and the whole concourse of spectators were cheering their particular selections on to victory, or stood hushed in the agonized silence of expectation; and as, up in the Governor's box, his staff and his guests, with field glasses to their eyes, watched with more aristocratic composure but excitement equal to that of the crowds below, the now rapidly impending decision, Sir Fowell (or so it was said) would tap them on the arm or shoulder, and in a courteous manner call their attention away from the race to the beauty of the scenery, or the nature of a cloud-effect, in fact to anything that distracted their mind from the principal matter in hand. All this (though no doubt much exaggerated for the purposes of a good story, which is at least as popular in Australia as in other parts of the world) caused a certain amount of good-humoured friction between Sir Fowell Buxton and his temporary subjects.

The consequence was, that directly our ship, the *Ophir*, reached Fremantle (the harbour of Western Australia) reporters, representing various South Australian newspapers, boarded the deck, and with true colonial frankness enquired whether the new Governor had the same objection to horse-racing and dancing as his predecessor. I think I have emphasized the fact that my father regarded my grandfather's opinion on all debateable subjects as absolutely final, and that it was largely owing to the old poet's devotion to the cause of Imperial union and expansion that he now found himself where he was—that is to say facing an eager body of cross-examiners in the form of Adelaide newspaper reporters. As the poet's idealism had carried him so far afield, it was not likely to desert him now or to cease to sustain him under the questioning of the Press. In fact, he was able to reply with perfect satisfaction to himself and to all others concerned, that the poet had danced at the age of eighty-two at a ball given at Farringford, and that what he thought right could not possibly be wrong. As regards horse-racing, too, was not the poet's love of horses well known? "Horse-racing," said my father, "is a great sport, of which I have been fond ever since I was a boy."

Everyone was enchanted with these very sensible views, and in a moment the wires hummed with the news that the illustrious Laureate had danced at an age when most ordinary folk, if alive at all, can hardly even walk; and that the new Governor thought horse-racing one of the finest sports in the world. All this prepared for him when we arrived at Adelaide a really cordial welcome.

Though it is now over thirty years ago, I can remember that reception as vividly as if it had happened yesterday—the cheering crowds lining the streets—the mounted escort of Light Horse with rifles, bandoliers, and swords clattering ahead of our carriages—my father in his plumed cocked-hat, scarlet uniform and

24

silver lace. I had, it must be remembered, been brought up entirely in the country, and had never even seen a procession till this date, much less figured in one myself. Then came the new Governor's first speech in the Town Hall, Adelaide, and a real triumph it was. His fine presence, voice, and eloquence made a most favourable impression on his audience. From the moment of his arrival in Australia my father was, in fact, a great success.

Absolutely unaffected, and with a keen sense of humour, my mother also very quickly captured the hearts of all the South Australians.

Having had six brothers, she understood men thoroughly, a very rare thing in a woman, and they all adored her. With her own sex she was all sympathy and eagerness to help, and they equally looked up to her as a confidante and wise friend.

No doubt her good looks helped not a little to gain her such great popularity. Her father, Charles Boyle, was reputed to have been the handsomest man of his time, and my mother had inherited to the full the gift of personal beauty. With her striking features and upright carriage, she looked the very embodiment of breed and spirit. She was also a good horsewoman, which, in itself, was a recommendation to every Australian, and I do not think I am far wrong in saying that she was the most popular Governor's wife that was ever known there.

My father's first private secretary was Captain Wallington, now Sir Edward, and not long retired, full of years and honours, from his post as Treasurer to Her Majesty the Queen.

Since leaving Oxford, where he was a cricket Blue, Captain Wallington had spent a quarter of a century in Australasia, as a Secretary. The consequence was that he was famous from one end of the country to the other, and knew all there was to know about his job. He was, in fact, the perfect Private Secretary, discreet, tactful, loyal, and infinitely industrious, with a complete knowledge of the tastes, peculiarities, and past history of every man and woman in Australia. In appearance he was tall, thin, grave and aquiline in features, but those who knew him best, realized that under this composed exterior he kept firmly repressed a very distinct sense of humour. How otherwise could he have seen all things and all men in such admirable proportion? To his friends he was always known as "Wall" or "Captain Wall," but by the profane he was usually called "Captain Better-Not." The origin of this somewhat mysterious nickname is easily explained. New Brooms, in the shape of new Governors, not infrequently arrived from home. These enthusiastic gentlemen were sometimes inclined to leap before they looked, and, all agog to carry out some cherished and particular project without counting the cost, imparted their notions to Captain Wallington. Rumour said that on these occasions Captain Wallington, who was a firm and convinced believer, after many years of first-hand experience, in letting sleeping dogs lie whenever possible, would reply gravely after a period of apparently profound contemplation: "Better not, I think, Sir."

To return now, however, to some of the things that I, myself, particularly remember! Our favourite place of residence when in South Australia was not Government House, Adelaide, charming though it was with its wide lawns and beautiful gardens, but the Governor's summer residence at Marble Hill, a largish stone-built house with wide verandas, about ten miles from Adelaide and up in the hills. All the family loved Marble Hill, and its free and easy life and atmosphere. Most of all we liked the rides, where we went by lakes swarming with wild swans, or through the bush alive with flocks of parrots and wild turkeys as well as with hares and rabbits innumerable. We often saw too, wallabys, opossums, and native bears, flying-foxes, cockatoos, laughing-jackasses, and lizards three feet from snout to tail amidst trees three hundred feet high and ferns ten feet long. Lest the country might seem a Paradise too beautiful for our sinful earth, I must mention that snakes of all sizes and the deadliest description simply abounded; and even in the gardens as one walked along, one could hear them rustling away under the leaves. Scorpions were also an unpleasant and plentiful type of insect. Beautiful though the bush was to ride through, it was no less alarming in case of fire. With a North wind, bush fires travelled at an incredible speed, annihilating everything in their path. February 1901, I remember, was terrifically hot and dry, and the bush-fires that month were terrible. I have seen thirty square miles of trees alight at night like a huge illuminated town. One day part of our garden at Marble Hill caught fire, and all the household, including my brothers and myself, turned out to extinguish the flames by beating them down with brooms. The only way of course to stop the onrush of a big bush-fire is by burning off a broad belt which the flames cannot pass.

An even more exciting adventure than fighting bush-fires befell my brother Aubrey and myself about this time, although at the moment we did not realize our danger. We slept in the same room, and one night woke up to see the face of a strange man peering at us through the mosquito curtains. Whether Aubrey called to me or I to him, I don't remember, but probably the fact of our waking up scared the intruder, and after a threatening grimace or two he disappeared. We had great difficulty next morning in convincing our parents that our experience had not been a dream, but a gardener having found some footmarks in a flower-bed underneath our window, the police and a black tracker set to work, and finally caught the nocturnal visitor in the small hours of the next morning just as he was climbing into another house. He proved to be a most dangerous homicidal maniac already responsible for several murders, who had escaped from an asylum.

Another unusual character that I remember (though *he* was no one's enemy but his own) was the man who taught us to swim at the Adelaide Swimming Baths. He had led a roving and adventurous life before adopting the business of bath-attendant, and while thus engaged had the incredible good fortune to win the Calcutta Derby Sweep, worth at that time about £65,000. This piece of luck did not, however, profit him much. He relapsed into his old reckless ways, and in two years was back in the position of bath-attendant, having spent or gambled away every penny of his winnings.

We had only been a few months in Australia when the South African War broke out. In the light of after-events and remembering the magnificent army, numbering tens of thousands of men and equipped with every modern engine and device of war, sent by the Australian Commonwealth a short fifteen years afterwards to fight in Gallipoli and France during the Great War, it is strange to look back on the small Forces which sailed from South Australia and other States in the autumn of the year 1899.

About 150 men left Adelaide in the first contingent. Even this little band only got under way after innumerable telegrams backwards and forwards between the War Office and the Colonial Office at home, and my father and his Ministers. For three days also there was an embittered debate in the South Australian Parliament in which the Labour representatives opposed tooth and nail the suggestion that their State should take part in the war, declaring that it would be ruined by the expenditure. The Prime Minister of South Australia, Mr. Kingston, was a Labour man himself, but he was a real patriot and a far-seeing one who, like Mr. Chamberlain and my father, knew that the time had come when the component parts of the Empire could no longer afford to exist in isolation, and that in time of crisis they must all act as one. Mr. Kingston had a terrific fight with his own party, whom, as a matter of fact, he had not consulted when offering a South Australian contingent to the Mother Country, and finally carried his proposal by a bare eight votes! Mr. Kingston was a great friend of my father's, who admired and respected him greatly for his massive good sense and force of character. He had had, I believe, a romantic career, and made his own way at the bar from a humble origin. The troops selected for service in South Africa, of course, became immediately national heroes who were fêted, dined, and wined all over the place in the intervals of preparing for the campaign, and not least at the two residences of Government House and Marble Hill. On one occasion, I remember, as my brother Aubrey and I rode back with the mounted troops after they had spent the day at Marble Hill, voices from the crowd were heard saying: "What a shame to send two such young boys to the war!" When the first contingent actually left for South Africa, the crowds that collected to see them depart were beyond description. When they finally got on board the transport they sailed out through a fleet of excursion steamers literally crammed with sightseers. It was a wonderful spectacle which one can never forget in a lifetime. Fifteen years later the Australians were to prove that all this loyalty and enthusiasm were not the outcome of a mere taste for sensationalism, but of great virtues deeprooted in the very heart of the nation.

Another event which happened towards the close of my father's time as Governor of South Australia, and one which stirred very deeply the loyal and patriotic feelings of the vast majority of Australians, was the visit of the Duke and Duchess of York (Their Majesties King George V and Queen Mary). They arrived in May of the year 1901 to open the first Commonwealth Parliament at Melbourne. My father and mother had gone to Melbourne to assist at this historical function, and whilst there my mother had asked Their Royal Highnesses to help her in a cause which she had very much at heart, and which in the face of considerable difficulties she had been working at practically since her arrival in Australia. My mother had seen and discovered for herself the troubles and dangers which expectant mothers living up "in the bush" experienced, and had determined to found a home for them in Adelaide. At the time of Their Royal Highnesses' visit, all the preliminary negotiations had been concluded, and she had succeeded in getting an excellent site for this Maternity Home. The Adelaide people had wanted it to be called Lady Tennyson's Home, but my mother herself wished it to be named in honour of Queen Victoria who had passed away in January of that year, and she therefore asked His Royal Highness if he would lay the foundation stone. The Duke of or most kindly consented, and with the Duchess came to spend a few days at Government House, Adelaide. Their Royal Highnesses made themselves endlessly popular and were charming to everyone. Unfortunately I cannot give any personal instance of their good nature, except a few nice words from a distance and a joke or two and a wave of the hand, because at the very instant of their arrival my brother Aubrey and myself developed whooping-cough and were isolated; in fact we were packed off to the seaside, and missed practically all the fun and excitement of their Royal Highnesses' visit. My youngest brother Harold, however, escaped the infection, and had the time of his life going everywhere with them.

Before finishing this chapter I must allude to my good fortune on the Adelaide cricket-ground in seeing the greatest and most scientific hitter of a cricket ball that ever lived score a century. The great G. L. Jessop, when playing for A. C. MacLaren's 1901–1902 side, made over a hundred runs there. At Farringford there is a cricket bat, signed on the back with the names of all the team, with which they presented me, and which is still a treasured possession.

CHAPTER IV

MY FATHER BECOMES GOVERNOR-GENERAL OF AUSTRALIA

MY father succeeded the Earl of Hopetoun (created during his term of office Marquis of Linlithgow) as second Governor-General of Australia.

All the State-Governors, senior by appointment to himself, had left after the establishment of the Federal Parliament, imagining, I believe, that political change to have lessened their former prestige as State-Governors. Amongst them was a very old friend of the family, the much-loved Lord Brassey. He had more than once lent my grandfather his famous yacht the *Sunbeam* in which by the way he had come to Australia. Lady Brassey was the most charming of ladies, and their daughter Lady Helen, now the wife of Colonel Murray, head of the famous publishing firm, was a close friend of ours.

As I have said, my father and mother had been immensely popular in South Australia, and on his new appointment the Adelaide newspapers united in praising his tact, common sense, dignity and wish to do the right thing, while prophesying that he would be an equal success as Governor-General.

The position, however, was rather complicated. Lord Linlithgow had been the most magnificent Governor ever seen in Australia, and the festivities given by him in honour of the Duke and Duchess of York had far eclipsed anything before known out there. He had, however, resigned because the Dominion Parliament and himself could not see eye to eye over matters of finance. So all concerned, especially the people of Melbourne, were feeling rather sore, and it was not by any means a certainty that they would welcome my parents with the same cordiality as the South Australians had shown.

On their arrival in Melbourne, in fact, the lighter Society journals were distinctly sarcastic. Their first party was called "frigid" and a falling-off after Lord Linlithgow's splendid entertainments. My mother, though her charm of manner was acknowledged, was taken to task because her appearance "from a sartorial point of view was modest in the extreme": whilst my father's hat struck the fashion expert "as two sizes too large with an extraordinary dip forward and aft." "Such a hat could not belong," so the journal in question asserted, "to one who was a great sport."

The cartoonists also were pretty busy exploiting a rather difficult situation, seeing that the new Governor-General was at the same time expected to be both hospitable and economical. They drew my father in all sorts of embarrassing positions—as a Master of Hounds in singularly ill-fitting attire, wondering if he could afford to keep the pack going—standing champagne to the unemployed but refusing to entertain a horde of aristocratic visitors from England—scanning the financial agreement by which the Governor-General's salary was secured, and so on. . . .

In this way and for a few weeks, my parents had to undergo an ordeal which must have been distinctly difficult. In those days the Australian Press certainly "called a spade a spade," and it seemed as if my father and mother were not destined to enjoy in their more exalted office the immense popularity achieved by them as a State-Governor and his wife. The remarkable thing was how quickly the change of feeling came about.

All at once we read in the Press of guests at Government House parties being enraptured by their reception. Here, for instance, is a quotation from the *Lyons Mail* of that period.

"The amiable and surprisingly pleasant greeting accorded by Lord and Lady Tennyson to all warmed the newcomers, and from the very beginning a cheery element prevailed which continued all the evening. Never do I remember a Government House function of so small and official a kind developing into such a bright affair. It was quite charming. Lady Tennyson talked to everyone with an air of interest. It was not the usual conversational small change that is current in the most fashionable circles. It was talk of the best kind, intelligent and illuminating. We are charmed with Lady Tennyson. I trust her natural manners may correct the stilted and artificial mincings of social dames who only realize an amusing automatic-like manner in their efforts to emulate the frigid. . . ."

(Here a lady's name at that time well known in English Society and lately on a visit to Australia was mentioned.)

Apparently, too, my parents created an excellent impression at their first race-meeting in Melbourne.

"It was, really," says the enthusiastic writer, "the first time the public had had the joy of staring at them, and the ordeal of gaping was suffered by them with a brave show of unconcern. . . . Lady Tennyson," he writes, "looked perfectly happy and acted as if she were the least concerned person in the enormous crowd and under no observation whatever. There is a delightful absence of self-consciousness about her that presents the stiff-necked matrons of society in unhappy contrast."

The gossip-writers found my father a slightly more complex problem, perhaps.

One of them described, in rather vivid terms, "how His Excellency fixed the crowd with his monocle and studied their faces with a careful air." Apparently, according to this writer "the smart people rather squirmed under the focus of that highly polished eyeglass, which, when the scrutiny had ended, dropped from its holding very abruptly and dangled as a reserve force on the chest."

To make amends, however, for what might be mystifying in my father's manipulation of his monocle, it was generally allowed by the writer in question that "he was nice to all the bores, who, by grace of office, found a way to an introduction." "I assure you," he ends up, "that we are going to like this Governor-General immensely. Already the feeling of aloofness has worn off."

Once, indeed, the tide had turned it started flowing with a vengeance in my parents' favour. Their every appearance in public was a triumph: every entertainment they gave was an unparalleled success.

Let me quote one more eulogy: this time from *Table Talk*.

"A small but very brilliant and enjoyable ball was given by their Excellencies last Monday evening. Hot as the night was the music was so excellent and inviting that the guests were incited to dance energetically and joyously. In fact there was an air of infectious gaiety pervading the whole function. . . . There was a welcome plethora of dancing men, a large suite of aide-de-camps, popular Naval and Military officers, to say nothing of civilians. The frocks were very beautiful . . . Lady R——— was the motherly soul of the party . . . There was Miss

R—— average in height, average in looks, average in style . . . There was Lady H—— with her peculiarity of manner . . . Lady Tennyson was the livelier figure, not in the least vitiated by heat or dust. Even responsibility as a hostess did not rob her manner of its engaging cheerfulness."

It is proverbial that straws show which way the wind blows: so these extracts from the lighter organs of the Press indicate clearly enough the rapidity of the conquests that my parents made. These effusions were, as I have said, nothing if not candid, and that is why, to throw into relief the nice things said about my parents, I have quoted the less nice ones about others, however suppressing the names. The shape and tilt of my father's hat, in fact, did not matter so soon as politicians and people discovered that there were brains inside it: and my mother's charm and wit compensated for the fact that she did not attempt to vie with the smarter Melbourne or Sydney women in the latest intricacies of fashion, or, as one gossip-hunter put it more briefly, "that she was, of course, no *frocker*." Very quickly, indeed, had the prophecies of the loyal and affectionate Adelaide newspapers come true.

———

It is now time to mention another character who played a great part in our lives in Australia.

When Captain Wallington left my father's staff to assist Lord Hopetoun on his appointment as Governor-General, and before he returned to my father, Lord Richard Nevill, on Lord Brassey's departure from Australia, had taken his place. Tall, elegant, handsome, and faultlessly dressed, Lord Richard was the pink of courtesy and the perfection of manners. A shrewd brain and an immense knowledge of his work lay behind an exquisite exterior, and successive governors during a long career in Australia had found him a tower of strength. While on my father's staff he was most kind to us boys and generally rode with us. He was a good and bold horseman himself and often hunted. The fences "down under" are formidable affairs, as the jumps are of solid timber which it would take a battering ram to remove. Lord Richard's nickname in Australian Society was "The Lord Who Knows" as he knew everything and everybody. I must also mention one other member of my father's household. This was Mlle. Dussau. This French lady had come out with us from England as governess. Good-looking and with great taste in what the paragraphists termed "sartorial matters," she created quite a sensation, first in Adelaide and then in the other capitals of the Australian States. She invariably formed one of the party at any function given by my parents, and was greatly in request at other peoples' houses for dances and dinners. To her smartness and good looks she added a wide knowledge of French literature, and somewhat to the astonishment of the inhabitants of Adelaide gave a course of public lectures on this subject in the city. Their present Majesties were much struck by her, when staying with my parents in Adelaide, and afterwards requested her to come as governess to H.R.H. the Prince of Wales and his Royal brothers, with whom she remained for many years. Mlle. Dussau is now no more, but the memory of her charm, vivacity and foreign grace must still linger in the hearts of not a few Australians.

To my brothers and myself, of course, the change from the quiet surroundings of Adelaide and Marble Hill to the stir and variety of scene that accompanied the comings and goings of a Governor-General were only the opportunity for increased amusement and excitement. In the two years my father was the Head of the Commonwealth, we managed in fact, in one way or another, to see a good deal of the country. I well remember our cruise in H.M.S. *Protector* to the Islands south of South Australia and to Port Augusta, where we went over an ostrich farm. We sailed down Gulf St. Vincent to Edinburgh and Yorktown, then by Spencer Gulf to Port Lincoln.

All this region was discovered by two Lincolnshire explorers, Flinders and Franklin (my father's great-uncle), and as in addition the Tennyson family is of Lincolnshire origin, my parents were much interested to recognize there many old Lincolnshire names of families and places.

My own recollections are, however, principally of wonderful fishing; and of beaches on the islands strewn with innumerable shells of every hue and size (some of them almost microscopical, others as large as soup-plates). I remember also being taught to steer the ship by compass: the sight of rows of penguins lined up on the beaches: the scanty and solitary population, nearly all fishermen, in the places where we landed: and a very rough sea coming home.

Another trip by steamer which we made was up the Murray River—the largest river in Australia. Just after starting we encountered a hurricane, an awe-inspiring experience. The steering got out of control and we ran ashore. The ship was blown into a tree, which made a large hole in the upper deck. In those days there were what English people would call enormous properties along the Murray River—stations of hundreds of square miles with tens of thousands of sheep running on them. I remember it took us fifteen hours at six miles an hour to steam past one of them.

A seaside place we loved was Port Victor, where there were wonderful sands and rocks of all sizes, first-class bathing, and good sea fishing.

We now began also to see racing on a larger and more splendid scale, the meetings at Adelaide, though very good fun, being more like those in provincial towns at home. The race-courses at Melbourne and Sydney, on the other hand, are palatial both in extent and accommodation, and equal to anything in the old country, whilst the crowds which attend them are really not much inferior. . . . I had "beginner's luck" at my first Melbourne Cup, won by "Wakeful." A friendly, though perhaps misguided, footman put on half-a-crown for me, and though I now forget the odds at which the winner started, I remember well my jubilation at my success. Opinions must vary on this, as on other subjects, as to whether horse-racing is a pleasant and amusing way of spending money, but after thirty years of experience, it is definitely my conclusion that it is certainly not a good way of trying to get rich. I have ceased for some years to do any serious or systematic betting, though from time to time a recurrent spasm of optimism seizes me and forces me to indulge in a mild speculation: but though I have parted in my time, like so many others, with very considerable sums to my good friends the bookmakers, it is strange that nearly all punters start with a winner, just as I did.

I suppose one remains true to type through life, and having already mentioned what an uncommon attraction dancing always had for me, and how uproarious I used to get even at the prospect of the annual Farringford Ball, it is not too much to suppose that such functions as State Balls at Government House would arouse some very considerable interest in my youthful bosom. In fact, they did. Of course, I was supposed to be in bed and sunk in dreamless slumber by the time they began, but this was not the case. I used, in fact, to climb out of my bedroom window and on to the next roof in order to get a look at them through a big sky-light. To do this involved getting over a gap between two walls three or four feet wide with a sixty-foot drop. This diversion, however, was at last put a stop to, as my tutor caught me one night, and, as a punishment, my Saturday half-holidays were stopped for a month.

———————

On looking through the press-cuttings giving an account of our departure from Australia, to which point I have nearly arrived, I see that my mother (as was natural enough) was very greatly affected, and retired to her corner of the railway-carriage in tears. By way of making things easier for the reporter who was interviewing us, however, and also of cheering every one up a bit, I seem to have expressed a hope to be back again in Australia before many years as Captain of an English cricketing side. Incidentally, perhaps, I might mention that though Captain of cricket sides both in England, the West Indies and South Africa, I never had the luck to take one "down under," and thus missed one of the greatest ambitions of my life. The real reason why I recall this forgotten story of my youthful days, is, however, because the newspaper concerned thought it apparently worth printing, which they probably would not have done, even in the case of a Governor-General's son, unless he had shown promise as a cricketer above the average. I had, in fact, a great advantage in having Captain Wallington as a cricket-tutor from an early age, to make the best of any advantages with which Nature endowed me. Captain Wallington, who had been an Oxford cricket-blue, was a splendid coach. He was, in fact, the man who during his secretaryship to the Governor of Fiji had introduced cricket in those islands. I played the first match of my life for the junior eleven of Melbourne Grammar School, and in the course of that cricket season made a couple of centuries. During my father's last residence at Government House, Sydney, Mr. P. F. Warner's 1903–1904 M.C.C. eleven came to play a Test Match there. In that match R. E. Foster made 287 not out for England, which remained a Test record till the young Australian, Don Bradman, recently beat it thirty years afterwards. On the Australian side the one and only Victor Trumper was playing. Beforehand the teams came up to Government House, and my father said to Mr. Warner with the paternal pride in which one must surely pardon exaggeration, "Come and look at my young Trumper!"—"Plum" Warner did as my father asked, and came and watched me batting. He was very kind and took a lot of trouble in showing me how to hold my bat, as apparently I was employing a method used neither by the immortal Victor nor by any other prominent cricketer.

There are numerous further reminiscences that I could give of our Australian life, visits to my parents' friends, for instance, such as the Barr-Smiths of South Australia—our paper-chases over a course of post and rails which Lord Richard Nevill used to organize—our acquaintance with the famous singer, Madame Melba, who was very fond of my youngest brother, Harold, and used to sing for him, and to help him with his violin—but all this would take more space than is at my disposal, and I must now bring this brief record of a wonderful period in my life to a close. My father, in fact, had accepted the Governor-Generalship for one year (subsequently extended to two) merely as a stopgap, and to assist the Home and Australian Governments. The reason for his being anxious to retire at that time was his wish to have my brother and myself educated in England. During that period of two years he had made a great name for himself in Australia as an administrator and a speaker. English people are apt to be rather incurious as to what happens outside their own little island, and I do not think my father ever had full justice done to his work, or that people at home ever realized what a force he had been at one of the most critical junctures of Imperial affairs. Perhaps I never realized it myself, before reading through the articles in the Australian Press written at the close of his term of office. In these there is absolute unanimity of opinion that he was one of the greatest, if not the greatest, representative of the Crown ever seen in Australia. As an orator, the Press said, he was, at any rate, supreme, and it is interesting to read his speeches of thirty years ago, delivered in all sorts of places—big cities, senates, little up-country towns, institutions, and festival grounds—and to realize what a great and ever-increasing hold he obtained over his audiences, and how at the end of his time as Governor-General he could strike a note rarely used by such august personages, and genially chaff himself and his audiences without any fear of loss of dignity on one side, or loss of temper on the other. Only on one occasion, in fact, was there an objection raised by any section of the Press to the matter of a speech. This was one delivered as a farewell to the Australian people. In it my father, greatly daring, took it upon himself to depart from his strictly impartial position as the Crown's representative, and to warn his audience of some of the dangers he saw approaching from the horizon and threatening the stability of the state. Amongst these he particularly emphasized the coming struggle between Capital and Labour, and indicated also the failure of the first Federal Parliament to achieve any legislation of permanent value.

The amusing thing was that, on the dissolution of this Parliament, he had at the instance of Mr. Deakin, the Prime Minister, in "the speech from the throne" warmly applauded its work; and so somewhat of a Constitutional dilemma was created by the Governor-General speaking from his personal point of view and from his official point of view in an exactly contrary sense. While the politicians (especially the Labour ones) fussed and fumed—having been put in a somewhat ridiculous position—all the saner elements in Australian life warmly congratulated him on his courage and patriotism; and as one outspoken journal put it "as long as the people trust Lord Tennyson, it doesn't matter a damn what the politicians think."

Let me refer to one other speech of my father's which created a profound impression throughout the Continent. This was an address at Ballarat on "Literature and the Literary Career" and was hailed as the most profound, comprehensive, and masterly contribution to thought on the subject ever heard in Australia. It was printed and distributed in pamphlet form all over the country, and for many months after its delivery was the theme of admiration and discussion in all classes of society in every state.

On 11th December 1903, leaving my father to await the new Governor-General, Lord Northcote, from Bombay, the rest of the family embarked in the s.s. *Ortona* from Adelaide.

My mother, on her departure, wrote the following letter to the Australian people for publication. As it expresses so simply and truly what we all felt on leaving that land of warm hearts and boundless hospitality, with its dislike of shams and affectations, and its dauntless sincerity and courage so nobly proved in the Great War, may I quote the letter here:

GOVERNMENT HOUSE,
ADELAIDE,
10th *December* 1903.

"DEAR, KIND FRIENDS,

"Before leaving the shores of Australia, my boys and I would like to say an affectionate good-bye—God be with you—to our numerous friends in every rank of life throughout the various States.

"It is with heavy hearts that we are going away, but it is a very great happiness to us all to feel that we have made so many true and loyal friends, who have bound themselves to us by ties of affection.

"The one and only regret we have in connection with our happy life in Australia is that it has passed only too quickly; indeed, we would gladly have it all over again.

"May God bless you, is the sincere wish of your affectionate friend.

"AUDREY E. TENNYSON."

CHAPTER V

CHEAM AND ETON

I RETURNED to my native land just in time for the Easter Term at a preparatory school, and I cannot truthfully say that I enjoyed it.

In the first place, there was the awful weather after the five years I had passed in Australia. Secondly, it was an anti-climax. Small boys are usually sent off to school at the age of about nine years, when they just accept the inevitable in a submissive spirit or, without really understanding what they are in for, feel a stir of rather pleasurable excitement in leaving the home circle and setting forth to see the world. My own case was quite different. I was fourteen years old when I first went to Cheam, and had seen a good deal of the world already, in fact more of the world and society than the vast majority of people in England do by the time they reach forty.

Mr. A. S. Tabor, the Headmaster of Cheam, could not be expected to realize this. Perhaps I might have explained matters to him if invited, but his ideas of discipline were extremely rigid, and I cannot ever (strangely enough) remember his asking me to do so. Instead of that it was his custom to throw fives balls and other missiles at one in the event of any difference of opinion or misunderstanding with regard to the declension of a noun or the translation of a verb. As he had been a first-class cricketer, and had retained, owing to an austere life, much of his former vigour and accuracy of eye, this practice proved extremely painful and terrifying for those he considered in the wrong, amongst whom I was, I regret to say, frequently one. In the use of the cane he was remarkably proficient, and a favourite remark of his was "You blithering little idiot, I'll flog your tail to ribbons!" I was in his class for the translation of Cæsar's Commentaries, and I remember thinking at the time that he was much more like Nero, and that Cæsar treated the conquered Gauls, whose defeats and misfortunes we stumbled through in terror and dismay, with far more courtesy and consideration than our teacher treated us. My temperament, owing perhaps to the mixture of poetical and Irish blood in my veins, has always been somewhat ebullient. I had not, then, even in the previous course of my education, which had taken place in Australia under the care of the Rev. E. Salisbury Jose (afterwards tutor to the Marquess of Camden's children and now a country Vicar at Lamberhurst in the county of Kent), escaped a fair ration of spankings from my father; as, for instance, when my brother and I played football outside in the passage when a State dinner party was going on, and with a mis-directed shot at goal I mixed up the cutlets and the ice-cream. The tyranny (and I really can call it nothing else) of Mr. Tabor was, however, a different affair. Probably we disliked each other at first sight, and he determined to reduce me to a suitably submissive level as quickly as possible. But, be this as it may, it was an enormous relief to me when I got the measles and was removed to the comparative comfort and seclusion of the sick-room. Cheam has since then altered enormously, and has now one of the most delightful of Headmasters, the Rev. H. M. Taylor.

So much for my one and only term at an English private school!

––––––––––

At the beginning of the summer "half" of the year 1904 I went on from Cheam to Eton.

Dr. Warre was headmaster of Eton for my first two years and an awe-inspiring and magnificently distinguished figure he was. So great a man in his profession was he that he could hardly help being conscious of his own universal fame.

On one occasion whilst staying in Scotland with the parents of one of his pupils, he was taken over to see an old woman living in a cottage on the estate.

When Dr. Warre was introduced to her she gazed in admiration at his massive proportions and splendid features; and the sentiment most common to all females rising in her mind, she inquired:

"An' hoo many boys hae ye, sir?"

The Doctor, however, who took it for granted that the old lady knew, like everyone else he had met, that he was Headmaster of Eton, replied:

"One thousand and nine, madam."

"By gum, what a mon!" exclaimed the old dame, retiring quickly into her cottage from sheer fright.

Dr. Warre, who had been at Eton for thirty years or more, was a very strong supporter of the old régime, and in consequence there had been very few changes in the customs and spirit of the place over a considerable period. Subsequently the

Headmaster was the Hon. and Rev. Edward Lyttelton, late Headmaster of Haileybury College, one of my father's oldest friends. Those were the days when the great clan of Lyttelton occupied positions of importance in almost every department of activity throughout the country. Alfred Lyttelton was Colonial Secretary, Neville Lyttelton a famous general, other Lytteltons or relatives of Lytteltons were bishops, admirals, prominent civil servants and leaders in Society. England, as well as Eton, may well be said to have been governed by Lytteltons.

At Eton I took Middle Fourth, a respectable though not highly exalted place, and, incidentally, was in consequence brought a good deal into contact with the Headmaster's deputy, the Lower Master, Mr. Edward Austen-Leigh, called by all and sundry "The Flea." Mr. Austen-Leigh was one of the most famous characters that ever were at Eton—as much an Eton institution as the Chapel, the Upper School, the Cloisters or any of the other prominent landmarks of the place. No one who knew him could ever forget him, so great was his personality and so pronounced his characteristics. Who, indeed, could forget his dry, explosive humour, his high nasal metallic voice, his slightly stooping rolling walk, and his ruddy countenance with the constantly puffing lips turning from side to side as he acknowledged salutes from acquaintances and boys? Full of brains, and a fine athlete in bygone days, he was admired on that account alone; but what especially endeared him to boys was his generosity and hospitality and his manner of treating and speaking to them. There was nothing of the superiority of the Schoolmaster about him although he was a stern disciplinarian. From my humble position as a Fourth Form boy, I greatly liked and admired "The Flea."

It was he, in his capacity as Lower Master, who "swiped" (*i.e.* birched) delinquents from the Lower School. During my second half as the head boy in Upper Fourth after my examinations and promotion from Middle Fourth, it was my duty to "hold down" for him. This expression would seem to imply that the culprits were accustomed to writhe in agony or to try to escape the penalties of the law by main force, necessitating the use by the Lower Master of a couple of hefty supporters to keep them in position while he performed the execution. Let me explain however (for the benefit of non-Etonians) that, whatever had been the case in mediæval times from which, I suppose, the expression dated, all that was necessary in my own was delicately to lift the tail of the victim's shirt, and to lay his posterior bare for the application of the birch. I was only "swiped" once myself, and that privately when I was in the Eleven and in "Pop", for telling a story to our "Dame" of which the point depended on a certain word having a double meaning. In my schoolboy innocence I thought "she" would only know the proper meaning, but she was a wiser woman than I imagined and complained to the Headmaster, and I, in consequence, was a sadder boy.

My House at Eton was Mr. A. M. Goodhart's. It had formerly been the house of that well-known literary man, the late Mr. A. C. Benson. Disappointed, however, at not being made Headmaster of Eton on Dr. Warre's resignation, Mr. Benson had recently resigned to become the Master of Magdalene College, Cambridge. Mr. Benson by his intellectual eminence and his prowess as a teacher had made a great name for himself amongst schoolmasters, and, in consequence, parents who were themselves interested in art or literature or who had clever boys, had been very eager to get Mr. Benson as their boy's housemaster and tutor. He had had therefore the best of England in a social and intellectual sense to pick from, and his house had been remarkably distinguished both in games and work.

To this house, with such high traditions in the school, Mr. Goodhart had succeeded the half before I arrived. If not a writer like his predecessor, Mr. Goodhart was an eminent musician. His compositions were frequently played at the school concerts, and he set to music some of the school songs. He was also a good footballer. As a boy at Eton he got into the "Field" (the School Football Eleven) and was invincible at the Wall Game, which he played passionately and undauntedly at an age when football to the vast majority becomes a memory rather than a pursuit. My housemaster was a blissful contrast to Mr. Tabor of Cheam, and I'm afraid that in the exuberance of youthful spirits I more than once took advantage of his kindness.

I started off very well at Eton both at games and work, playing for my house both at cricket and football in my first two "halves" and getting "my shorts" for the latter. I also played in first "Lower Sixpenny" my first summer half at cricket. My first form-master was Mr. "Tuppy" Headlam, a member of the North Country family of that name, and a Guards Officer during the war. Urbane and debonair, he had a distinct gift for teaching and interesting boys, and a slightly cynical manner and humour of which it was hardly possible for a boy, however naughtily disposed, to take advantage. I worked very hard "up to" him, and nearly took a "double remove" my first half. After that promising start as a "highbrow," I fear that my scholastic successes and attainments hardly deserve the trouble of being recorded. For the rest of my time at Eton, although I only actually once failed in "Trials," I confess that I devoted more time to games and amusements generally than to my work. I did, however, (which is more than most Etonians do) win three or four French Form prizes, and two Form Mathematical prizes for being top boy at the end of the half. This, perhaps, was not quite so considerable a feat as it sounds, because I had a great advantage over most other boys in French in having been thoroughly well grounded in that language early in life. The really remarkable thing about my winning these French prizes, however, was not so much that I *did* win them, but that I actually beat a *Frenchman* (my friend the Duc de Mouchy, then Henri de Noailles), who was always in the same form for French as myself. How this occurred, or what came over the French masters at the critical moment and made them give the prizes to me, I cannot even guess. At any rate, if my victories did me no other good, they have given me something to laugh over when I meet Mouchy, as I not infrequently do either in London or Paris.

―――――――――

Two years after my arrival at Eton I began to make some real mark in the school as a cricketer, getting my Lower Club Colours first choice. Playing for the Second XI, I made two centuries, and also did fairly well in Upper Club games. C. E. Hatfield in fact, who was Captain of the Eleven, told me one day to my frantic joy that he wanted me to play for Eton against Winchester. I was really in the seventh heaven of delight, and was just going to order my First XI Colours, when Hatfield met me in the street looking very confused, as if something had just come into his mind. With many apologies he confessed that he had totally forgotten to include a wicket-keeper in the team, and that he must therefore cancel his former selection to play me against Winchester. Like all other mortals, I have had some bitter moments in my life, although my philosophy is to try to remain cheerful in all circumstances, and, at any rate, not to show my feelings in public. I must, however, acknowledge that on this occasion all my self-control was needed to keep a cheerful countenance in Hatfield's presence. I muttered something and tried to smile gaily; then hurried back to my house and to my room, where I remained for a long time in floods of tears, so agonizing had my disappointment been.

The next year, 1907, things came right, and I got into the Eleven. I say things came right, because, after all, getting into the Eleven was what I had always set my heart on doing, and I had the great disappointment of the previous year to atone for. All the same, the season was rather an in-and-out one for me. It was very wet and cold for one thing, which never suited my cricket after the hard and true Australian wickets, and my batting, perhaps for that reason, was for the greater part of the so-called summer hopelessly at sea. I developed, however, as a fast bowler, and as one was needed in the Eleven, was played in that capacity at Lords, going in to bat last.

The next year, 1908—my last at school—my batting came on again. I went in seventh in the Eton v. Harrow match and scored 13 and 26. The match on a wet wicket and under leaden skies was a rout for the School, who were beaten by ten wickets. The only satisfaction from my point of view was that I did not do quite so badly as some of the rest of the Eleven.

To complete some account of my athletic performances at Eton, I played several times in the "Field game" but never got my school colours for football. Also I won the House quarter-mile in 1907 and 1908, beating each time my great friend The Hon. G. W. ("Billy") Grenfell, who actually won the school quarter those two years. I was, unfortunately for myself, ill on each occasion, and therefore unable to run in the School event, which, on form, it is possible I might have won. This was a disappointment to me, not only on my own account, but because I should have liked to carry on my father's record who, as a boy at Marlborough, won the school quarter there more than once and had a big reputation as a runner over this distance, although I think he never ran on the track afterwards when at Cambridge. Also, in 1906, I rowed for my House when our boat made two "bumps." I did not row my last two years at Eton, as I found it interfered too much with cricket.

As I am writing my own memoirs, I suppose it would be wrong of me to suppress the fact that other friends and I at Eton did not always confine our amusements and enterprises to those recognized by the School authorities. There was a practicable way out of "my tutor's" after "lock-up," which, however, I shall not divulge here for fear of leading astray any youthful

Etonian happening to read this book. This was through windows and over roofs and down fire-escapes, and other members of the House and I sometimes used it when our good and worthy housemaster must have thought us safely asleep. We had, by arrangement, a horse-cab waiting for us (taxis and motor-cars were not available in those days) and, hidden inside it, we would drive to Slough Station and take the last train to London, where we attended three Covent Garden Balls and occasionally other diversions. Luck must have been on our side, or perhaps our dispositions were more than commonly skilful; at any rate we were never caught. We had, however, a very narrow escape one night when about to go to one of these Covent Garden Balls.

Knowing that the authorities were always watchful, I suggested that some of us should make the attempt to get to London disguised as ancient men with beards, and board the 11 p.m. train, thus attired. This idea was well received; and three other boys, "Billy" Grenfell from my tutor's, Edmund Turton from Broadbent's and John Earle from College, as well as myself, having met at a pre-arranged rendezvous, donned the longest and fuzziest beards we could order from Clarkson's, and set out for Slough Station. What none of us had reckoned on, however, was that the School authorities had specially warned the police to be on the lookout. In consequence of this a detective, highly trained in the art of piercing disguises, was stationed on Slough railway platform. This acute officer instantly detected, in spite of our bowed figures, long and hairy beards, and palsied fingers tremblingly grasping the walking-sticks that with difficulty supported our tottering footsteps, a body of youthful Etonians. Fortunately his zeal and the excitement of his discovery made him leap forward in our direction before he had us thoroughly cornered. A miraculous transformation instantly took place in the case of those four greybeards. In the twinkling of an eye and as one man their youth was restored, and casting away their walking-sticks and anything else that might impede their flight, they dashed out of the railway station and across the fields in the direction of Eton. The detective who had discovered us, assisted by other policemen who had come in answer to his whistle, chased us for quite a long time, but fortunately in vain. We were young and in good training, and had got too long a start. This happened towards the end of a winter half, and luckily our names were never discovered.

———————

47

My last year at Eton I was very fond of a girl. She was extremely pretty and a young schoolmistress in Windsor. I met her walking on the terrace of Windsor Castle one afternoon and listening to the band, which it was the custom for large numbers of Eton boys and inhabitants of Windsor to do. Her Christian name was "Rara", so my pet name for her was the "Rara Avis" which, for the benefit of those who have not had a classical education, I might freely translate as meaning "a bird in a thousand." Rara seemed to like the name. In the holidays she used to meet me sometimes in London, and I used to take her out to dinner and afterwards to the theatre, whence she would return by the last train to Windsor. Rara was, I am sure, worthy of commemoration in anyone's pages, with her lovely dark hair and eyes, wonderful smile and pleasant conversation which, by the nature of her vocation, could not help being highly intelligent. It is not, however, exclusively on account of her many charms that I mention her here, but rather because owing to the peculiarity of their system of education public schoolboys seldom, I suppose, have a pretty girl to talk to in the intervals of their work and games.

SIDNEY HERBERT, THE HON. J. ELIOT (LATER THE EARL OF ST. GERMANS), AND THE AUTHOR

THEIR LAST HALF AT ETON

[Image credit:] *Alfred D. Kissack*

E. W. S. FOLJAMBE, G. W. CATTLEY, R. ST. L. FOWLER,
HON. L. H. TENNYSON, G. H. M. CARTWRIGHT, R. L. BENSON,
R. H. TWINING, HON. A. WINDSOR-CLIVE, W. A. WORSLEY,
R. O. R. KENYON-SLANEY, F. W. GULL

[Image credit:] *Hills & Saunders*

There were a very clever and amusing lot of boys at Good-hart's. Particular friends of mine were Lord Cochrane, John Craigie, Lord Alistair Leveson-Gower, afterwards an officer in the Blues, who died since the War, and "Bird" Eliot (afterwards called "Mousie") who became Earl of St. Germans. He was famous for his great sense of humour and rather reckless character. He also died young. Very great friends of mine also, then, as later, were the two brothers Sidney and the late Michael Herbert, whose father and mother had a lovely London house in Carlton House Terrace where I sometimes used to stay. They were both of them witty and amusing and remarkably able. Michael's brilliant brain brought him a partnership in a big City firm in his early thirties, but just when the ball was at his feet, illness and premature death took him from his numberless friends and admirers. Sidney has suffered much from ill-health all his life. He was in the Blues during the War, then entered Parliament and became Mr. Baldwin's Political Secretary, but alas! his most promising political career was sadly interfered with by illness, although he has just lately entered Parliament again as Member for Westminster. Captain J. Craigie, son of the lady well-known to thousands of readers at that time as the novelist "John Oliver Hobbes," was a neighbour of ours in the Isle of Wight. He was a magnificent fives and racquets player at Eton, being keeper of both, and afterwards got a blue for golf at Oxford. He served for some years with distinction in the Guards, and also became one of the best bridge players in London. Another friend of mine at Eton was Duff Cooper, the author of the recently published and brilliantly written *Life of Talleyrand*, an extremely clever and amusing boy who was awarded one of the best D.S.O.'s in the war. He is now Under-Secretary for War, and husband of the beautiful Lady Diana Manners, to whom he has been devoted from his schooldays. Lady Diana Duff Cooper and I, with many other Eton friends and their sisters, were more than once guests together at Taplow Court, the home on the banks of the Thames of Lord and Lady Desborough. Their two sons, the Grenfells, were, I think, the most remarkable boys at Eton in my time. They both fell in the War, Julian with the Royals, Billy with the Rifle Brigade; and by their death in action it is certain that the country had to mourn the loss of two young men of genius. Julian's two poems, "To a Black Greyhound" and "Battle" will not be forgotten, and it is only possible to surmise what fame he might have earned had he been spared. Billy, my greatest friend at Eton, whom I have already mentioned once or twice, was distinguished by a combination of talents that were Elizabethan in their variety. In addition to being a first-class athlete and boxer, he had the most marvellous brain-power that enabled him to assimilate in an inconceivably brief time any subject he chose to take up. His record in school work simply staggered his less gifted contemporaries. He won the Newcastle Scholarship and every other school prize worth winning, and afterwards got a Balliol Scholarship. With all this, he remained absolutely simple and natural, and always ready for a gay adventure or a bit of fun with an element of risk about it.

What happy days those were at Taplow Court! The Grenfells were the most united family, and their affection for each other shed itself like a benediction over all the guests, old and young, beneath their roof. Men and women, famous in the great world, and youthful friends of the Grenfell brothers and sisters met together during those never-to-be-forgotten week-ends, every hour of which was made vivid by Lady Desborough's keen intelligence, beauty and charm, and by that great sportsman and accomplished man-of-the-world, Lord Desborough, who has seen and done almost everything worth doing. What interesting people I met at Taplow Court in days gone by! And amongst them more than once the Rt. Hon. W. S. Churchill.

Let me tell a story of Mr. Churchill in the old days there, which redounds much more to his credit than to my own.

One lovely summer evening during the session of Parliament he had come down from London still attired in what was then the usual Parliamentary costume—top hat, frock coat, stiff shirt and collar. Standing on the banks of the Thames which runs past the foot of the garden, before the dressing bell rang, Mr. Churchill was talking to Lady Desborough, with all his customary flow of language, upon some topic of the day. The sight of him orating and gesticulating in these clothes so near to the water was too great a temptation for us to resist. Charging all together from behind, the Grenfell brothers and myself sent him flying with a mighty splash far out into the river. . . .

Mr. Churchill behaved in the most sporting manner imaginable about it, and on regaining the shore, dripping and hatless as he was, interceded for us with Lady Desborough in an address which I have never heard excelled for humour and the arts of advocacy.

CHAPTER VI

TROUBLE AT HOME OVER MY FUTURE CAREER

My Eton days were now practically over. I had had a splendid time and made lots of friends. Only, it must be confessed, I had not been very industrious and had also shown a tendency to be harum-scarum, a good deal to my father's disappointment. I'm afraid it was with the knowledge that he was not quite satisfied with me that I now climbed the winding stair to his study and, cautiously turning the door handle, entered that famous room. I say *famous*, because it was there that my grandfather had composed most of the poems of his later life, when the high moral and philosophical tone that so much appealed to the end of the Victorian age was most in evidence. To myself, at any rate, there always seemed an atmosphere about Farringford, which it was extremely difficult to live up to. Perhaps no one without a similar experience could understand exactly what I mean. It was the sort of atmosphere which makes one whisper in a church even when it is quite empty, and no service is going on. There was nowhere about the place where this peculiar sensation was more evident than in the aforesaid study.

Trees planted by the old poet grew right up to it,—a giant ilex, of which he was inordinately proud, pushed its great arms almost in at the windows, and on windy nights tapped the panes with its fingers—the walls were lined with his books—framed manuscripts of his poems and pictures of other famous poets filled the gaps between the bookcases—the sofas and chairs were strewn with volumes about himself.

Taking a long breath (as I always did when I entered what had been the poet's study and was now my father's), I picked my way through the mass of furniture to where, at the further end of the long room, the top of my father's bald head was just visible above the back of a chair covered in flowered red chintz. I was pretty sure that the interview that was about to take place would be conducted with a certain amount of constraint on both sides. I had advanced a proposition with regard to my future career through the medium of my mother, who was always my best and most faithful advocate; and she, after submitting it to the proper quarter, had informed me that my father would talk to me on the subject, but that, at the present moment, he was reluctant to entertain it. Nervously, but with an assumption of jauntiness,

I approached the chair where my father sat, pipe in mouth and *The Times* newspaper on his knees.

"Well, Lionel," said my father, "your mother said you wanted to see me."

"Yes, Father. She told you what I wanted to see you about, didn't she?"

"About your future career."

"Yes. I hope you approve."

"You want to go into the Guards, I understand, and what are your reasons for wishing to join them?"

"A lot of my Eton friends are going into them."

"Probably a frivolous and extravagant lot of fellows."

"Not at all, Father."

"I very much doubt it. I should have preferred, if you wish to go into the Army, that you should join some quieter regiment."

"But the Guards are the finest regiment in the service. If we ever have a war. . . ."

"At the present moment we are at peace. The Guards are most of their time in London, and I know what temptations there are for a young officer to be extravagant in London. I am not a rich man, Lionel, and though I can give you a reasonable allowance, I can't afford to let you live like a millionaire's son, or pay extravagant debts. I do not want you to go into the Guards."

After a few more words he then put his pipe back in his mouth and returned to his reading of *The Times*, and I understood that the interview was over and that for the present, at any rate, there was no chance of my being allowed to join the Brigade as was my wish. It was obvious that other methods must be tried to win him over to the idea.

My father was always in the habit of referring to himself as a poor man, but he never told anyone, much less myself, what his actual income was. All things are relative, and, though he was in actual fact, of course, a poor man, compared say with the Duke of Devonshire or the Duke of Westminster of the period, I, who (amongst the other gifts with which Providence was pleased to endow me at birth) had never a very pronounced sense of the value of money, always imagined him to be a much richer man than he was, from the fact that we lived comfortably enough, and never seemed embarrassed for the want of anything.

My father's arguments, then, that he was unable to afford me the life which a good number of my richer friends were leading, I brushed aside both at this moment (and afterwards), and then returned to my mother, took her into my confidence, and told her what my father had said.

"Oh! I am sorry, Lionel. I was afraid your father would be against it. I told you so, before you went to see him."

"I know you did. Would it be any use if you spoke to him on the subject again, do you think?"

"Oh! Lionel, I don't think I can. I've talked and talked to him already, but he won't hear of it. You know he is not a rich man, and then he's afraid you'll be a naughty boy and run up debts."

"But what *is* father's income?"

"I don't know, darling, he's never told me."

"Why look at K—— and C—— and D——. They're going into the Brigade. Surely their fathers aren't richer than father is."

"Perhaps not. But nobody knows what your father's income is."

"Well I'm *sure* he can afford it. I'll go and see him again and make him see reason."

"Oh, Lionel dear, don't have another quarrel with him. It won't be any good just now."

"I know! I'll write to Uncle Willie and ask him to come down and talk to father about it."

"Uncle Willie! That's a good idea. I'm sure if anyone can get round your father, he can."

"Yes. And we'll ask Uncle Ernest to come too, and back us all up."

So that was that. My mother, who adored and rather spoiled me, I'm afraid, fell in with these ideas and the plot began.

Before he well knew where he was my father was surrounded by many members of the family, all of them endeavouring to persuade him on my behalf against his better judgment. My poor father! Let me say here in all justice that he was probably quite right in the line he took up, and that it would have required a different temperament from my own to resist the combined temptations of excitement, pleasure, beautiful ladies and notoriety that in those few pre-war years were to assail me. It would have required again a different character from his to withstand completely the combined assault of so many members of the family. Though he had somewhat of a reputation in certain quarters for being stern and unbending, that was mostly his surface appearance. In reality, he was shy, nervous, good-natured, and hated being bothered. In such circumstances my Uncle Willie Boyle was a trump-card in himself. Let me here say something about him. In the first place, like my mother, he was extremely handsome with his hawk-like features and blue eyes. He had an imperious nature, and never cared what he said to anybody, and seeing him approach with his dignified walk, one realized that he was not a person to be trifled with. My Uncle had been successful in life, in which he had played a good many parts, being famous, I believe, in his young days as a consummate horseman when in the West of America, and in later life as an equally bold financier. Once or twice, as must happen to those who play the big financial game, he suffered reverses of a serious character, but his spirit and enterprise for long defied the tricks of Fortune. For some years he was the Member of Parliament for Mid-Norfolk, where he lived *en grand seigneur* in an exquisitely beautiful old Manor House. He was, in fact, a *grand seigneur* all over, in his mode of life, in his appearance, and in the way he thought and spoke.

My uncle and myself were always very good friends, and had a good deal of sympathy with one another, despite the fact that I was unable sometimes to resist the temptation of pulling his leg.

On one occasion, some time before the episode which I have just been describing, and when my brother Aubrey and myself were both junior schoolboys, my Uncle Willie was also stopping at Farringford.

It chanced that in the neighbourhood there were staying some beautiful and amusing ladies whom my uncle was very anxious to meet, so my mother asked them over to tea one day.

The drawing-room at Farringford is at one end of the house, and the house itself is long and rambling. In this room the ladies in question were sitting with my parents, talking and looking at the lovely view of the park, and the cliffs of Freshwater Bay with its sea of Italian blue. The butler brought in tea, everything was present and ready, except my uncle.

"But where can Willie be?" said my mother. "Surely he must know it's tea-time."

"We won't wait for him," said my father, drawing his chair up to the table and turning to his guests. "What may I offer you—hot-cake or bread-and-butter?"

"How naughty he is to be so late," said my mother, herself handing the tea-cups to the strangers. "And I know he was so anxious to meet you too. I don't understand it."

The tea went on: cakes vanished, cups were replenished; but still no Willie Boyle appeared, to the consternation of my parents, and the vast disappointment of the fair creatures who had come to meet him. For some little time, however (I have mentioned that the house is long and rambling and the drawing-room right at the end of it), a strange, dull, booming, bumping sound had been audible.

"What a queer noise that is," exclaimed my father, putting his monocle in his eye and listening attentively. "Do you hear it, Audrey?"

"Distinctly," said my mother.

"Distant thunder perhaps," observed the guests. "I thought the sky looked threatening as we drove over this afternoon."

"More likely to be the guns firing at the Needles Fort," said my father. "And yet, it doesn't sound to me exactly like guns."

"No more it does," exclaimed the guests: and then my mother added: "But what on earth has happened to Willie?"

"I'll ring the bell for Waters," said my father, "and tell him to find Willie at once."

The butler having arrived said that he had not seen my uncle, and was retiring at my father's bidding to search the house, when the latter exclaimed: "And, Waters, when you have found Mr. Boyle, please find out what that extraordinary noise is. 'Pon my soul, it seems to be getting louder and louder. I hope that the cistern hasn't burst, and that that isn't the noise of water flooding the house."

The chorus of exclamations from the ladies at such a supposition had hardly died down, when back came the butler with a face from which every vestige of expression had obviously been carefully banished, bent down, and whispered something in my father's ear.

"What!" exclaimed my father, letting his monocle drop heavily on his chest.

"It was the young gentlemen, my lord," said Waters as he followed my father, who with some sort of scrambled and hasty apologies to the guests, was hurrying from the room in the direction of the clamour that with every step seemed to be assuming positively stupendous and awe-inspiring proportions.

Astonishing to relate, the noise had all been made by my uncle in his fury. He had all tea-time been bottled up inside the lavatory in the Hall, kicking the door, buffeting it with his fists, and yelling without being able to make any one hear sooner. My brother Aubrey and I, seeing him go in to wash and brush up before tea, had quietly turned the outside key in the lock and gone off with it. Oliver, the estate carpenter, had to be fetched to let him out again.

I think I had better draw a veil over the subsequent proceedings so far as they concerned my brother and myself.

My Uncle Ernest was a very different character from his brother Willie—reserved, quiet in disposition, and without any of the latter's dash. After many years in a public office in London he retired to a beautiful estate in Jamaica, which I have often visited during my recent trips to that most enchanting of islands in the British Empire. When the War broke out, despite a somewhat serious ailment which, as well as his years, rendered him quite unfit for active service, he rejoined the Honourable Artillery Company in which he had served previously to his retirement to Jamaica. He was killed later, fighting most gallantly in command of his battalion.

As my Uncle Cecil was killed with the Imperial Yeomanry at Boshof in South Africa, and another uncle, whom I never saw, in one of the Zulu Wars: and as both my own brothers lost their lives in the Great War, it is due to me, I think, to mention this family record in their honour.

I seem, somehow, to have digressed at considerable length from the original purpose of this chapter which was to retail the sequence of events by which I came to be a Cambridge undergraduate. To cut a long story short, my father, though he held

58

out for some time, was unable, as I had supposed, to resist the combined pressure of so many relatives; and finally came to a compromise largely in my favour, by which I was, before joining the Guards, to go first to a university and see something more of the world.

In conclusion of my Eton career, it might be well to mention that I had a very good report from my housemaster, Mr. Good-hart, who wrote to my father that during my last year I had done sufficiently well in school work, exerted myself energetically for the honour of the House, and in particular had shown great interest in the junior cricket, helping and coaching the younger boys most assiduously. Being myself in "Pop" and in the Eton Eleven, I had brought some prestige to the House.

CHAPTER VII

MY LIFE AT CAMBRIDGE

As arranged after the family manœuvres related in the last chapter, I went up to Trinity College, Cambridge, in the year 1908.

Before leaving Farringford for the university, I had another interview with my father in his study.

"You are going into the world now, Lionel," said he, fixing his eyeglass on me with an expression in which hope and doubt were equally mixed. "At least, if Cambridge is not actually the world, you will now be your own master to a greater extent than has ever been the case before. You will no longer be a schoolboy to be treated as such. I sincerely hope that with increased liberty there will come an increased sense of responsibility on your part. Your mother and I have often been distressed at your levity and at the way you sometimes will not treat even the most serious things seriously."

"I'm sorry about that, Father."

"That's all well enough, but it is no good being sorry unless you will earnestly try to do better in the future. I hope you will now read more than you have done hitherto. Do you ever open a book unless actually made to do so?"

"Oh, yes, Father."

"I doubt it. However, I really do hope you mean to do better now and bring credit to the name of Tennyson."

"That's rather difficult, Father. Think of grandfather and all the marvellous things he wrote: and then there's yourself, the most famous Governor-General that ever was in Australia. . . ."

"Well, my boy, if you only do your best, your mother and I will be more than satisfied. I hope you will try."

From the nature of this conversation with my father, and those given in the previous chapter, which represent, as nearly as I can recollect, what took place between us, it may be deduced that our relations were not always entirely harmonious.

Despite, then, these paternal exhortations to the higher life, my first care when arriving at Cambridge was to select the most comfortable "digs" I could find. I shared them with Reggie Abel

Smith, a friend of mine from Eton with whom I have hardly come in contact since. These lodgings were over the Bank exactly opposite the Gate of Trinity and therefore remarkably convenient. That they were also decidedly expensive and consequently known as "The Ritz" was a pity, but it could not be helped. There we led a carefree and festive existence.

As he kept in regular communication with my tutors at the University, it was not long before my father began to be worried about me again. I do not honestly know that I was much idler or more extravagant than many others, though away from Farringford I was always apt to kick up my heels a bit. Even at Cambridge, however, the name of Tennyson required a lot of living up to. Does not a large and life-like statue of the poet seated in company with Sir Isaac Newton and other illustrious members of the College meet one at the entrance to the Hall in Trinity? A hundred years ago, almost exactly, he was in residence as an undergraduate of the College, and there he lived in company with a band of kindred intellectual spirits, known by the name of the Apostles, whose laudable ambition it was, on leaving Cambridge, to remedy all the evils of the world. The name of his greatest friend at Trinity, Arthur Hallam, was borne by my father and descended to myself.

On reading through the letters, papers, diaries and other documents connected with my life, the most important of which it has always been a habit of mine to preserve and bind together, I seem indeed to discover a whole posse of tutors and crammers in correspondence with Farringford; and one and all exerting themselves in a manner almost undreamt of in their previous connection with undergraduates, to bring me up to an intellectual level that would not disgrace my name and all its associations with Cambridge. There appeared, from perusal of all these notes and letters, no particular danger of my compromising myself later in any social sense from too ardent a desire to reform this wicked world; on the contrary my instructors thought that I found the world uncommonly pleasant, and to be enjoyed to the full whenever and wherever possible. There was racing at Newmarket—the allurements of London not so very far away—shooting parties at well-known houses in the neighbourhood—in fact the hundred and one pursuits that are apt to tempt a young man of sporting tastes on the threshold of manhood from the paths of industry.

It was in vain that I urged upon this body of stern-willed and indefatigable advisers in that spirit of inextinguishable optimism with which I was born, that things were not so bad as they seemed. Their reply was that, though shrewd in conversation and pleasant to deal with as I took all their rebukes in such good part, I did not seem able to concentrate my mind on some of the tasks which it was imperative to master, if I wished to pass the second part of my entrance examination, the "Littlego." I might add that I had succeeded in getting through the first part with flying colours while still at Eton, much to all my masters' astonishment.

My greatest stumbling-block was that well-known work (now, I think, abolished from the Cambridge curriculum)—Paley's "Evidences of Christianity." There was something in my intellectual equipment that positively refused to allow me sufficiently to master the details of this scholastic and theological masterpiece in order to obtain the requisite number of marks to defeat the examiners. Midnight electric light, miserable hours of toil, prayers or execrations of tutors all were in vain. At length I was sent (missing the Easter Term) to a crammer, by name Mr. Norris Elye, who lived at Utterby Manor near Louth in Lincolnshire.

Lincolnshire is the county from which the Tennyson family came and where my ancestors had, in fact, lived for about five hundred years. Had I gone to cram in Kirkcudbright or Glamorganshire, it is possible that my brain might have given a sudden start and acquired all the knowledge of Paley that was necessary. As it was after three months of arid and exhausting toil, supplemented by unremitting efforts on the crammer's part combined with weekly letters to Farringford on the progress I was making, I returned to be examined at Cambridge once more and got precisely two marks out of a hundred.

Let me add that in the spirit of "never say die" I did eventually pass this examination, getting thirty-four marks, the minimum being thirty.

While living at Utterby Manor as Mr. Norris Elye's pupil, I paid my first visit, amongst other houses in the neighbourhood, to Bayons Manor, the residence of my cousins the Tennyson-D'Eyncourts. Bayons Manor is quite one of the show places of England, and were it situated in a more accessible spot, would really be famous with sightseers. Built in a fine park with beautiful trees, and on a rising slope above the village of Tealby, it is approached by a long drive winding in and out amidst the folds of the park.

Those who see it for the first time and are unacquainted with its history, exclaim that it is the noblest specimen of Norman castellated architecture preserved in this country. As their car for the last part of the way turns in amidst high and frowning walls, passes under vast portcullises and crosses more than one thundering drawbridge to pull up at length in front of a part of the building which has obviously been modernized, they wonder what fierce Norman baron built these massive keeps and feudal fortifications.

In such speculations, however, the visitor goes astray. It was no mediæval baron who built this splendid castle, but my great-great-uncle, the Rt. Hon. Charles Tennyson-D'Eyncourt a well-known politician at the beginning of the nineteenth century about the time of the Reform Bill. It is supposed to have cost him about £100,000 and was erected from designs entirely his own. Legend says, that if he was dissatisfied with any part of his creation and thought it did not look as well when actually built as it had done when merely on paper, he just ordered the workmen to pull it down again and rebuild it according to a new design, which might strike some of us who live in harder and sterner times as somewhat extravagant.

My cousin, the late Edmund Tennyson-D'Eyncourt, was a most accomplished man, being a very witty speaker and a talented artist. While a boy at Eton he drew on the whitewashed walls of one of the classrooms such a speaking likeness of old Johnny Young, a well-known master of his day, that it was left undisturbed for some thirty years. I hope it is still there. Mrs. Tennyson-D'Eyncourt was also, as she still is, very kind and hospitable, and her sons and daughters inherit the good looks and good qualities of their parents. The Tennyson-D'Eyncourt twins were both in the Eight at Eton and then joined the Guards.

Another relation of mine lived near Louth, Captain Julius Tennyson. He was immensely strong and somewhat of a petulant nature. One night returning home late, he found a burglar lying in the conservatory who had cut himself and fainted from loss of blood. Stooping down, he picked up the fellow and threw him over the ten foot high garden wall.

On returning to Cambridge for the Summer Term, I was of course, apart from anything else, extremely busy playing cricket. I was invited to play in the Freshman's match and made 38 not out and 51 not out. There was some heavy scoring in the match, three centuries and a number of scores over 50 being made in addition to my own in the second innings. The critic of *The Times* was quite complimentary about my batting, giving me credit for clean hard hitting, but I had gone in ninth and was considered in those days principally as a bowler. As a matter of fact, the same gentleman was quite complimentary about my bowling, and said that I had bowled well and with any luck should have taken many more wickets than I did.

I also played for Perambulators *v.* Etceteras. On this occasion, despite my two innings in the Freshmen's Match, which several critics had described as the "brightest displays of the match," I was put in absolutely last. I was still, I presume, considered in the light of a bowler pure and simple. My scores on this occasion were 3 and 21. I was not at all successful in bowling, sending down 19 overs in the two innings for 64 runs and 1 wicket. For the rest of the Term I played regularly for the Trinity First XI and for the Crusaders. I made some useful scores but except for one century, did nothing outstanding. I also took about 25 wickets in the course of the Cambridge season.

I have already mentioned that my temperament is optimistic. Tutors and coaches had, intermittently but fairly continuously, throughout my stay at Cambridge been prophesying woe, writing that I should never be able to pass my exams. [*sic*] to get into the Army, and frightening my poor father into fits. One highbrow don went so far as to say that even if I did get in, I should be kicked out again in six months for being so infernally casual.

As far as I remember, these gloomy forebodings did not particularly perturb me. I had sent in an application for a probationary commission in the Coldstream Guards and, with complete self-confidence, felt perfectly sure that it would turn out all right. So it did, as things happened. Colonel (afterwards General Sir Ivor) Maxse, who was then commanding the Coldstream, had asked me to come up and see him. The interview went off remarkably well, and he told me that he would be glad to have me in the regiment provided the reports on me were satisfactory. Judging by those he received I could not have been so very bad in those days after all. One came from the old Master of Trinity, an intimate friend of my grandfather's, who wrote on my behalf the following charming letter:—

"DEAR SIR,

"Allow me to say a few words in favour of the Hon. Lionel Tennyson, whom I have known from his birth. He came to us at Trinity last October with a high character from Eton, and his conduct with us has been blameless. He has passed Part I of his 'Little-Go,' but he has had difficulties in getting through the Mathematical part of the Examination. He is a young man of winning manners and in his own line energetic. He seems to me quite certain to make a good soldier, and I should not be at all surprised if he became even distinguished, he is so manly, so sensible, and so attractive.

"I am, dear Sir,

"Faithfully yours,

"H. MONTAGU BUTLER."

Another letter in my favour was sent to the War Office by Canon the Hon. Edward Lyttelton, Headmaster of Eton, whom I have already mentioned once or twice in these Memoirs. It ran:—

"I hereby certify that Mr. L. Tennyson showed himself at Eton a boy of unusual energy and exceptionally fine physique and to be possessed of qualities which would fit him to become an officer of distinction. He is absolutely trustworthy, has good organizing power, and plenty of common sense. I much hope he will be successful in obtaining a commission."

There was, Colonel Maxse had written, only one vacancy for a probationer in the Coldstream Guards, but I got it.

So here—despite parental hesitations, despair of coaches, my own intermittent attention to the books I was supposed to study, and vacancies in that most celebrated of regiments reduced almost to vanishing point—was the second of my youthful ambitions fulfilled. I was to be a Guardsman!

Much water has flowed under the bridge since those days but I still recall the thrill of pride and pleasure which my good fortune gave me.

I joined my regiment at Aldershot in August of that year (1909).

CHAPTER VIII

I JOIN THE COLDSTREAM GUARDS

It was in the Guards, before the Great War, more than in any other regiment that the stern and bitter lessons of the South African War had been learnt. From the point of military training the Brigade were more up to date than any other unit in the British Army, and instruction was enforced amongst all ranks (men, N.C.O.'s and officers) with the very strictest discipline on parade and in the field.

I was "on the square" three months myself, and had to be word-perfect in the training manual, as well as wholly conversant with every detail of drill, before being allowed to handle men.

Needless to say, smartness in word of command and personal appearance was absolutely essential. To indicate with what insistence this latter important aspect of an officer's education was impressed upon subalterns who had the honour of serving in His Majesty's Guards, I remember my captain, Christie-Miller, who was a very strict disciplinarian, sending me off parade one day to change my boots, because one of the heels was slightly worn down!

The adjutant was Captain Vaughan, nicknamed "Little Man," who was afterwards killed in the War. He was a tremendous martinet with inexhaustible energy and a lynx-eye for any laxness on the part of junior officers. Nothing except perfection would satisfy him, and we all liked him for it.

As a matter of fact, I have always been fairly efficient where absolutely practical matters are concerned, and I think that, in a comparatively short space of time, under the stern and unrelenting supervision of Captain Vaughan and aided by a certain natural gift that way, I became tolerably capable as regards the initial duties of a young officer. Our Colonel, The Hon. W. Lambton, at any rate seemed fairly pleased with me except, I am bound to say, on one occasion when I was reported to him by my Company Commander, and got in consequence a tremendous "telling off". I had been ordered to read a selected portion of "Field Service Regulations," and then in order that they should acquire some elementary notions of the principles of strategy and tactics, to lecture on it to the men of the Company. Now, extracting information out of books has never exactly been a hobby of mine; and those acquainted with the masterly military work just referred to will perhaps agree with me that, whilst reading it, the attention is apt to wander.

A fortnight was given me to prepare this lecture, but despite all attempts to study the particular passages on which I was destined to instruct the Company, after reading a few sentences, my mind invariably began to waver and lose grip and my eyes would soon shut in a refreshing doze.

When the allotted fortnight had all too swiftly expired, and the moment came when I must stand up in front of rows of soldiers perfectly drilled to silence, my mind was as completely blank as it had been fourteen days before. In order to carry off the situation, I was obliged to read to my audience a page or two of "Field Service Regulations" in all their naked sublimity, and after two minutes of this improvisation Captain Christie-Miller in a voice of thunder told me to stop and sit down.

After the close of the 1909 Autumn Manœuvres in Berkshire, the battalion moved to winter quarters in the Tower of London.

I find, by the way, in my collection of Press cuttings, a description of these manœuvres by that famous journalist and war-correspondent Robert Blatchford—most interesting in view of later events. Mr. Blatchford had only just returned from witnessing the manœuvres in Germany, and in this article he draws comparisons between the two armies, in which our own emerges with much credit.

As a soldier of a previous generation, Mr. Blatchford notes the vast improvement made in the personnel during thirty years or so:

"The old country isn't played out yet," he exclaims, and seeing the 1st Grenadier Guards and the 1st Coldstream Guards coming in after a march of twenty-five miles with their chins up, singing, adds: "there was not a single *canteen* face amongst the men! They looked fine and fit. There were no stragglers, no passengers in the carts; not a lame duck amongst them. They seemed to me absolutely first-class infantry, much better soldiers than the men of the *seventies*. They look more intelligent, more alert, keener at their work, and steadier men too. As for the officers, they are also evidently much improved since my time. They seem more business-like and more in earnest. On the whole I was very much encouraged and reassured by what I saw to-day."

It did not, however, need Mr. Robert Blatchford (valuable as his opinions from long experience were) to tell me that the 1st Battalion Coldstream Guards was a magnificent battalion. Casual and unreflecting as I was, in many ways, at that early age, association with such splendid men and with such good comrades and fine officers as Percy Wyndham, David Bingham, Humphrey de Trafford, Francis Gore-Langton, Byng Hopwood, Jack Brand, and others, fired me with genuine ambition to be one of the zealous young officers of whom this well-known journalist penned his praise.

I hope, therefore, my readers will not think it inconsistent with this last confession if I admit that, during my earliest soldiering days, the love of pleasure was not totally extinguished by my desire to do well in the regiment. As the famous educational authorities who supervised (sometimes vainly) my school and university career observed, I was born with great physical strength, a most robust constitution almost insensible to fatigue, the highest of spirits and a superabundance of energy. That these gifts of Nature might sometimes have been employed by me more profitably in other ways cannot be denied, but I had, at any rate, one advantage over my fellow-mortals which, indeed, I still retain to a considerable extent—the need of very little sleep. I can do with five hours or so and wake up in the morning feeling perfectly fit, even now; and when I was twenty-one and for many years after that, one or two hours a night for quite a long period did not seem to hurt me. So while the battalion was at Aldershot, going up to London nearly every evening in the week and coming down again just in time for parade next morning had no appreciably damaging effect either on my general health or capacity to carry out my duties. When, in the late autumn, we moved to the Tower it might be thought that our nearer approximation to the ballrooms of Mayfair (to which, in that happy period of time, there were generally two or three invitations a night awaiting a young officer), or to other slightly more Bohemian entertainments in the West End, might have induced me to take a longer and more regular ration of sleep. As a matter of fact, the contrary was the case. It was a hectic life, but I do not remember being any the worse for it, or ever feeling my spirits flag. My brother-subalterns were a most gay lot, and together we kept the ball rolling quite happily.

On one occasion, I remember, two of us by a stroke of bad luck had to be on guard and picket at the Tower on Christmas night. As, however, several other young brother-officers living in barracks were also in London and (or so we imagined) all the senior officers were naturally on leave, we resolved to celebrate Christmas in the Tower in quite a new and original fashion. It is, I presume, fairly generally known that male friends are sometimes invited to lunch and dinner at the Officers' Mess in the Tower, but on this occasion we subalterns having decided to extend our hospitality somewhat more widely, asked some half-dozen lovely members of the opposite sex from the Gaiety chorus to brighten our evening. Christmas night arrived; the time-worn stairs, the grim old walls echoed to the peals of feminine laughter and the rustle of the most exquisite frocks of the period, whilst our young and sprightly guests were welcomed and made at home by my brother-officers and myself in all the glory of full mess-kit. The waiters drew back the chairs, and we sat down to the festive meal. The champagne circulated briskly, eyes gleamed more brightly, and those who had been merely acquaintances at first, under the influence of the shaded lights and the whispered compliments of their neighbours, very quickly became more than friendly. But just as the fun was growing fast and furious, who should suddenly open the door of the ante-room and stand there for a moment rooted to the spot with amazement, but one of our senior officers who, after all, had not gone on leave as we expected! Only for a moment or two he gazed at our party, and then, hardly knowing what to do, retired to his own bedroom. But opening that door also, he found two members of the party who had recently preceded him thither and were now clasped together in an affectionate embrace. After this our evening ended abruptly. The next morning we were all run in before the Colonel, and confined to barracks for a fortnight. Unofficially, however, I believe he would have liked to have been at our dinner himself.

One of the earliest and most impressive ceremonials in which it was my privilege and honour, as an officer in the Guards, to take part, was the lying-in-state of His late Majesty King Edward VII in Westminster Hall, May 1910.

As a matter of fact, I nearly missed it. A day or two before, having severely torn some muscles playing cricket, the doctor strongly advised me not to exercise my leg in any way till the injury was somewhat healed. To carry out his advice would have meant missing my part in such an historic event, and I determined, despite the pain any movement caused me, to carry on.

The King's coffin lay in Westminster Hall, surmounted by the Royal Regalia and flanked by massive candelabra. All the Household Regiments (the Horse Guards, the Life-Guards and the four regiments of Foot-Guards) took it in turn to mount Guard over His Majesty's body, and the period of duty for each officer was for half an hour in each hour-and-a-half. During these thirty minutes one had to remain absolutely motionless like a statue, with the head bowed and the hands resting on one's drawn sword. In my case, this attitude of unrelieved tension was productive, long before my period of duty terminated, of an almost unbearable pain which, however, I luckily managed to stick out. As a much-prized memento of this solemn and historic scene, I have the portrait of His Majesty King Edward VII which His present Majesty signed and presented to all the officers who took part in the ceremony.

It is worthy of record that while I was mounting guard over the King's body in the small hours of the morning a terrific thunderstorm burst over London. Through the high narrow windows of the time-honoured hall the lightning flashes glared and glanced without intermission, while tremendous peals of thunder crackled and volleyed seemingly just above its venerable roof. This gigantic storm, combined with the solemn duty on which one was engaged, was a really awe-inspiring experience. Had one been able to go forward a few years and become aware that the death of King Edward was the close of an epoch; and had one known that so many evils and such great changes were to be so soon let loose upon the world; one might well have believed in listening to the storm that night, that it was in some way connected with the disappearance of so potent and loved a personality, and a portent of woes to come.

The Brigade, of course, had a great deal of their time occupied in ceremonial duties of all kinds; lining the streets of London on the occasion of State Processions; mounting guard at Buckingham Palace, St. James's Palace, and Windsor Castle; attendance at Courts and Levees, and so on. To a young officer such as I then was, there was no doubt something particularly inspiring on these occasions in the fact of serving in such close personal attendance on the Sovereign, and in being in command (even in a lowly capacity) of such perfectly trained, perfectly disciplined, and perfectly turned-out troops. No one can savour the real pomp and circumstance of military life who has not marched along the Mall carrying the Colour between rows of admiring spectators, while with glittering arms and in faultless alignment the bear-skinned and scarlet-tunicked ranks kept step and time to the crash and thunderous music of the band. Duties such as these, it might be thought, would have handicapped the Brigade as a whole on field exercises in comparison with other regiments which were naturally able to work oftener as complete units. Their training and discipline, however, enabled them to overcome all difficulties on such occasions. I remember well the 1912 interdivisional manoeuvres which took place over a large area of the Eastern Counties. The 1st Coldstream Guards were in the 4th Guards Brigade, composed besides ourselves of the 2nd and 3rd Grenadier Guards and 2nd Coldstream Guards, and commanded by that great soldier now Field-Marshal the Earl of Cavan. The divisional commander was Major-General H. M. Lawson. The idea was that our division represented a raiding force moving from the direction of the Wash in Norfolk upon the flank of a mythical Brown Army marching into the Midlands. The flank guard to the Brown Army was the 2nd Division, which it was our object to defeat and drive back. The weather was very wet, and we spent some days under canvas in a large camp at Swaffham, which resembled a lake more than a camp. On our approach to the field of battle we were soaked to the skin again, so much so that an attaché from the Japanese Imperial Staff expressed his admiration and amazement that the men remained so cheerful, willing and effective in the face of such discouragements. The actual day of the battle, which took place in the region of Brandon and Mildenhall, was fine enough. Under the eagle eye of the Director of Operations, Sir Douglas Haig, a very spirited engagement was fought between the 1st and 2nd Divisions which, as far as I remember, ended in a draw.

I believe that, on the outbreak of war two years later in 1914, both those famous Field-Marshals, the late Earl Haig and the late Earl Roberts, advocated a manoeuvre such as we practised that autumn in 1912, but by that time the British Army was committed to a frontal attack on the advancing Germans.

OFFICERS OF THE FIRST BATTALION, COLDSTREAM GUARDS

M. BECKWITH SMITH, R. BEWICKE-COPLEY, R. ARKWRIGHT, L. H. TENNYSON

R. CLUTTERBUCK, J. WYNNE FINCH, LORD PETRE, R. ROWLEY, L. M. GIBBS, F. GORE LANGTON, J. SOMERS-COCKS, J. BOURNE MAY

CAPT. J. E. VAUGHAN, CAPT. MAITLAND, CAPT. MACGREGOR, MAJOR THE EARL OF LANESBOROUGH, COL. H. G. SUTTON, D. BINGHAM (*Adjutant*), CAPT. J. CAMPBELL, CAPT. J. E. GIBBS, CAPT. E. CHRISTIE-MILLER

[Image credit:] *J. Russell & Sons*

THE AUTHOR CARRYING THE COLOUR

[Image credit:] *Mrs. Albert Broom*

Let me now say a word or two concerning some of my brother-officers in the Coldstream and the Brigade of Guards.

One of my greatest friends, as he is still, was Sir Humphrey de Trafford. His wife before her marriage was Cynthia Cadogan, sister of Lady Stanley, Lady Hillingdon, and Lady Blandford. It would be impossible to find four more delightful sisters. They have always been most kind and hospitable to me, although they have constantly tried to "pull my leg." Humphrey de Trafford joined the Brigade two years after myself, and quickly made his mark as an unusually capable officer and a remarkably fine horseman. He won the Household Brigade Cup at Hawthorn Hill on more than one occasion, as well as many other steeplechases in various parts of the country. His mother, the late Lady de Trafford, whom a former generation considered one of the most beautiful women of her time, was like a second mother to me. Their house in Portland Place was always open to myself to dine or stay, and she was one of the most loyal friends a young man in London could have. Her second son, Rudolph, is also a particular friend of mine. He has great business ability, and is now a partner in Higginson's bank. Other friends in the Regiment were Percy Wyndham and David Bingham, handsomest and best-dressed of men. Their good looks were the outward sign of a dauntless mind and resolute will. Even in peace time all men and women recognized their quality. They were killed early on in the Great War, but their names will never be forgotten in the Regiment.

General Crawley de Crespigny, Grenadier Guards, was somewhat senior to myself, being a captain when I first joined. He was a good horseman and rode in and won many races. He was one of the most renowned officers in the Brigade during the war, and his name was a household word on the Western Front for gallantry and skill in commanding men. There was no man who would not follow him, or who did not have implicit faith in his leadership. If ever a man deserved the Victoria Cross, Crawley de Crespigny did. He has since then earned considerable fame as a big-game hunter in East Africa.

Another very gallant officer and horseman of my time was Colonel George Paynter of the Scots Guards. The night he won the Grand Military Race at Sandown he gave a great party at Princes Restaurant to which I was invited. The most beautiful ladies of the stage were there, and everybody became very happy. The climax of the evening was when a raid was made on the band, who defended their instruments stoutly. In attempting to seize the big drum on which I have for many years fancied myself as a performer, I remember, in the rough and tumble that ensued, having it smashed down over my head, to the consternation of the drummer.

————————

There will be a word or two in a later chapter about my own cricket whilst with the Brigade, but before passing on to this I should like to mention a few very good cricketers with whom I served in the Guards between 1909 and 1913. In 1911 the Household Brigade had the most successful year known hitherto in their annals. A glance into such of the cricket records of that period as happen to be in my possession shows that the Guardsmen do seem to have made exceptionally large scores, even granting the excellence of the wicket and the comparatively small size of the ground at Burton's Court, Chelsea.

Our matches were against the I Zingari, the Butterflies, the Eton Ramblers, the Green Jackets, Old Wykehamists, Harrow

77

Blues, M.C.C. and Free Foresters, schools like Harrow and Winchester; and other regiments.

Scores of three and four hundred in an innings were then often made by the Brigade, and sometimes we made even over five hundred, while numerous centuries were scored by individual batsmen. The side had, in fact, an exceptionally fine array of really first-class players, nearly all of whom, before joining, had figured prominently in Eton Elevens of the past dozen years. One of the best batsmen and a most prolific scorer was Colonel Lord Francis Scott. He was several years older than myself but a great personal friend, and we played much cricket together. Francis was very badly wounded in the war. After it was over, he and his wife, a daughter of the late Lord Minto, went out to Kenya, where they have lived ever since.

Another very fine cricketer from a famous cricketing family was the Hon. A. E. Mulholland, who was killed in the war. P. Pearson-Gregory and T. Curtis also scored freely for the Brigade, as well as Ralph Cavendish and Colonel Guy Edwards. The late Capt. Payne-Gallwey was our best bowler, who in his time took numbers of wickets. What splendid fun those Brigade matches were!

I plead guilty to having always enjoyed personally the publicity of County and International Cricket, the exciting and tense atmosphere associated with them, and the stir and enthusiasm of applauding crowds, but for sheer pleasure and for playing good cricket on the result of which too much did not depend, these Brigade Matches among friends in the days before the war were the most enjoyable.

Colonel J. N. Horlick, who was in my regiment and another very fine Brigade cricketer, reminds me that perhaps I did not always take the cricket at Burton's Court very seriously. According to his story I arrived on the ground one day five minutes before the opening of the game, not having shaved or been to bed at all. Our skipper, Guy Edwards, who had been busily practising at the nets for half an hour or more, was perfectly furious, and said that this was the last time I should represent the Brigade. Unfortunately, however, after having won the toss he was bowled first ball, and I made 170 in an hour and a half. I still, therefore, curiously enough, retained my place in the side!

CHAPTER IX

SOME QUAINT EPISODES

THE great houses of London, as they existed in pre-war days, are now only a memory to the middle-aged like myself. Stafford House, where I often went as a young man in London, has become a museum. Devonshire House, the scene of so many sumptuous balls and festivities, has vanished altogether. Throughout Mayfair and all through the West End, for night after night during the London season, hospitable doors were open wide till the small hours of the morning; champagne flowed like water; and the most beautiful girls in England came to be danced with. Life can, I think, never have been pleasanter or gayer in the whole history of the world than in those days just before the war, if one was young and resolved to enjoy oneself. A few short years—and then the large majority of the young men who danced and supped and laughed so light-heartedly were lying still on the battlefields of France, Flanders and Gallipoli. A year or two more, and the enormous increase of taxation had swept away the whole scheme of things which made such hospitality possible. Not in our own time, and perhaps never again in our history, will there be a class that can afford to spend money so generously on the mere process of entertaining their friends.

It is, I know, the fashion amongst those who write their memoirs for an indulgent public, to supply a list of the important and interesting persons they met in the period of Society that they adorned. It suits me better, however, as this is by way of being an unconventional record of an unconventional life, to tell a story or two, not of the friends and acquaintances I made in the great world, but of how I unfortunately made one or two enemies or (rather more accurately) impaired one or two friendships in a way that, if one looks back on it, was not devoid of humour.

I was one evening at a ball at Derby House. There was a big crowd there that night, including the loveliest girls in London. Loveliest of them all, perhaps, was Violet de Trafford, renowned for her classical Greek features, flawless complexion, and graceful carriage. She had, though still very young, inflamed the hearts of numberless admirers, many of whom were at the ball that night. It was, therefore, quite a difficult matter to secure a dance with her, but—such was my good fortune—I succeeded in getting one.

"I'm lucky to get a dance with you this evening, Vi," said I, as I captured her from a whole horde of dancing men.

"It *was* our dance, I suppose, Lionel?"

"Of course it was. Do you suppose I would say so, if it wasn't?"

By this time we had got about three-quarters of the way round the room; the floor was crowded, and progress was slow. As we came more or less to a standstill, I was aware of someone regarding me with a look of overpowering indignation. The next instant a large and bearded individual came over towards us, and said in a very authoritative and slightly foreign accent:

"This is my dance with Violet."

"Your dance," replied I. "Certainly not."

"I say it *is* my dance," exclaimed the bearded person again, looking extremely angry. "I have engaged it with Violet at the beginning of the evening."

"And I," said I, "engaged it two days ago. Didn't I, Vi?"

"There is such a crowd here, I may have got mixed," replied Vi looking very upset.

"How," said I, turning again to the foreign gentleman, "do you expect to keep your dances with a girl everyone wants to dance with, if you don't go and wait your turn at the end of the room like other people? After the difficulty I had in getting this one, I'm not going to give it up for you or anyone else."

"I tell you it is *my* dance," he began once more, but by this time my partner and I were moving on again and out of earshot.

"Who on earth was that old blighter, Vi?" asked I, when we reached the other side of the room.

My partner did not reply at once, and on looking at her I saw that she was in fits of laughter. When, at length, she had recovered herself sufficiently to inform me of the name of the elderly gentleman I had "told off" so unmercifully and deprived of his dance, I discovered somewhat to my own confusion that he was a famous foreign Royalty.

Lord Petre was a subaltern in my regiment. After I had been in the Coldstream about two years, Petre "The Painter" as he was called after the chief actor in the notorious Sydney Street affair (though I need hardly say without any personal application), became engaged to Miss Kitty Boscawen. There was no reason for delaying the matrimonial ceremony, as he was very well off; so the happy pair were married at the end of the season, and Petre was kind enough to ask me to be his best man, which important office I fulfilled to the best of my ability.

On their return from the honeymoon, which coincided with the opening of the hunting season, they asked me down to stay with them at Thorndon Park, their country place in Essex. This was an immense house built in the Palladian style of the eighteenth century. It stands high upon an eminence considerably above the level of the surrounding country, and is encircled by a large park several miles in circumference. This park is full of very fine old timber, principally oaks, some of which are of immense antiquity. The ground slopes with a decided fall to the south, and through it runs a broadish winding ditch with sloping banks on either side that drains into a large lake at some distance from the house.

My poor friend Petre was killed in the war only a year or two after he married, and his huge family mansion and park are now the headquarters of the local golfers. Playing round the course a few years ago, I had the opportunity of seeing once more the exact place where the most unlucky adventure I am about to describe took place.

Petre and his lady could not do enough for me when I arrived as their guest. In the first two days we had some first-class shooting in the park; and on the third day of my visit, there was a meet of the local foxhounds on the large gravelled sweep before his front door.

I had brought no horses with me, and was quite prepared either to attend the meet on foot or to try to hire a horse in the neighbouring town. Petre would not, however, hear of either proceeding. He insisted on mounting me.

There was in his stable at the time a very fine animal, nearly thoroughbred, a magnificent jumper and very fast, besides being up to a good deal of weight. Either he had recently bought it to run in point-to-points and steeplechases, or some rich relation had given it him as a wedding present, I forget which.

For the sake of friendship and the part I had played at the wedding, Petre insisted on lending me this horse to ride the morning of the hunt.

His covers were the first to be drawn; there was a big one quite close to the house which had been left undisturbed during the previous two days' shooting. A fox was found at once and broke straight away across the park, crossing the ditch which I have mentioned above at quite a short distance from and in full view of the house, where my lady and some of the other guests who were not hunting stood looking on. Whatever the reason (inexplicable to me then as afterwards) my magnificent chaser blundered in jumping. This ditch was nothing of a place really; and such of the field as happened to be in front of me had negotiated it without the slightest difficulty.

The horse pitched me forward on to the sloping bank on the further side as he came down on his knees, and then himself rolled over.

Quite unhurt, though rather annoyed at being pitched off right at the beginning of the hunt and under the very eyes of my fellow-guests, I was on my feet in an instant and tugging at the rein to pull my mount to his feet again. He lay there like a log, however, and positively refused to move. I shouted and cursed and tugged harder than ever, but devil a bit would the annoying brute budge from the position in which he had fallen.

"What the devil's the matter with the horse?" cried I, not noticing two rustics who had come up at my elbow during these frantic struggles.

"He's dead, sir," said they.

It was too true. In some extraordinary way this priceless animal had broken his neck within two minutes of the fox breaking cover. My friends accepted the whole thing as an unavoidable accident, but still there was a slight coolness. In fact I didn't visit their house again till the day I played golf there many years after the war.

———————

During the time referred to, I went to stay with Lord and Lady de Saumarez at Broke Hall in Suffolk for the shooting. Their son Vincent in the Scots Guards was a friend of mine. It was the last night of my visit, and about half-past eleven. We had played a rubber or two of bridge, the ladies of the party had already gone up to their rooms, and now my host rose and said that he was sleepy and tired after his day's sport, and was going to follow their example.

"Well, Lionel, you've got to go off early in the morning, haven't you?" said he.

"Yes," answered I. "I'm afraid I must catch the early train. Eight o'clock isn't it?"

"All right. I'll send you there in good time: and as I probably shan't see you in the morning, good-bye."

"Good-bye, and ever so many thanks for a very nice time."

"Anyone else for bed?"

The other members of the party announced their readiness, and after more good-byes Vincent and I were left alone.

Now I have never (once up) been very fond of going to bed, and when Vincent suggested one more whisky and soda I was nothing loth. We talked a little, and then as I was not a bit tired I said:

"I'll play you a game of billiard-fives, Vincent."

"Oh no you won't," replied he. "Father would have a fit if we played fives on our table."

"That's all right," replied I, "he won't ever know. He's sound asleep and snoring by now."

"Yes—he is," said Vincent, "but still . . . ."

"One game couldn't possibly hurt the table, do it good on the other hand, I expect—harden up the cushions a bit. If they weren't so soft the balls wouldn't keep on sticking under them as they do."

"Do you really think so?" asked Vincent.

"I know it," said I. "Come on then! Just one game."

"All right, but mind, Lionel, no hard hitting! Father would be mad if he found we'd been playing at all."

"Play you for a fiver," said I.

Playing billiard-fives without hitting hard is many times more difficult than sparring with a man and not irritating him occasionally with a blow that he considers has too much weight behind it. Vincent and I started mildly enough, but as first one got ahead and then the other, our strokes got more and more vicious till I eventually won the game with an absolute fizzer that went into the pocket with a bang like a cannon-shot.

"Here, I say, Lionel, steady!" exclaimed Vincent.

"Well," said I, "it was no harder than the last one of yours. It nearly knocked the top off my fingers trying to stop it." And then the usual argument began and lasted quite a considerable time.

"Well, I'm going to get my fiver back," said Vincent. "Gosh! This fives does make me thirsty. Wait a minute, Lionel. I'll just get the whisky and soda from the library and we'll have a drink. Then I'll play you again."

"Righto," said I.

Our thirst appeased, we started another game, this time without any camouflage about soft hitting. The ball hummed up and down the table, our hands ached, the pockets rattled as our returns rocketed in, and this time Vincent won.

"Good Lord! It's after one," said he, mopping his brow. "I knew I could get that fiver back. One more drink and we'll go to bed!"

"We simply must have a conqueror," I replied. "There's plenty of time."

"Well, you're getting up, not me."

So we had the conqueror and I won, and then another and I won again.

"Here, I believe you've got the best side," said he. "Change over."

It was now about three o'clock in the morning. Except squash rackets, high-speed billiard-fives is the hottest and most exhausting pastime ever devised by man. We had played about half-a-dozen games on end, hitting as hard as we could and running like madmen to intercept each other's shots; and in consequence to quench our outrageous thirst we had got outside quite a respectable number of stiffish whiskies and sodas. Our brains therefore were not so cool, nor were our bumps of caution so much in evidence as earlier in the evening. The play now became positively fast and furious and the most desperate shots were attempted and frequently successful. In trying to cut off one of Vincent's most powerful blows and get an outright winner myself, I committed the unforgivable sin at billiard-fives and did a "scoop." The ball rose from the table and flew into the shadows at the end of the room with dramatic swiftness.

"My God, Lionel," cried Vincent, "mind the mirror!"

Hardly was this agonized cry out of his mouth, than it was drowned by an appalling crash and fragments of glass came flying into the room.

"Now," said Vincent, with an expression of awe, "you *have* done it."

There was no doubt about it. I *had*. The mirror that this unlucky "scoop" had smashed was about six feet high and twelve feet long, and composed of very valuable glass. In such a position as mine the most experienced and most tactful man in the world might well have been at a loss. What was to be done? . . . After half an hour's debate which brought the time to nearly five o'clock in the morning, I decided that the only possible thing was to take all the blame on my shoulders, approach my host the next morning after deferring my start, and offer to make whatever restitution he would accept. This was, no doubt, all very well and the only thing to be done, but when seven o'clock came—the hour at which it was arranged I should be called—in spite of all my unusual capacity for doing without sleep, I arose and dressed in an absolute daze. All recollection of what had happened during the night had temporarily escaped me. I ate my breakfast, drove to the station, and got into the train still much more asleep than awake. Once there I fell into a really profound slumber and did not wake up again till the collector came for my ticket at the next station to the London terminus. . . . Then, suddenly, I remembered everything, and that after all I had gone away from the house without apologizing or even mentioning to my host what had happened.

There was only one thing to be done—to write now. So down I sat at the earliest possible moment pen in hand and began to cudgel my brains as to what to say. The longer I sat, however, the more impossible it seemed to write the letter with even a passable account of our behaviour. At last, after making four or five attempts and tearing them up, I decided the task was impossible and never wrote at all.

How Vincent explained the reason of this gigantic and priceless mirror being broken I don't know, but strange to say I was never asked to the house again.

CHAPTER X

IN 1911, two years after my entry into the Coldstream as a probationary officer, I passed the examination for a permanent commission. When the result was communicated by the War Office I was much pleased to find my name at the top of the list of candidates.

To show that this was not entirely a fluke, however, I set down here a copy of my confidential report, 10th October 1911, from Lt.-Col. H. C. Sutton, who was now commanding the 1st Battalion Coldstream Guards.

> "This officer has greatly improved. Has energy and self-reliance. A good horseman and fond of sport. Is popular with all ranks. Takes pains at training. Requires to read up his books more and take his duties somewhat more seriously. Is rather inclined to be too contented with his efforts.
>
> "There is, however, no reason why he should not make a very good officer."

The pity of it all was that a year was hardly out before I left the regiment. I will now explain how this came about.

The confidential report given above states that I was fond of sport. This was no more than the truth, and at that time of my life I devoted every spare minute to the joys of horse and hound. Starting in a smallish way by hunting with the Household Brigade Drag and the Garth when on duty in London during the winter of 1909–1910, I was not satisfied for long with such a modest taste of the supreme delights of fox-hunting but, pining for the real thing and the cream of the country, took a small hunting-box in Warwickshire from Ronnie Holbeach, which I shared for two seasons with my second cousin Ulick Alexander, also in the Coldstream. By now I had four or five pretty good horses, and not having attained my present size, in those days could easily ride 12 stone. I used to get up in a lot of point-to-points, and in 1911 often acted as second whip to the Household Brigade Drag, the master being Captain Byng Hopwood, a fine and fearless horseman, afterwards killed in the war. Some of my best horses were "Zulu," "Doctrine," "The Ferret," "Togo

IV" and "Sunstar II." I came in second and third on "Togo IV" and "The Ferret" in several cross-country races, and represented the regiment in the Household Brigade point-to-point which the Coldstream won the two years I rode, four officers being selected to ride from each regiment. I was very unlucky not to win the Coldstream Plate at Hawthorn Hill on "Togo IV" in 1911. When well ahead, he came down at the last fence, breaking my collarbone. The race was won by "Noble Roy" belonging to Captain Banbury, who afterwards won the Grand Military on the same horse. Mr. G. Lambton's "Suffolk" was second. "The Ferret" had a mouth like iron, and I was generally a quarter of a mile ahead in the first mile. I think the race I enjoyed most, and in which I rode every year, was the open race of the Berks and Bucks Staghounds. In this I once finished third.

[Image credit:] *Sport & General*

[Image credit:] *J. Russell & Sons*

Now the hiring of hunting-boxes, the purchase of the best oats and hay, wages to grooms, boxing horses, and all the other expenditure connected with the grand sport of fox-hunting, especially in countries like the cream of Warwickshire, where a horse must be able to gallop and jump, undoubtedly costs a good deal of money. Moreover, if, like young Lochinvar in the ballad, I was fond of the chase, like him also I was "no laggard in love." A succession of lovely ladies held first place in my heart, and towards them all in turn I was far too generous. It is not to be wondered at that before long I began to find myself somewhat embarrassed financially.

Before I joined the Coldstream, my father had written to Colonel Maxse on the subject of a suitable allowance. The Colonel had replied that a young officer should never have a superfluity of cash, and should be made to calculate what everything would cost him. He therefore named £400 a year as probably the right amount. My father, indeed, did better than Colonel Maxse suggested and allowed me £500 a year.

Ah! If I had always been able throughout life to calculate what everything would cost me, my days would have been somewhat easier. The only fact that is certain is that I have never been able to calculate what anything would cost me, and that a superfluity of cash is exactly what I have always needed. Some people are able from earliest youth to reconcile themselves to doing without the things they want. I, on the other hand, have always resolutely determined not to be poor. When, therefore, I discovered that £500 a year plus £200 pay and allowances as a subaltern in His Majesty's Guards was insufficient to defray all these expenses, I thought the best plan would be to augment my income by a little judicious betting on race-courses. This discovery had all the simple majesty of a great idea. After all, the best ideas are the oldest, and why should I turn up my nose at this one because similar methods have been used by persons in similar circumstances since the beginning of time? As a matter of fact, I do not suppose the pros and cons of the idea ever entered my head at all, and the whole operation seemed dead easy.

Dead easy it was too! My readers can hardly imagine how easy—in the beginning. The goddess of Fortune seemed to have fallen in love with me, or at any rate heartily to sympathize with me for being in want of a few hundreds a year to lead the kind of life I particularly wanted to lead. I had only to take up a hand at cards for aces and trumps to tumble into it; I had only to step on a race course to name my selection and see it romp home first past the post. My natural tendency to optimism therefore was so much increased, that no thought that Fortune might ever desert me crossed my mind.

Little did I know that the treacherous goddess was fooling me to the top of my bent.

Every time I was in want of a few hundred pounds, I remember—during the three or four years that this merry and exciting existence lasted—I would go to Alexandra Park on a Saturday and back the horses of a certain well-known bookmaker of those days—Charlie Hibbert. His horses had a singular knack of winning during the period referred to, and usually started at remunerative odds. The bookmakers I used to bet with most were Ladbroke's, H. Slowburn, Junior, Joe Thompson, Cooper & Rowson, Pickersgill and M'Lean. May I say that in after years when things have not been quite so rosy with me, many of these gentlemen have behaved to me in the most kind and generous way.

At the zenith of my success, when money was coming into my hands in an apparently inexhaustible supply and in the manner, as it were, that oil gushes from the earth in a newly bored well in America, I, of course, went home on leave to Farringford more than once. As I crossed the Solent standing on the little steamer's deck, and saw the picturesque little port of Yarmouth with its red roofs and mediæval castle draw closer and closer; and watched growing clearer the long outline of the Downs on which stood the old poet's monument, with Farringford lying hidden in the trees below, I felt, in very truth, superior to circumstances. Despite my own self-confidence, however, there was a feeling of constraint in the air during these visits home. My father, of course, knew that I hunted and raced, and possibly he had also heard that these were not the only ways in which money slipped through my fingers. It was always, no doubt, running through his head where on earth the money could come from for me to lead a life of this kind. I caught his monocle fixed upon me more than once with a doubtful and gloomy expression; and his manner was often somewhat reserved. He must, surely, have had a feeling in his bones that all his doubts about sending me into the Guards were about to be justified; and that some penalty was in store for allowing himself to be over-persuaded. Heaven knows what fairy tales I concocted at this time in the attempt to pacify his alarms. My mother perhaps believed them, or did not want to disbelieve them (which, in the end, comes to the same thing) but my father I feel sure (though he never said so) did not. Though he lived remote amongst his downs and trees practically from year's end to year's end, he was a shrewd man in essentials, one in fact who never did badly anything he tried to do, and but for a certain mixture of diffidence and indolence in his character might well have done a great deal more. So, being what he was, I think he just gloomily disbelieved and awaited the evil day. It was not, alas! now long in coming.

Playing a little game of roulette one evening I had taken a bit of a knock and lost about £200. As I had more than £5000 in the bank at that moment, and all the more urgent of my bills had been paid up, it was nothing to worry about. The winning vein, however, had been so constant with me of late, that I was faintly irritated and determined to get it all back the next day at Hurst Park—so thither I went.

Tragic events are best recounted as briefly as possible; and it will suffice therefore to say that, by the end of that day's racing at Hurst Park, I had not only not succeeded in recovering my £200, but had lost about another £1000 in addition. At this moment, so far as I recollect, though faintly shocked at such a check having been administered to me, I felt rather as Julius Cæsar or Napoleon must have felt after one of their minor defeats—that is to say, completely confident in the memory of former victories and in the resources at their command, to recover all the ground lost and immediately to put themselves in a stronger position than ever. My next campaign (to pursue the military metaphor) was to be fought at Newbury. There, full of renewed confidence after the disagreeable shocks of the previous days, I arrived. At Newbury the result was even more disastrous than it had been at Hurst Park. At the end of the three days that the meeting lasted, I had lost all the money I had in the bank, and a bit more. My readers may, perhaps, not believe me, but it is a fact that I could hardly credit what had happened. It seemed like a nightmare! Everything had appeared so easy, and now in three or four days the whole of the fruits of my enterprise had been swept away. Could this really have occurred? The gambler's mind is a curious one, and in the intense moments he lives his actions are not to be impartially judged by persons without his temptations. My luck, it seemed to me, had been phenomenally bad. I don't think it occurred to me that to enable me to win so constantly it must previously have been phenomenally good. I simply considered (after what appeared to me as sober reflection) that by perseverance all my losses must be won back again. So now on to Windsor was the cry! On that Thames-side course, however, things went worst of all. I was in the grip of one of those runs of bad luck which every gambler has from time to time and did not pick a single winner, losing in my desperate efforts to right myself even more that I had done at Newbury. In a little over a week, in fact, £12,000 had gone. The inevitable had happened, and instead of my breaking the Ring as I had fondly hoped, the Ring had broken me. £5000 had been to my credit in the Bank before starting operations, but I finished £7000 short, which had to be found before settling day.

This was, in truth, one of the most awful experiences of my life. I had started some weeks before the final crash with comparatively small amounts, but the fact that I had won for so long almost continuously, made me think that I had really discovered some secret about horse-racing not known to the general world of punters. When the luck began to turn against me, I had still thought it only a temporary setback, and then, before the truth became obvious, it was too late to stop.

There were only two courses open to me—money-lenders or my father!

At the age of twenty-two I did not know enough to go to the former. With regard to my father, my readers are by now as well informed as myself about his views of my entering the Guards and his forebodings in this matter. In addition to that, he had a perfect horror of any form of betting. The old poet, of course, had denounced gambling as the canker of civilization and the root of all demoralization, and what the poet said went with my father. He had never, in fact, had a bet of a sixpence in his life either on a card, a horse, or a dog. This was perhaps enough to ensure a stormy interview, but there was more. My father was not niggardly. He could be generous. Nevertheless money meant a good deal to him, and, as I have shown, he shrouded in secrecy from everyone except his lawyers, in what position he stood as a dividend-holder, and lived on a carefully calculated budget. £7000 was a good lump sum of money, disconcerting even for a regular operator in stocks and shares, whereas my father simply lived carefully on investments. Nevertheless—appalling as the prospect was—I had to collect all my courage, go home, and make a clean breast of everything.

The storm was so dreadful—so far worse than anything I could have imagined—that I cannot think how any members of the family (except that human beings, as a general rule, seem able to survive pretty nearly anything) managed to survive it.

My poor mother was in tears. She was always fond of me, too fond of me perhaps, and tried to shield me, in pity, from the wrath that brooded up in the poet's study.

My father, indeed, would speak to no one; muttered incoherent words to himself as he stumped in solitary agony through his shadowy copses or along the foot of his downs: groaned that he had known all along what would happen, that I would be the ruin of him yet.

When the first horrible day or two had passed, another family meeting was summoned and my future fate was debated. Should my gambling debts be paid? Should I be declared a bankrupt? Should I be dispatched as an agricultural asset to Southern Africa or Northern Canada? Should I be taught a real lesson, or was the lesson I had just had real enough? Had I no sense, or if any, how much? In the course of these daily debates there arrived letters from my Colonel and about sixty of my brother-officers in the Brigade, asking my father to keep me in the regiment and give me another chance. This he was adamant in refusing to do. One other thing, however, he determined on at last, namely, to keep as high as ever the honour of the family name. The bookmakers were all paid. Moreover, the letters from my brother-officers influenced him in thinking that I must have something in me as a soldier. But no return to the Guards! I should go, as he had always wished, into the Rifle Brigade.

CHAPTER XI

MY TRANSFER TO THE RIFLE BRIGADE: AND FIRST CRICKET TOUR
IN SOUTH AFRICA

THE 1st Battalion, The Rifle Brigade, was then at Colchester and commanded by Colonel Biddulph. My father's idea was that I should join it pending transfer to the Battalion then at Dagshai in India. After I had been a month with my new regiment (about which, of course, much will be said later on) I found Colonel Biddulph distinctly averse to the idea of parting with me as soon as had been intended. The officers of the Battalion were extremely nice to me from the first day, and I felt thoroughly at home, and having a good knowledge of drill, although the Rifle Brigade drill is different to the Guards drill, I was able to justify my existence. My prowess as a cricketer may also have influenced the Colonel's views. So in the 1st Battalion I stayed.

Now let me say something as to how I came to be known as a player of our national game after modest beginnings. At Eton and Cambridge for some strange reason (possibly because I had really laid the foundations of my game as a boy in Australia, and was for a long time at sea on wet wickets) I never fulfilled my early promise. As soon as I joined the Coldstream, however, whatever was lacking in my batsmanship before suddenly seemed to develop. I scored heaps of runs for the Brigade in army and club cricket during 1911 and 1912, my batting average being 45 and 61 respectively in these two years, and my highest score 258 not out against the I Zingari.

Naturally, with a reputation to keep up as an army cricketer, and not wishing to belittle Colonel Biddulph's faith in me after his kindness in retaining me in the Home Battalion, I was anxious to do my utmost for the regiment in cricket as well as at hockey, football and military duties. Club and country-house cricket was then in full swing all the summer throughout the country, and a large number of amateurs could afford to play for their counties during the season. Cricket was *the* summer spectacle with no competition from dog-racing and dirt-track riding, and a successful young cricketer was a little god in the eyes of a very large section of the population. The opening months of the season of 1913 showed that my success in army cricket during the two previous years had been no flash in the pan, and I continued to score fifties and centuries. One day—a red-letter day in my life!—to be precise 16th June 1913, I had a card from Sir F. E.

Lacey, Secretary of the M.C.C., asking me to play against Oxford University on July 3, 4, 5 at Lord's. There was no difficulty about getting leave from the regiment, and so to Lord's I went.

The match in which I had been invited to play was the last of Oxford's Trial Matches before they met Cambridge, and in consequence a fine array of cricket pundits of all ages were gathered in the pavilion to note rising talent and criticize the play. The M.C.C. side was supposed to be somewhat weak, and Oxford to have an excellent chance of winning the match, as they had a bowler of really high class in B. G. von Melle, a South African Rhodes scholar. In this match I went in first and scored 28 and 110 in the second innings (the latter in 100 minutes). I had some luck, it is true, being missed three times (Dame Fortune was beginning to be tired of having treated me so roughly); but despite what the cricket reporters call "blemishes" my innings pleased all the critics. At the end of the game I was invited to play for Hampshire, and, barring the interval of the war years, have played for that county ever since.

It was the beginning of July when I took part in my first match in first-class cricket, and by the end of the month I had become famous, as one journalist put it, "from Castle to Taproom." The journalists indeed did run riot a bit with their pens in describing me and my cricket. Here are some of the epithets I inspired. I was called "a Star," "a Meteor," "a Bombshell," "another Jessop," "the famous grandson of a famous grandsire," "the maker of cricket-poems," "the greatest army bat since Teddy Wynyard," "a polished and scientific hitter," "the marvellous Etonian," "the Hampshire prodigy" and dozens of other terms and phrases all in the highest key of superlatives.

Here is a list of my performances for the aforesaid month which were responsible for such praise in the Press.

M.C.C. v. Oxford University	28	and 110
Hants v. Worcester	28	
Hants v. Essex	38	and 116
Hants v. Notts	111	and 4
Hants v. Yorkshire	96	and 19

Total = 550 runs; 9 completed innings; average 61. The number of runs scored in so short a time was, indeed, more than respectable, but that, in itself, was not all. Did not my old friend and colleague, Philip Mead, alone score 8 centuries for the county that year? The real thing was that I was a novelty, with the happy knack (not always possessed by better cricketers than myself) of playing cricket as if I enjoyed it and hitting the ball hard and often. To this my temperament (which, when it errs, errs on the side of confidence) contributed, perhaps, not a little, whereas not a few fine cricketers when introduced to first-class games are immediately seized with mental cramp and cannot play in their natural style. At any rate, Press and spectators were "tickled to death." The evening papers "featured" me day after day as "the Laureate's amazing grandson"; Jack Hobbs was complimentary enough to rank me high amongst the leading amateurs; and telegrams and letters of congratulation followed me about in shoals. As was to be expected, considering my name and ancestry, the poets themselves had a go—though to judge from their verses they were, perhaps, not in the highest flights of their profession. I set down here, as a matter of interest, one of these effusions which was more remarkable for enthusiasm than for art.

There's a sound of smiting, smiting,
    Willow clumping leathern pill—
Hark! the noisy crowd delighting
    In fierce lusty strokes that thrill.
Do you hear it? Loud and shrill;
    For spectators love the fun,
And their joy they cannot still,
    Furnished by a Tennyson.

When a man is fighting, fighting,
    'Gainst great odds adverse, until
Fate's harsh balance he is righting
    Making warmth where once was chill,
Making safety of peril;
    Then all gloomy thoughts we shun,
Sweetest strains our bosoms fill,
    And we bless our Tennyson.

When a bard is writing, writing,
  With an all too-feeble quill,
Much he feels that he's inditing
  Lines of which some may think ill,
  Quite a feeble squeaky trill.
Then his lyric word he's plighting
  'Tis the best that can be done,
For ballades would test the skill
  Of a Laureate Tennyson.

Princes put him on the grill,
  Blow him from a Maxim-gun,
But his homage you can't kill
  For a Hampshire Tennyson.

I kept up my form to the end of the season (during which I played 19 innings) and finished fifth in the all-England batting averages with an average of 45.22.

Germany was sharpening her sword; the Balkans were seething with hatred, intrigue, corruption, and bloodshed; big trouble was brewing in Ireland; and distant ripples of the maelstrom which was so soon to convulse the world were already touching the shores of England. All this, however, at that time meant nothing to cricketers, or to the tens of thousands who followed their fortunes. The only question, now the season was ending, was as to who should represent the old country in South Africa during the coming winter. Several of the newspapers, in view of my "meteoric rise to fame," were suggesting that I myself should be chosen. I had, personally, no expectation of such an honour, but whilst on autumn manœuvres in Buckinghamshire with my regiment, after which I was specially complimented by the General for my work as Transport Officer, a telegram arrived from Lord's inviting me to accompany the M.C.C. side abroad. Another soldier-cricketer and wicket-keeper, D. C. Robinson, had also been invited, and the War Office very generously gave us two soldiers leave of absence to play in international cricket overseas.

Before I set down the names of the rest of the team, let me here say something about the Captain, my old friend the late J. W. H. T. Douglas. Famed as boxer, footballer, and all-round cricketer, he was even more remarkable for his indomitable determination and dauntless courage either on the cricket-field or in sterner contests. Johnny literally never knew when he was beaten. This trait, though there is no space for them here, was the source of many anecdotes about him, some very quaint and amusing, but far more of them inspiring. He was in very truth a great Englishman, loyal in every inch of his tough frame, and unquenchable in spirit. His end was as fine as his life had been. My readers will no doubt remember how he perished in the wreck of the S.S. *Oberon* in the North Sea, while attempting to save his old father.

Enough for the present of Johnny, though I shall have more to say of him later.

The rest of the team were a formidable combination, as these names will show:—

J. W. H. T. Douglas (Essex)
Hon. L. H. Tennyson (Hants)
M. C. Bird (Surrey)
D. C. Robinson (Gloucestershire)
M. W. Booth (Yorkshire)
W. Rhodes (Yorkshire)
C. P. Mead (Hants)
F. E. Woolley (Kent)
A. E. Relf (Sussex)
J. B. Hobbs (Surrey)
H. Strudwick (Surrey)
J. W. Hearne (Middlesex)
S. F. Barnes (Staffordshire)

This selection was somewhat criticized at home, not on the score of merit, because few more powerful teams have left these shores and the South Africans were believed to be weak, but on account of their number being only thirteen, and therefore somewhat at the mercy of casualties. The superstitious may be interested to note that ill-luck beyond the average *did* pursue the team. Robinson was taken so seriously ill on reaching the Cape that he had to return immediately to England, and was replaced by "Tiger" Smith of Warwickshire. Hobbs was ill all the voyage out, and never in the best of health during the tour. Jack Hearne was laid up in South Africa for several weeks. Barnes was never really well, though he bowled like a demon. Strudwick was sometimes unable to keep wicket and Bird had to deputize for him before the arrival of "Tiger" Smith: while he, Hobbs and Booth had a terrible motor smash from which, though they emerged with painful injuries, they were very lucky to escape with their lives.

By the way, I had nearly forgotten an unpleasant adventure of my own on board the S.S. *Saxon*, in which we travelled to the Cape. Johnny Douglas and myself always used to run a mile before dinner in order to keep fit. One evening a little boy about ten years old shot out his leg as I turned a corner and tripped me. I fell on the deck nearly knocking myself silly and got two gashes on my face, one on each arm, and injured my knee!

Our first South African experience (barring, of course, the sight of the sun rising over Table Mountain, which I rose early to enjoy) was a luncheon of welcome at which the Mayor of Cape Town, Mr. John Parker, presided. Old speeches somewhat lose their savour, and I will not, therefore, quote from His Worship's, admirable though it was. I must, however, revive a paragraph or two from Johnny Douglas', both because it was typical of him and also because it made some quiet fun of himself and myself.

In his reply to His Worship the Mayor, Johnny said:

"We have three members of the team who last season scored over 2000 runs, namely Hobbs, Mead and Hearne. Several others of the team scored over 1000 or thereabouts. We have one whose name is Tennyson. You said, sir, I think, that you liked to see the ball hit out of the ground. Well, provided Tennyson gets going, I think you will see him do that all right (cheers). And if he has the same good season out here as he has had on board the *Saxon*, I think he will also come out on top of the averages (loud laughter).

"Now I come to the bowling! We have Barnes, whom many good judges think is the best bowler in the world . . . also Booth, who took more wickets than anyone else last season, Rhodes, Relf and Woolley. . . . As regards myself, you have mentioned one story about me. Now I'll tell you another.

"I was playing at Melbourne where the railway line runs past one side of the ground. I was batting and trying to keep my end up. One spectator in the Pavilion said: 'Now Douglas is going in. We shall see the ball fly.' His neighbour replied: 'I'll bet you more trains pass the ground whilst he is at the wicket than he makes runs'" (laughter).

A voice: "Who won?"

Johnny: "The trains won by 23" (loud laughter).

Our Civic welcome and entertainment at Cape Town over, the real business of the tour began at Newlands a few miles from Cape Town, and in my experience the loveliest cricket ground in the world, lying as it does embowered in trees and amidst grand mountain scenery. Before writing further about our South African tour, let me say that Johnny Douglas (whilst frequently chaffing himself and others in after-dinner speeches) was the keenest and most business-like of captains, and could also hit the ball much harder and oftener than he sometimes pretended, although he had a positive genius for "closing up the game" at will. To win the Test Matches was his object, to which everything else was subordinated. This was the cause of a little friction at one period of the tour, and Johnny came in for some rather foolish criticism for having refused, perhaps a little bluntly, well-meaning people who wished to entertain the various members of the Team rather more than he thought suited their cricket. These things are better understood now, and touring teams are generally strictly disciplined with regard to late hours, and this saves trouble all round. Apart, however, from the tense atmosphere always associated with Test Matches, it must be remembered that at that time only ten years had gone since the close of the South African War, and this fact was bound to complicate matters. We were regarded, even more than is usually the case, as ambassadors from the old country. Whilst, therefore, there might still be those up and down the land who did not much love England, there were also those whose feelings were before long somewhat ruffled by our easy succession of victories both in local matches, in State matches, and in the Tests. So there arose, in certain quarters, two mutually contradictory sets of opinions, first that we regarded our task too lightly and enjoyed ourselves too much between matches or even during them; secondly, that some of us unjustifiably refused parties to which we were invited. As these views were equally unreasonable and confined to a few; and as, of course, the vast majority of the South Africans we met were as sensible as they were hospitable; after one brief and rather violent storm they vanished and were not heard of again. This storm, which was responsible for several letters to the Press embodying the feelings I have described, and which caused a good deal of sensation not only in South Africa but in England also, really had its origin in an unfortunate episode at Bloemfontein where, of course, racial feeling could not help being high. After the series of matches at Johannesburg, the team were due to play in the former city. I had gone on ahead to stay with friends, and John Douglas had also preceded the others to meet his father and mother who had just arrived in South Africa. The team was left in charge of Bird, the Vice-Captain, and he on arrival at the station, not knowing that the Mayor of Bloemfontein was waiting for him on another platform with a magnificent speech and an escort of 300 of the city notables, simply went off to his hotel without seeing the Mayor, accompanied by the rest of the team. For a short time, as I have said, feeling ran very high over this incident, not only in Bloemfontein but all over South Africa; and although the Mayor at once accepted John Douglas' apology and explanation, there were a certain number of wiseacres who refused for a considerable time to be comforted. Perhaps it was as well that a certain ludicrous incident that had happened to myself shortly before in Johannesburg, remained shrouded in secrecy, otherwise I should certainly have been accused of regarding Test Cricket too lightly, although the contrary was the case and I was striving to do myself justice on matting wickets.

I must explain, however, before telling this story, that our cricket tour in South Africa nearly came to an untimely end shortly after the third Test at Johannesburg. This was due to no fault of ours, but to a most menacing and formidable strike that broke out in the Mines. For some time it was touch-and-go whether the railways and other transport services would not also go on strike and paralyse the life of the country. The Governor-General, Lord Gladstone, and his Ministers took prompt measures to avert such a catastrophe. The newly organized South African Defence Force, numbering 60,000 men, was called out, and some of their mounted troops, consisting chiefly of Boers, rode in and picketed the streets of Johannesburg. One night I dined in one of their messes and met several fellows who had fought against us in the late war. Their one desire now seemed to fight for us in a new war. As all the world knows, that wish was granted, and right nobly these gallant troops showed their courage and loyalty both in East Africa and France. During this state of tension when no one could say what would happen, though fortunately the wise measures taken by the Governor-

General were not long in restoring order, the team all volunteered to serve as special constables. It was one evening when things were at their blackest, that the absurd adventure occurred to which I have alluded. The city was under Martial Law, and everyone required a pass to be out after 8 p.m. Having promised to dine with a married couple I had recently met, who lived two or three miles away in a suburb of Johannesburg, and not wishing to disappoint them, I obtained a pass and went out to their house. I was somewhat surprised when arriving there, rather late as usual, to find the lady alone.

"I'm so sorry," said she, coming forward to greet me, "owing to the strike it was impossible to get any other guests to meet you, and now my husband has been called out on duty at the Mines. We shall be quite alone. Do you mind?"

Being, I trust, the essence of politeness, and as she was very good looking, I, of course, replied that though deploring the husband's call to duty, the prospect of an evening without him did not utterly displease me! My hostess suitably acknowledged my compliment, we went to dinner, talked, became friendly, finished our meal, talked still more pleasantly together, and finally felt as if we had known each other all our lives! It was a very hot night, and for greater ease I sat in my shirt sleeves, my kind hostess waiving all ceremony. Neither of us noticed, however, that time, as is its wont, was creeping on.

Suddenly there came a tremendous bang at the front door, rapidly followed by others no less violent.

"Oh! My God!" cried my hostess, turning deathly pale. "We are lost."

"Why, what on earth's the matter?" said I, startled.

"It's my husband," whispered she, looking as if she was going to faint. "You must fly—fly at once."

"Fly!" I exclaimed. "Why?"

"Don't linger for God's sake," exclaimed she. "You don't know how jealous he is. You and I together at this time of night! It would drive him mad. And he has his revolver too. You are a dead man if he finds you here."

The banging at the front door continued more violently than ever, and alarmed by the lady's distress, I hastily snatched up my hat and coat and began to look for the most suitable means of exit.

"Not that way!" said she in an agony of apprehension. "Upstairs! It's your only chance." Upon which she half-pushed me up the staircase, and opening a bedroom window at the back of the house, told me to descend by way of a trellis-work all covered with rambler roses. By the time I reached the ground my life was safe indeed, but my clothes were in ribbons and blood was pouring from almost every part of my body, while my arms and legs were absolutely lacerated. I had to knock up a doctor on the way back and get him to dress my wounds. On the morning of our next match, which took place after all, the strike situation having become easier, my fielding in the deep was greatly praised by the spectators and Press. The more charitable amongst them would have praised it even more had they known the difficulties under which it was done.

As I have already intimated, we won the first three Test Matches off the reel; the fourth was drawn in favour of South Africa: and the fifth and last ended in another crushing victory for England. My own part in our victories, in spite of being chosen for all five Tests, was not a very large one, though I had the satisfaction of making a fifty in the first of the series. The matting wickets, on which, of course, I had never played previously, had me all at sea to begin with, though towards the end of the tour I became considerably more used to them and did better. Without wishing to detract from the performances of other members of our extremely powerful side, all of whom on occasions did magnificently, while John Douglas himself was in great form with bat and ball, the tour as far as we were concerned was almost a "two-man show." Jack Hobbs in batting, and Sydney Barnes in bowling were "out by themselves." Hobbs scored six centuries and had an average of 75 for 25 innings. Barnes in 27 innings took 125 wickets for an average of 9.64. With his height, strength and magnificent delivery, bowling fast-medium, and breaking from leg and off with a spin unplayable on the matting wickets, he ran through local sides as destructively as a fox in a poultry yard, and had even South Africa's Test representatives practically at his mercy. They were nearly all young cricketers with the faults of youth—impulsiveness and inexperience—and though several of them showed considerable promise, notably Newbury and Blanckenburg, and Dave Nourse gave us glimpses of his true form, the M.C.C. side, as a whole, carried too many guns for them, and their cricket was too much in and out for them to have a chance in the Tests. These factors make the work of their captain, the famous H. W. ("Herbie") Taylor even more impressive than the figures show. Except in one instance, the return match against Natal (the only match we lost and which Herbie may be said to have won off his own bat), he was always on the losing side, and up against the finest bowler who ever lived, while the wickets of his comrades were often falling like corn before the sickle; and yet, marvellous, nay miraculous to relate, these were his batting performances against us.

	1st Innings	2nd Innings
Natal v. M.C.C. (Durban)	83 not out (out of 124)	54 not out
1st Test (Durban)	109 (out of 182)	8
2nd Test (Johannesburg)	29	40
3rd Test (Johannesburg)	14	70
Natal v. M.C.C. (Durban)	91	100
4th Test (Durban)	16	93
5th Test (Durban)	42	87

In Test Matches, by reason of this really wonderful batting, which caused Jack Hobbs to say that he was the finest player on matting the world had ever seen (though cricketers generally would place Jack himself at least on an equality with him), Herbie Taylor had an average of 50.80.

———————

It was my intention at this point to write something about South Africa itself, a country which I love for its vast sunny spaces, wonderful scenery, and warm-hearted, hospitable people. As, however, I had the good fortune to visit South Africa again in 1924–1925 as Captain of the late Mr. Solly Joel's touring side, and this chapter is already long, I will defer these impressions to the pages dealing with that very pleasant and interesting experience. Let me wind up here with a remark or two belonging exclusively to my earlier trip. Amongst my recollections of this time are visits paid to the South African battlefields—Magersfontein, Colenso, Ladysmith, and Spion Kop—names which were then full of poignant interest to a young English soldier, but which, in the case of the modern generation, have probably been almost forgotten in the roll of others of much vaster and more tragic significance.

Nor can I close the chapter without some reference to the amazingly generous and cordial hospitality the Team received from one end of South Africa to the other. It would take a volume to do justice to all the kind people who opened their homes to us, and spared neither time nor trouble to make our visit out of cricketing hours pass happily. I can, however, here for reasons of space name only a few, and ask others to believe that I shall never forget the splendid welcome they gave us. First, then, let me mention the Governor-General and his wife, Lord and Lady Gladstone, who invited us to a magnificent ball at Government House, Pretoria, and when due honour to the King's representative has been done, let me also recall the kindness of Sir George Farrar, who entertained us at his beautiful place, Bedford Farm. My memories include a most pleasant stay with Sir Abe Bailey and a dinner given by him to the members of the Team, while many Clubs in Johannesburg, Cape Town, Durban, Port Elizabeth, Kimberley and other places, entertained us royally.

I was not as successful cricketing in South Africa as I had hoped to be, scoring only one century at Ladysmith; nevertheless owing to my successful season in 1913 in England, I figured in the 1914 publication of Wisden among the best five cricketers of the year. This means that my photograph can be found in its pages, an honour reserved only once in their lives for a limited number of first-class cricketers, and therefore greatly coveted.

CHAPTER XII

SINCE the date of my return from South Africa on 31st March 1914 in the S.S. *Kinfauns Castle*, a voyage which, I remember, was not so amusing as the outward one as there was only *one* lady on board, I had been kept hard at work at military duties. I had taken part in the match at Lord's at the end of June to celebrate the centenary of the famous cricket ground, in which the M.C.C. South African side (without Barnes) played the rest of England and got beaten in an innings owing, partly, to rain. Beyond this, however, I had figured only in regimental matches most of the season. Some leave came in July and I played a couple of matches for Hampshire, and on the night of the 3rd of August was staying in my flat at Princes Hotel in Piccadilly, preparatory to taking part in the August Bank Holiday match against Essex at Leyton the next day. It was about two o'clock in the morning and I was sound asleep, and dreaming one of the dreams that ardent cricketers know. It seemed to me that the Leyton ground was packed to its utmost capacity; the turf was hard and green, and I, with one of my Hampshire colleagues, was at the wicket. As the bowler walked back preparatory to delivering the next ball, I looked up at the score-board and saw my score standing at 94. Down came the ball, my bat swung and caught it truly, and then it soared far away over the heads of the crowd on the leg side to give me my century. A tremendous outburst of applause followed which, though I acknowledged it in the orthodox fashion by repeatedly raising my bat, refused to stop. The scene of my dream grew dim, and I gradually awoke to the fact that the noise was that of someone banging loudly on my door.

"What the hell's the matter?" said I, turning on the electric light and shouting "come in!"

This invitation was quickly followed by the appearance of the night porter's head in my open doorway.

"A telephone message for you, sir," he said.

"A telephone message!" I exclaimed, "at this time of the night! Who is it from?"

"From Captain Liddell, sir, Adjutant 1st Battalion The Rifle Brigade."

"'Snipe' Liddell," said I. "What the devil does he want at two o'clock in the morning?"

"The message says," replied the night porter, "that war has been declared on Germany and that you are ordered to return to duty immediately."

War! Of course I and all my brother-officers had been expecting it for some time. This summons in the middle of the night had been, however, in the nature of a surprise. All trace of sleepiness nevertheless vanished directly at the news. I leapt out of bed.

"Run down and get me a taxi," I said to the night porter, "and then come back and help me to pack my bags like a good fellow. As quick as you can!"

I remember dressing and packing with the night porter's help in feverish haste, so anxious was I not to run any chance of missing the war; and a very few moments later saw me speeding through sleeping London on my sixty-mile taxi drive back again to Colchester. This was a drive pretty familiar to me as a matter of fact, although the special circumstances of that night have particularly fixed it in my memory. My father had, it may be remembered, arranged for me to be stationed at Colchester with the Rifle Brigade, so that I should have more difficulty in getting up to London where were so many men and women friends of mine, especially one of the latter, then prominent on the London stage, to whom I was exceptionally devoted. I have always had a talent for overcoming difficulties of that kind, however, and the simple expedient of a flat at Princes and a taxi back in time for parade kept me adequately amused, although, I fear, it resulted in an increase of expenditure rather than in a decrease, as my poor father desired.

To return, however, to the night of the declaration of war! All the way down, as the taxi rattled through the darkness, urged on by my fear of missing the war, I kept telling the driver to hurry. We jerked and pounded along to such good purpose that I arrived to rejoin my battalion, six hours ahead of anyone else.

The next day and those following were days of feverish preparation—packing of mess-furniture—arrival of reservists—route marching to get the men fit—an open-air service on Sunday the 16th in the Abbey-Field at Colchester where the Bishop gave a most impressive address—good-byes to relations by all and sundry, and amongst them my own farewells to my father and mother who came down to Colchester to see me—and then on 18th August the battalion left for Harrow by train and encamped that night in the school playing-fields. Three days afterwards as I was walking down Harrow High Street with Captain de Moleyns, an old Harrovian and a brother-officer, we met our General, now Sir Aylmer Hunter-Weston, M.P., who informed us that we were off to the front the next night. Then came my first shock in the war.

Instead of going overseas with the battalion, I was detailed to take charge of the first lot of reinforcements. I was terribly disappointed and could hardly bear going back to Colchester. I sent a telegram to the men of my platoon in B Company, and they sent me back another wishing me good luck and saying they were sorry to lose me. I think they meant it. At any rate a brother-officer told me later on that the men kept on saying to him, "We miss our officer."

At Colchester I had some trouble. The reinforcements were very unruly and I started off by giving three of them what I afterwards discovered was an illegal punishment. It had a good effect, however, which was the principal thing!

On Sunday the 23rd, 150 of us, with all the battalion and officers' kits, left for Southampton. We reached Havre at 1 p.m. on 24th August after anchoring off Sandown Bay all night in a thick fog, and there on the wharf to greet us were crowds of Frenchmen shouting, "Are we down-hearted? No" and singing "Tipperary." In blazing hot weather we marched the eight miles to Harfleur and then, after receiving three days' rations, marched back to Havre again, and with reinforcements for several other regiments entrained for Amiens. We arrived there about 2 p.m. next day *via* Rouen, and encamped in fields north of the town without blankets or overcoats, shivering with cold consequently for the two nights of our stay. In the middle of the night of 27th August an Inniskilling Fusilier had a nightmare and jumped up yelling: "The Germans are on us." Everyone else awoke and seized what weapons they could lay hold of in tremendous excitement. I, however, having taken off my boots, and not being able to find them in the pitch darkness, was powerless—a horrible sensation! Next morning we moved back to Rouen with the intimation that we might be attacked in the train by German Cavalry, but nothing happened though we could hear the battle in the distance. At Rouen we heard that my battalion had had 600 casualties at Ligny, and that many officers had been killed and wounded. We stayed there under canvas till the 30th, and then entrained for Le Mans. On 2nd September we left for Versailles and after a short rest outside the town went on to Colombiers expecting to meet our battalion there. We could hear the battle raging about five miles off and the noise was terrific, but on being told that the battalion was now forty miles away, set out once more in quest of them.

We reached them at last at 2 p.m. on the 5th at Lagny, having marched forty-three miles in twenty-two hours with only ten-minute halts, except for a two and a half hours rest at Crecy. In spite of route-marching every day since our arrival in France, the men were terribly done and footsore, and I had great difficulty in preventing them throwing away their packs. None the less, only four fell out next day, whilst in the East Lancs., Hampshires and Somersets in my brigade about twenty-five to thirty fell out in each regiment. These must all eventually have been captured by the advancing Germans.

I was on outpost all that night, and to our surprise orders came during the early hours of the morning for a general advance.

This was the last day of the famous retreat from Mons, and we had caught the battalion up in time for the Battle of the Marne.

The first two days of the battle my brigade never came into action, though we marched steadily in pursuit of the retreating Germans. On the afternoon of the 8th September, however, we reached the village of La Ferte, beneath some hills overlooking the River Marne. The half of the village beyond the river was still in German hands. Our shells were bursting amongst them, setting alight to farms and houses, which seemed to me then a marvellous and awe-inspiring sight, and for many miles now the road had been littered with the decomposing carcasses of horses. "Fat Boy" Micklem in my battalion (now Brigadier-General J. Micklem, D.S.O., M.C.), here put in some deadly work with his machine-guns. I was really in the war at last. Our wounded were being brought back, and after a day of scorching heat rain was coming down in sheets, till everyone was soaked to the skin. That evening I was sent as Orderly Officer to General Hunter-Weston, and next morning was awakened by his orders at 2.30 a.m., to take a message to our Colonel that we would attack at dawn. The Brigade, accordingly, moved down through La Ferte at about 3.30 a.m., my own battalion to the right of the village, while the General and his Staff remained on the hill to get a good view of operations. It was about half an hour afterwards that I received my own baptism of fire from German machine-guns, having been sent on a bicycle down the hill with a message to the Colonel of the East Lancashire Regiment. A minute after I left him to return to General Hunter-Weston, the Colonel was shot through the head and killed. An hour after this I was again fired on by machine-guns, this time in company with the General who had gone down into the Square of La Ferte. The General, however, didn't appear to notice the firing at all, although the bullets were spattering the bank just above his head. At last, to my intense relief, he moved away. That evening about 8.30 he said:

"Tennyson, go and get in touch with the Hampshires and bring them down the hill, and into La Ferte."

"Very good, sir."

"And, Tennyson. . . ."

"Sir."

"I think you'll probably come across a few Uhlans on your way, so have your revolver loaded, and be ready to shoot at a moment's notice."

On receipt of this order, I saluted, and sallied forth into the night.

To reach the Hampshires the way led through a thick dark wood for a distance of about two miles. I think, despite the fact that the night was as black as ink, I walked quicker than ever before. I met no one, however (except an old French peasant who bade me good night), till I reached the Hampshires' sentries, who very nearly shot me.

The Germans had destroyed the bridge over the Marne at La Ferte and, while the R.E. worked during the night at a pontoon bridge, parties of eight men at a time ferried themselves across in boats by means of ropes the Engineers had fixed up from bank to bank. At 6 o'clock the next morning, 10th September, the General sent me off again to get into touch with my own battalion. I was about a quarter way across the Marne pulling myself along with one of these ropes when I heard a shout.

"Hey! young fellow, wait a minute for me."

There on the bank I had just left, was an officer in staff uniform. I pulled back, and lo and behold! Colonel Jack Seely (now

General Lord Mottistone), our neighbour in the Isle of Wight and the ex-War Minister, got into the boat.

"You don't recognize me, sir," said I. "The last time we met was playing golf."

"I remember your face perfectly well," said the Colonel, "but not your name."

"Tennyson," said I.

"What, Lionel!" exclaimed he. "Of course! It's very interesting to think we should meet here again."

By this time we had reached the farther bank, and as we stepped from the boat he asked:

"Is your revolver loaded? We might meet some Germans here. By the way, what are you doing?"

"Orderly Officer to General Hunter-Weston, sir. And you?"

"I," replied the Colonel, "have been sent by General French to report on the present situation. Perhaps this man can tell us something."

Unfortunately the sentry he spoke to seemed to find the situation beyond him altogether, as did all the other troops we met, although confronted with Colonel Seely's august credentials. Some French civilians, however, who had sheltered in the cellars of La Ferte during our bombardment said that the Germans had retreated, leaving many badly wounded and having buried seven hundred dead. Colonel Seely and I then mounted the hill on the farther side of La Ferte, and about a mile on reached the little village of Le Limon where the East Lancashire Regiment had taken up a position under their senior Major. Colonel Seely had some breakfast there which he evidently appreciated, although he strongly disagreed with the Major over his outpost line and dispositions generally: after which he departed to report to General French, I to find my battalion. After walking some way and seeing several dead German officers and men, I found them happy and comfortable in a farm by the river which they had crossed after a slight engagement. That afternoon we marched on, as we did the next day and the next, in pouring rain, but without actual contact with the enemy. Then, on the night of the 12th, after an awful march of twenty-seven miles still in torrents of rain to the village of Rozières, we were ordered to advance once more just as we got ready to billet for the night, and arrived after yet another drenching at Venizel on the River Aisne.

That night the whole of the 11th Brigade crossed the river. This was the manner of their crossing, which at the time seemed to us the riskiest and most slap-dash proceeding ever seen. The Germans had meant to destroy the bridge, but had left a single girder standing on the left side. In the midst of the inky darkness, and although the men were so tired with their forty miles march in the rain that they went to sleep as they stood or marched, they crossed this girder one by one. It was sixty feet above the river and quivered and shook all the time. As soon as all were across (and for some reason not a shot had been fired by the enemy) the whole Brigade passed through the village of Bucy-le-Long to the summit of the ridge beyond. Though the Battle of the Aisne lasted three weeks, this was the farthest point reached by our Brigade. The Germans were strongly entrenched with artillery some five hundred to eight hundred yards to our front and it was impossible to get on. On the afternoon of the first day, Sunday 13th, after my Company had by mistake been shelled by our own guns in the morning and lost a dozen men, killed and wounded, A and B Companies were, it is true, ordered to advance, but were soon compelled to retire after heavy casualties, which included three officers wounded. Sergeant Walker, who had been recommended for the D.C.M. and Medaille Militaire at the Battle of Ligny, had his leg almost blown off and only left hanging by a bit of bone. It is hardly credible, but he severed the remnant of bone with his pocket-knife as he lay, bound up his leg himself, and was still conscious when brought in at dusk. After this reverse we started entrenching and were heavily shelled from 5 a.m. to 10 a.m., during which time I was hit by a spent piece of shell but not injured. After a lull in the firing I was astonished to see our Colonel, Biddulph, and Sir Evelyn Bradford, the old Hampshire cricketer, who commanded the Seaforths, come up in the open behind our trenches and call out Jimmy Brownlow, my captain. They all three stood looking at a map, and I heard the words "General Advance." At that moment two shells burst in rapid succession right by them. Bradford was instantly killed and Brownlow desperately wounded, though he eventually recovered, but our Colonel only had his cap blown off. The next day, by the irony of fate, the Colonel was accidentally wounded by a signaller cleaning a rifle and had to go home, leaving the command to Captain "Tip" Prittie a very fine officer, afterwards killed. The command of C Company now devolved on myself.

Every day the shelling grew more violent, and we were continually losing men as the Germans were using very heavy guns. We therefore dug and improved our trenches each night. Battalion headquarters were in some caves in a wood behind our lines, and in one of them I found the sort of person one reads about in a fairy tale—an ancient hermit with a long white beard down to his knees and great long nails. As our reliefs were shelled each time they came up, we were continually on the lookout for spies (though we never caught one) and for a time suspected this hermit. He had, however, as we found out, lived in this cave for years, and certainly we never discovered anything incriminating about him.

From the 18th to 21st my Battalion moved three miles away to a rest camp just above the town of Soissons. The first night we lay out on the hillside in pouring rain (my diary says, "the most miserable night since we left England") but then built ourselves little huts of brushwood roofed with bushes and earth. This camp was supposed to be concealed from the German guns, but on the 20th three shells landed in it, and wounded several men. The next day we returned to our trenches. They were in pretty good shape by now, and though the Germans continued to shell us heavily till the end of our stay there, they did not do much damage. On 1st October we received the order to take over the trenches at La Montagne Farm from the Dublins, about a mile to our right.

There was a large turnip field in front of these trenches, and on the beautiful moonlight nights during our occupation of them these turnips looked exactly like hordes of advancing Germans. It was creepy work going out into them on a listening patrol, with their leaves always rustling and their look as of an army approaching.

We now dug a new forward trench, and staked and wired it heavily. On their side, the Germans had started sending up Very lights practically all night to light up the ground in front of them. This part of the line was even worse for spies than the one we had left. Every night a light from the direction of Venizel used to signal to the enemy. We failed to catch the culprit, but heard afterwards that it was a woman from Venizel and that she was eventually shot. Also, on several nights before we could turn a

116

rifle on him, a great white lurcher dashed through our lines towards the opposing trenches, but never could we trace how he returned or in what direction. One of my men once said that he saw him going into La Montagne Farm, but though the house and all the barns were searched, no dog could be found. The farmer there had, apart from this, aroused our suspicions, firstly, because his farm had never suffered in any way, and secondly, by having suggested a place for our guns which we did not adopt, and which was heavily shelled the next day. Later we learned that our suspicions had been correct. The French, when they relieved us on 6th October, saw the white lurcher again, traced him to La Montagne Farm, and shot the owner to whom he had just brought a message.

The B.E.F. was now being transferred from the centre of the Allied line to the left flank as part of a great turning movement, and to shorten their lines of communication. Travelling by road and railway for five days we arrived at Blendecques, a village three miles from St. Omer, and from there the whole Battalion were taken in fifty French motor-lorries to Hondighen, which we reached at 6.30 a.m. on 13th October. I had now handed over C Company to my senior, Freddy Blacker; and "Chaucer" Sturgis was commanding the battalion, vice "Tip" Prittie also his junior in rank.

A few hours later, with our Brigade in reserve, the 10th and 12th Brigades got into action and turned the Germans out of the villages of Meteren and Flêtre. It was of course, as usual, raining cats and dogs all the time. After billeting for the night in a stinking farm at Flêtre, my battalion led the Division through Meteren and on to Bailleul, which the Germans had evacuated, and where we had a tremendous ovation from the inhabitants. At Bailleul, with my platoon, I was detailed by a Staff Officer to search one of the streets for prisoners. I captured sixty-eight, including a German doctor who must have been one of the fattest men in the world. As, however, a considerable number of these prisoners were either wounded or extraordinarily drunk, I got rather chaffed on rejoining the battalion. That night my company was on outpost duty in front of Neuve-Eglise. It was, needless to say, deluging with rain again, and our ration parties had to reach us by a lane in which the mud was more than knee-deep. Their language, I believe, was really wonderful.

The next morning my company, which was now commanded by Oliver Sutton-Nelthorpe, had orders to clear some woods to our front. We had no opposition, and reached the main road running north and south from Neuve-Eglise in safety. Sutton-Nelthorpe told me to take up an outpost line with platoons No. 5 (my own) and No. 7, Sergt. Cording's (which had been mine in England), and if possible to reconnoitre the village of Rumarin which the enemy were believed to be holding with machine-guns.

Approaching this village across a field, we came almost instantly upon some wonderfully good dummy trenches manned with rows of turnips cut to resemble German helmets. There were also two tree trunks mounted upon old gun carriages. This pretty piece of work we, of course, immediately destroyed before moving on. We were now in extended order and fairly close to the village, having had only a few shots fired at us, when I had a sudden brain-wave.

"Sergeant Cording," said I, going across to him, "I don't believe there are any Germans in this village to speak of."

"It doesn't look like it, sir."

"What about trying to take it ourselves?"

"Seems a very good idea, sir."

"All right then, we'll have a shot at it."

At this moment two of our own shells burst remarkably close to us, which was rather disconcerting.

"I really think we'd better advance as quickly as possible," said I, "if they're going to shell us from behind. Take your platoon round to the left of the village, and I'll take mine to the right."

So off went Sergeant Cording and his men. Our exploit, however, though completely successful, was quite a bloodless one. There had been, we learnt from one of the inhabitants, about 150 Germans in the village but taken completely by surprise at our advance, they bolted after firing only a few more spasmodic shots. By nightfall we were five hundred yards to the south of Rumarin, with strong pickets in the village and also down the roads towards Ploegsteert and Nieppe. Meanwhile my battalion seemed to have disappeared, at least none of my orderlies could get into touch with them; so there was nothing to do except hold on. Later in the evening the 1st Battalion, East Lancashire Regiment, as well as two Companies of the Hampshire Regiment, arrived to capture Rumarin, and were rather annoyed to find us already in possession. Soon afterwards some of our own Cavalry also appeared on the same errand. Next day the battalion was located at Steenwerk where we rejoined them after twenty-four hours absence. Owing to losing touch they had supposed us killed or captured. On the following day we marched through Nieppe and Armentières and halted in a field beyond the latter town, in reserve to the 10th and 12th Brigades which were fighting just ahead of us. Several shells passed over us into Armentières, much to the alarm of some kind nuns in a convent for imbeciles to whom these fields belonged, and who told us the Germans had rested there two days before. During this firing, a spy was detected signalling to the enemy from the top of a gasometer, and immediately arrested and shot the next morning. That night was almost as bright as day, the Germans having set light to houses and farms and haystacks as far as one could see. There was a network of villages here, L'Epinette, Fresnelles, Verlinghem, Le Rouage, Hooplines, and we spent the next three days digging trenches, being heavily shelled, and trying to turn the enemy out of their positions, the key of which was the town of Frélinghien.

On one occasion Nelthorpe and I had gone back to our battalion headquarters, five hundred yards in rear of our trenches in the village of Le Rouage. As I was washing myself upstairs in a state of nature, the Germans started a night attack. Shells came howling and bursting in all directions, one even through the room underneath mine, but did not burst. Rifle and machine-gun bullets also flew past like hail. My servant Welch and I were thankful when we could get out of the house and take cover in rear of it with the other officers. (By the way, Welch had a curious experience on the Aisne. He was nearly blown up by one of our own Lyddite shells, and the fumes of it dyed his hair canary-yellow for weeks.) The German attack that night was brought to a standstill after an hour, but my diary says: "It was like hell on earth while it lasted, and the worst night attack we have had so far during the War."

At 1 a.m. that morning, 22nd October, as we were trying to get a little sleep, we were ordered to go in support of the 12th Brigade on our left just across the River Lys. They had been faring badly. When we relieved the South Lancashire Regiment, in fact, at 6 p.m. that evening, they told us that these trenches were the most terrible place they had been in yet. Nor was this description much amiss. I really wish I could quote my diary in full with regard to what we went through in this frightful position. It was a full fortnight before we were relieved and how the men stuck it out I cannot think. Nevertheless they remained willing and reasonably cheerful the whole time.

To begin with, we had not nearly enough troops to defend it properly. In my own section of trench there was only one rifle to every ten yards, nor were the other platoons better off. If the Germans had only known, they could have broken through at any time, as we had no wire in front and only one Company in support.

Our first night there was awful, blowing like fury and hailing incessantly, so that it was impossible to hear anything. I had a listening patrol about a hundred yards out in the inevitable turnip field. Twice they came in and said the Germans were advancing. I was very angry and then took them out again myself. Suddenly some bullocks came charging at us through the turnips, whom we could not see till they were right on top of us. I then gave the order to open fire, knowing something must have alarmed them. It was lucky I did so, as the Germans were there behind them, hoping to rush our trenches under cover of the driven beasts.

Opposite us, about a hundred yards away, was the village of Le Touquet, the houses of which were full of German snipers and machine-guns that gave us no peace; and three nights running the Germans attacked us, but did not succeed in penetrating our lines. By day they shelled us incessantly with high explosive, and at 8 p.m. on the night of 23rd, by way of variety, the church of Frélinghien was set on fire by our own guns. "The night was lit up like day," my diary says, "and up till midnight one could hear great chunks of masonry falling. This blaze to-night passed all imagination."

During the night of the 25th (I quote my diary once more), "owing to the ceaseless rain we stood the whole time in about 2½ feet of water. By the morning my feet were so cold that I had no feeling in them at all, and my overcoat literally weighed about a ton, being a mass of mud and water."

On the 26th my company had a brief respite, being relieved at 4 a.m. by our reserve company, and we marched "very miserable, cold and wet" to a farm in rear. There we spent two days resting in company with a couple of Belgian refugees who had escaped from Frélinghien. One of them was very angry with me because I would not volunteer to fetch a new pair of boots which he had dropped between the German lines and our own in the hurry of his escape. I wanted a rest badly, as I had been without sleep for five nights running.

At 3 a.m. on the third day we relieved A Company in their trenches. Frélinghien was now to our right, and Le Touquet to our left front. So here we had the pleasure of being sniped at from two practically opposite directions. To avoid being too obviously enfiladed we used two different sets of trenches by night and day, one being at right angles to the other. There was, however, an agreeable change of scenery, our trenches being sited amongst tobacco plants instead of amongst the usual turnips. The weather had turned bitterly cold and we were absolutely frozen. A cheering spectacle occurred on our second evening. A party of Germans were sitting round a fire at the edge of the town of Frélinghien singing "Das Vaterland" to a gramophone. Suddenly a tremendous shell (probably from the guns of the 7th Division which we had heard coming up to the north of us all the previous night) burst right in the middle of them, and as a fellow in my platoon remarked "they went to 'Das Vaterland' a bit quicker than they expected!"

The next day, after a terrific shelling, which lasted from 8.15 a.m. to 3 p.m., the enemy attacked B and C Companies in force. (C Company were still holding the trenches across the road opposite the village of Le Touquet where they had relieved us two days before.) The Germans advanced across the open in two solid lines with their officers in rear of the men. Our rifles and machine guns, however, simply mowed them down, and they broke and fled in all directions. One poor devil, I remember, ran right across our front, but just as he was reaching safety, a bullet hit him fair and square. Our casualties were heavy, considering our small numbers, both in officers and men, but the Germans left three hundred dead between their lines and ours.

The next day, as if enraged by this fiasco, the German gunners went absolutely mad and fired hundreds of shells all over the place without apparently hitting anything: and the day after that, after shelling our positions heavily in the morning, they again went mad from 3 p.m. to 5.30 p.m.

On Monday, 2nd November, congratulations "on our courage and tenacity" arrived from General Hunter-Weston, which cheered us up a bit; also a rumour that French reinforcements were on their way. "About time too," says my diary, "we have had to hold on now with a handful of men since the 19th, and it is a bit of a strain."

On the night of the 3rd, after two false alarms, a strong night attack started. The enemy's machine-gun and rifle fire was terrific and bullets came over in thousands. The right trench of my platoon was also enfiladed by a machine-gun which the Germans had managed to get into a house. By a real miracle, however, we had nobody hit at all, and drove them back with loss. The next night was quiet, and I was able to get up some wire, but when morning came shelling began again and went on all day, the noise being deafening. The report was that a lot more German guns had come up. We were shelled also all the day after. My diary says: "sometimes one literally feels as if one was going mad."

On the following day, the 6th, there was a thick fog, and from 6 p.m. to 8 p.m. the Germans once more attacked unsuccessfully. In the middle of it, Captain Geoff Toynbee arrived with 60 men as reinforcements to the 1st Battalion. They had been shelled with shrapnel on the way up and had had several casualties. A pleasant introduction to the war for them!

"*My birthday!*" records the entry in my diary for the next day, 7th November, "and long shall I remember it! The Germans attacked us once more this morning from 5 a.m. till 9 p.m., but we managed to drive them back again. A terrific day's shelling of our trenches took place to-day. . . . Literally hundreds of shells have been bursting all round us, as well as machine-gun fire directed at us. A German prisoner we took last Thursday informed us that he had been told by his officers (1) that London was a heap of cinders, having been destroyed by aeroplanes; (2) that our fleet had been done in by the German one; (3) that the few English soldiers now left in France and Belgium were only the remnants of Kitchener's Army. When we told him that this was all nonsense, he laughed and would not believe us. The battle continued to-day till about 5.30 p.m. when a night attack started. The Germans used a fair share of their Very lights, lighting up all the ground between our trenches and theirs to-night. About 7 p.m. I was standing on a road which ran between Montford's and my own platoon, showing my platoon sergeant where to dig a communication trench between the two trenches, and he being very dense could not understand where to start it. Therefore I got down into the trench to show him. I had not been down there ten seconds before six shells burst in quick succession exactly in the place where I had been standing on the road. . . . There was a heavy fog again to-night and constant alarms that the Germans were advancing, so we spent a very disturbed night, keeping on continually standing to arms, but eventually reached the morning safely. Never shall I forget this 7th November and my twenty-fifth birthday . . . one of the worst days we have had since we left England."

For the next two days there was fog and rain, but it was tolerably quiet except for sniping and another abortive attack by the Germans on C Company on our left, and on 10th November we were relieved by the King's Own Liverpool Regiment amidst a perfect fusillade of sniping which, marvellous to relate, hit no one, as all the bullets went high.

"We had," says my diary, "been fourteen days now in this one trench without a relief, which was very trying for the men, and they badly needed a rest. The only way we were able to wash, was out of our water-bottles and most of the men had grown beards, but I managed to shave and wash every day out of my own water-bottle."

We now hoped and were told that we should have a proper rest, but it was not to be. "No rest for the weary!" remarks my diary pathetically. After only a few hours, we moved to Ploeg-steert Wood, a dreadful place full of bogs and pits and holes, with trenches facing in every direction and full of water. Torrents of rain were falling, keeping on and on without intermission. The trenches we took over were about half a mile from the firing line and, despite the weather conditions, we did our best to improve them. On the afternoon of the 12th, by way of comic relief, I killed a cock pheasant sitting in a tree about 100 yards off with a borrowed rifle, much to the excitement and amusement of the men who had several wagers on the result. That night—and a pitch black night it was—we went up to the firing line to dig trenches, and my platoon, while acting as a covering party, was very badly sniped as well as shelled. On our return after getting a bullet through the leg of my trousers, I fell, in the inky darkness, into a deep trench or ditch and injured my leg so severely by tearing all the ligaments that I had practically to be carried the rest of the way. When the doctor had examined my leg next day he sent me back in the horse ambulance through Ploeg-steert village to Rumarin, the village we had captured on 15th

October. There was a private in the East Lancashire Regiment with me, with a great hole blown in his cheek by shrapnel so that you could see all his jaw. Showing astonishing fortitude, he had thirty-five stitches put in it. When I commiserated with him, his only reply was:

"Lor', sir, it didn't 'urt. Just like sewing up a sack, wasn't it?"

I never saw a braver fellow.

Next day a motor ambulance took us to Bailleul pending transfer to Boulogne and England. There I had my first bottle of champagne for months, and met the Rev. F. H. Gillingham, the famous Essex cricketer, who was chaplain in the hospital. He was awfully nice and kind, came and talked to me, and wrote home to my parents about me. I passed the night of the 15th at the Hotel Splendide at Wimereux which I had visited in peace time and which was now a hospital. There I found Miss Evie Gore, a neighbour of ours in the Isle of Wight, who was nursing and was very kind to me. I also found in my ward Stewart Richardson who had come down from the line for a new set of false teeth. His own he had lost in rather a singular fashion. Whilst shaving one morning, he had put them on the back of a mule. The Germans started shelling. The mule ran away. Stewart Richardson's false teeth disappeared with the mule! ! !

The day after we sailed in the s.s. *Carisbrooke Castle* for Southampton. I knew both the captain and the first officer, and met also a number of friends on board who chaffed me a great deal on looking like the complete scarecrow, as I was a mass of mud all over and my clothes were full of holes. Amongst these was Lord Francis Scott who had been very badly wounded. He was astonished to see me and said the papers had reported me killed. The first thing I did therefore on landing at Southampton was to reassure my parents on this point.

On reaching London I was taken to Mrs. Claude Watney's hospital at 20 Charles Street, Mayfair, where, funnily enough, in the next bed to me, was Francis Gore-Langton, one of my great friends in the 1st Battalion, Coldstream Guards. He had been very badly wounded in the arm.

Says my diary: "I soon fell asleep, but kept on being awakened by fellows yelling and talking in their sleep, all imagining that they were still fighting. Nobody knows what the feeling of being at home and comfortable is, after so many hardships! But

124

there is no nicer feeling that one can imagine, when one has seen what war is really like."

CHAPTER XIII

I BECOME A STAFF OFFICER: BATTLES OF LOOS AND GUILLEMONT: I AM WOUNDED

I RETURNED to France on 16th July 1915. This time I was a staff officer—staff captain in fact to General Roy of the 60th Light Infantry Brigade.

The injury to my leg, caused by the fall into a ditch in Ploegsteert Wood at the end of November 1914, had taken a long time healing, and it was not till March of the next year that I was passed fit for service. Even then, after having been on crutches for ten weeks, the doctor would only pass me fit for mounted duty.

In these circumstances, General Colville, who was at that time at Hindhead commanding the 60th Infantry Brigade (a formation entirely composed of the new "Kitchener" battalions of which the 12th Rifle Brigade was one), applied for me as his staff captain. From Hindhead we went to Larkhill on Salisbury Plain to complete our training. On the eve, however, of the Brigade's going on active service, General Colville—naturally to his great disappointment—was superseded by General Roy. It was bad luck for General Colville, but war is emphatically a game for the young!

Our Brigade formed part of the 20th Division; and on my arrival in France ahead of the Brigade to make all the arrangements for billeting them, I found both on the boat and in the hotels, in addition to many other staff officers in my division, quite a number of old friends much higher in rank than when I had last seen them. The old regular army had now, after nearly a year of war, been practically wiped out. Such officers as had survived the general massacre, were mostly either in command of battalions or serving on the staff of the new formations.

On the 17th of July I left Boulogne for St. Omer; and on the next day with the other staff captains and supply officers of the Division met Colonel Dundas, the A.A.Q.M.G. Then, in company with the French interpreter, a man named Lieut. Lebraly, I motored out billeting in the surrounding villages. Billeting for a Brigade, that is finding accommodation agreeable to the General, to his staff and to all the Colonels and Company Commanders each with their different messes—discovering convenient rooms for the sergeants' messes—making suitable arrangements for the men, as well as for the transport, guns, signallers, engineers, horses, mules and all the other miscellaneous odds and ends that composed a brigade equipped for war, was never a very easy job. When in addition to the other difficulties, one found in each village functionaries such as the French mayors were, who carried on their shoulders all the majesty and authority of the Republic, and were jealous to a degree of the slightest possible infraction of their dignity (which meant that to begin with, at least, they would on principle object to everything one proposed), the task became indeed no light one. However, after five days extremely hard work, Lebraly and I managed to get everything satisfactorily arranged, and all was ready for the Brigade's arrival on 23rd July.

During this week, on one occasion at St. Omer, I met His Royal Highness the Prince of Wales just as he was going into the Headquarters of the Commander-in-Chief, Sir John French. My diary notes: "His Royal Highness looked younger than ever. He spoke to me for a few minutes, and asked me on whose staff I was, and several questions about my Brigade in general. He also enquired the latest news about my youngest brother Harold, and in what ship he was then serving."

For the next three or four days the Division was arriving in our billeting area, and I was kept hard at work riding round and seeing that all those for whose comfort I was responsible were happy and adequately provided for. Amongst others I met at this time was my cousin Charlie Boyle, now in the 1st Battalion of the Rifle Brigade. Going to his billet one day, I saw a familiar face, that of Rifleman Fowler who used to be in the 1st Battalion with me.

"Hullo, Fowler," said I. "What are you doing here?"

"I'm Mr. Boyle's servant, sir," he answered. "I got wounded in November 1914, just after you came to grief."

"Not badly I hope?"

"No, sir, just a blighty one through the arm: and now here I am back again, sir."

"And how's the 1st Battalion?"

"Not much of it left, sir. That's to say not much of the old battalion you and I remember. All the officers have gone—killed or wounded, or promoted like yourself, and only six men left out of the original thousand that came out to France with us."

"Good God, how awful. Well, good-bye, Fowler, glad to have seen you again. I must now hurry back to my General."

"Good-bye, sir, and the best of luck."

———————

The Division now moved up nearer the line with their headquarters at Merris, whilst our Brigade's headquarters were at Oultersteene. During the move I was again kept tremendously busy, billeting for the advancing troops, and had little leisure for brooding over Rifleman Fowler's information that my old battalion had, in one way or another, been completely wiped out; or over the death of friends like Billy Grenfell, who fell in action just about this time in the 8th Battalion. Such, indeed, is war!

Just before we left Totinghem, our first Brigade headquarters, a German aeroplane flew over about midnight and dropped five bombs on St. Omer some three miles away with a terrific noise, and narrowly missing, I believe, the Commander-in-Chief's headquarters. These were the first bombs I had heard. I got up and looked out of my bedroom door, and there I saw five trembling women all standing in the passage in their nightdresses and crying with fright. My diary says: "Tried to comfort them as best I could, and then went back to bed."

One morning a day or two afterwards, I was walking through the village of Oultersteene with Hodson, our Brigade machine-gun officer. Our General was just in front of us, busy talking to another officer. Along came a car with Australia in large letters written on it and inside two fellows in Australian uniform. They passed without any kind of salute for the General, and with only a very inquisitive stare first at him and then at Hodson and myself.

"Damned casual fellows these Australians are," said I. "I wonder if the General noticed that they did not salute him."

"Don't suppose so," replied Hodson. "He was busy talking."

A little later in the day information came from the Division that these supposed Australians were in reality German spies, and that we were to keep a sharper lookout in future. We were now back in the area fought over by the 11th Brigade in the previous October, that, namely, of the villages of Caestre, Flêtre, Meteren and Bailleul, and it was interesting to revisit scenes of past adventure. I had escaped scatheless during the fighting

129

there, but, though the battle had rolled farther off, other enemies of the human race, besides the Germans, were at work.
The mosquitoes, in fact, were dreadful, and I was twice so badly
stung by wasps, that the combination of attacks from these insect plagues nearly drove me mad.

We were now in the 1st Army under Sir Douglas Haig and
in the 3rd Corps commanded by General Sir William Pulteney.
The latter came over one day with General Romer of his staff
and his A.D.C. Lord Castlereagh, now Marquess of Londonderry.
General Pulteney inspected the billets, with which he appeared
well satisfied, as also with the men. To them he spoke a good
deal individually during the inspection, and afterwards made a
speech complimenting the Brigade and bidding it in all circumstances to remember discipline. A day or two later Sir Douglas
Haig also came over to have a look at the troops, and I had a
short talk with him about the officers and men in the Brigade,
who, as I think I have before pointed out, were practically all the
new Kitchener Army.

I was delighted, very soon after this, to come across my
brother Aubrey, who was now commanding a Company in the 4th
Battalion of the Rifle Brigade. We had always been so much together and were so much of an age, that one of the worst experiences of the war had been parting from him. Till, however, his
Division, the 27th, was ordered off to the Amiens front about the
middle of September, we managed to see quite a lot of each other, I riding about fourteen miles to dine with him in Armentières,
or he coming to lunch or dine with me in my billets.

The Brigade now, at length, began to do their part in the war.
It started by being attached in the trenches to the 25th Brigade.
Our billets were at Fleurbaix, a village which had been very badly damaged by shell-fire as the German lines were only one and a
half miles away. On 11th August I went into the 2nd Rifle Brigade
trenches and dined with them at their battalion headquarters,
finding three old friends. Frank Nugent was commanding, with
Chichester-Constable adjutant, whilst Ham Riley, who had also
been with me in the 1st Battalion at the beginning of the war,
was there as well. After dinner we went round the trenches,
which were from eighty to a hundred yards distant from the German lines.

My diary says of this visit:

"Such excellent trenches I have never seen, and they are all called by the names of different London streets. The amount of sandbags, etc., that they have now is something wonderful. Everyone seemed very happy."

My memories were, of course, confined to the haphazard, hastily improvised, and badly provided entrenchments of the first few months of the war.

The Brigade were under instruction for a week in the line near Fleurbaix where they had several casualties, and then returned to Oultersteene. Roger Brand, an old friend in the 2nd Battalion Rifle Brigade, whom I also met at Fleurbaix, told me that his battalion took over there in May from a Territorial battalion to whom, as it appeared, the Germans used to talk and call out for cigarettes and beer. The 2nd Rifle Brigade, however, started shooting the first night they arrived which made the Germans furious. Whereupon one yelled out:

"Don't you know I've a wife and children in Liverpool?"

And a Tommy on our side answered: "Yes, and if you go on sitting up there you'll bloody well have a widow and children in Liverpool."

A surprise order now came to the Brigade whilst in reserve at Oultersteene, that we were to take over the trenches of the Garwhal Brigade, part of the Indian (Meerut) Division, instead of going back to Fleurbaix in due course as we had anticipated. The Brigadier was General Blackader; and his A.D.C. the young Maharajah of Cooch Behar, was in my form at Eton, and then known to us as Hitty Narayan. These trenches were about eleven miles away, near the village of Laventie. I had been working very hard at all the arrangements for taking over the trenches at Fleurbaix; settling the billets in the shell-battered streets of the village and in neighbouring farms; drawing maps of the area and taking them round to the Division; checking trench stores; settling disputes with the local inhabitants; doing, in fact, the hundred and one different jobs that fell to the lot of a staff-captain, and now this sudden change of plan appeared to make all my work useless. However, that is the little way of the Army! Everything had to be done over again. To make matters worse, the Brigade-Major left owing to a breakdown in health and I had to do both his work and my own. Fortunately Toby Curtis, a most competent officer and adjutant to our Divisional Cavalry, the Westmorland and Cumberland Yeomanry, came in to give a hand, otherwise I should never have got through all the work devolving on me till the arrival of a new Brigade-Major, Major Blount, D.S.O. of the York and Lancaster Regiment. It is not difficult to imagine that in these circumstances I was very much pleased when one day General Roy showed me the following confidential report on myself and my work that he was forwarding on to the Division for transmission to the War Office:

"This officer is intelligent, quick at taking anything in, and capable. He is always ready for any hard work there is to be done. He is an excellent horseman."

Our Headquarters at Laventie were in a tall three-storied, brick house with a high pinnacled roof. This house was called "La Carpière" and belonged to a M. Dumont-Dormion, and stood in full view of the German lines. Hence it was known throughout the Army as "Cockshy Hall." The extraordinary thing was, that although the rest of the village of Laventie had been pretty badly shelled, this house had never been touched despite the almost irresistible target it must have presented. Various legends arose to account for this, as for instance that the Crown Prince had stayed there and had promised not to shell it.

We had not been more than a day or two at Laventie before the rumour of a great attack being imminent spread through all ranks. Optimism was the keynote. The Germans were to be pounded for ten days and nights by shell fire, assaulted irresistibly, and driven out of France. The war was to be over by October. It is easy to be cynical after the event, especially considering that the ill-omened actions of Festubert and Neuve Chapelle had been fought practically on this very ground, and that in front of our lines along the plain stretched three miles away the long low Aubers Ridge, for the possession of which, only in the previous May, a desperate and unsuccessful battle had raged. But in war, memories are short. Besides, who could fight unless he was an optimist? Captain Liddell Hart says that the authors of this Artois-Champagne 1915 campaign (Joffre, Foch and French) "are the greatest examples in history of faith divorced from reason." This may be so—at any rate their sanguine views filtered down through all the ranks of the Allies, and neither in our Brigade nor in the others on the Loos front was there any doubt that this time we should conquer.

My journal till the opening day of the battle is mostly the record of the routine of trench warfare: notes of listening patrols; reports of movements in or behind the enemy's lines; counter-battery work; reliefs; a prisoner or two captured and examined; activities of snipers; personal visits to the forts which supported our firing line during which I had one or two narrow escapes from machine-guns and whizz-bangs; and of course, running through all, the ever-lengthening and melancholy list of wounded and killed. On the whole though, our part of the line during this period was reasonably quiet.

The story of the fight at Loos on 25th September and the following days has by now often been told: how the Commander of the 1st Army was dubious of his resources in men and guns and refused to advance unless the wind was favourable for gas: how on the evening of the 24th the wind was veering and changing, and then at 5 a.m. the next morning Sir Douglas Haig bade his A.D.C. light a cigarette and decided from the drift of the smoke that the attack should after all take place: how the wind changed again, and part of our assaulting troops were caught in their own gas, but despite this handicap, made progress especially on the right and captured the German first line positions: and how, finally, all these partial and preliminary successes were nullified by the slow arrival and inexperience of the two new Army Divisions in reserve, while to the South the French assault was badly timed, and almost at once brought to a standstill. All these dismal mistakes and disasters have long ago become history. My memoirs are concerned only with our small part in the battle on the extreme left flank of the 1st Army.

Supported by a bombardment which started after a dead silence of half an hour and was "such as I had never yet seen, and looked as if no human being could live in it," our Brigade (the 12th Rifle Brigade, the 6th Shropshires, 6th Oxford and Bucks and the 12th King's Royal Rifles) with the Meerut Division on our right, attacked at 5.50 a.m. Up to noon we made some progress, but after that the Germans counter-attacked, and with heavy shell and machine-gun fire drove us out of their trenches and back into our own. By 6 p.m. that evening we were all (save for those who had fallen) in the same positions as we started from in the morning. The 12th Rifle Brigade, who received the special thanks of our Divisional General, General Davies, for the way in which they fought, suffered the most severely. They had four officers killed, and three officers wounded, and about three hundred and fifty of the rank and file were killed, wounded or missing.

My diary says: "It was a great shock to me Joyce Bonsor being killed, as he was one of my greatest friends. He was shot dead right over near the German wire. . . . The sights one saw to-day one will never forget. They were too horrible and dreadful. In the Battle of the Aisne they were bad enough, but the bits of men, clothes, rifles, etc., in the trenches after this battle, with men dead and dying and mutilated, are better left unthought of and untold. . . . So ended September the 25th."

Our own little attack had been a complete failure! Nevertheless no one knew for a day or two, as the battle south of the La Bassée Canal was still proceeding, and encouraging reports kept coming in of French success in Champagne, whether we should not try again on our sector. Although I had had no sleep for forty-eight hours I spent from 9.30 p.m. to 3 a.m. on the night of the 26th–27th supervising the conveyance of ammunition and trench mortar batteries on the trench-railways up to the front line. The Germans remained very jumpy for some time, despite the fact that they had repulsed us so easily, and a lot of shelling continued till after 13th October when there was another big attack south of the La Bassée Canal, preceded by what seemed to us then a tremendous bombardment. After this had ended as abortively as the first phase of the Loos Battle, our sector returned to the routine of ordinary trench warfare. Meanwhile several of the more elderly officers of our New Army Battalions had been sent home. Poor old gentlemen! The conditions and stress of war had been too much for their physique and nerves. The older one was, the more one felt the strain! My General, however, all through our time in the La Bassée sector, remained undaunted and unperturbed.

So the war went on. As far as I personally was concerned, I was extremely busy again, as our Brigade shifted their section of trenches more to the right and I had a fresh task of billeting to carry out. My birthday, 7th November, came round again. I was now twenty-six and still alive, which was something to be thankful for. What was still more extraordinary perhaps, was that although hit several times by spent pieces of shell, I had never been actually wounded. My diary recalls my previous birthday spent in the trenches opposite Le Touquet in Flanders when the rain poured down in ceaseless torrents and the shells whined and crashed into our lines. It really seems wonderful that anyone survived that day, and now on my next birthday I was to have another extraordinary escape. I was going in one of the divisional cars to Estaires, and just where the Rue de Paradis joins the La Bassée road two enemy shells burst, one exactly behind and one exactly in front of the car, without touching it or us.

I had by now been promoted Captain, and after doing a machine-gun course at Wisques, the Corps Commander General Pulteney, a connection of my family's, ordered me to join his Staff as temporary assistant G.S.O.3. I enjoyed immensely working for the General, who was a most capable soldier, and would have been glad to continue on his staff, but my Brigade was now ordered up to the Ypres Salient and General Roy asked for me back again.

That Christmas, just before we left for Ypres, the 2nd Battalion of the Rifle Brigade gave a dinner to which they kindly invited me. I give the Menu here, as it seems, considering it was war-time and that we were all on active service, to have been a pretty good Christmas dinner.

Potage

QUEUE DE BŒUF

Poisson

MAYONNAISE DE HOMARD

Roti

DINDON ROTI
OIE ROTI

Entremets

PLUM PUDDING
MINCE PIE

CAFÉ

DESSERT

The back of the menu-card, which is in one of my albums, is signed with the names of a dozen or so officers of the battalion who were dining that night. Nearly all these poor fellows were afterwards killed.

We were nearly six months in the Salient, and from the time we marched up from Poperinghe under a bombardment to the day we left, it was a period of almost unrelieved beastliness.

No-Man's land was generally half under water, and the slightest movement of a patrol was apt to draw fire. The cold was terrible. The trenches were haunted by legions of rats which got their teeth into everything they could find and scuttled over one when asleep, and which we hunted after dark with sticks and electric torches without any apparent lessening of their numbers. I have killed as many as sixty by myself in one night. Sniping went on continuously. In the trenches men stood up to their knees in water, and suffered terribly from the disease of "Trench-Feet." It rained; it snowed; it sleeted continuously. Enemy bombing 'planes were unpleasantly active, while as the spring drew near their artillery fire increased in volume and lachrymatory gas-shells in large quantities began coming over. Our line ran in front of the Canal opposite the Pilckem Ridge, and consisted on its left flank principally of detached trenches about fifty yards long holding a few men and a machine-gun. One of these, F.34, was only twelve yards away from the enemy's front line. My job was to visit four of these detached posts at night about twice a week, and one evening, five minutes after I had left, this F.34 was captured by the Germans, and an officer and twenty-five men were taken prisoners. Mines, trench-mortars, and bombs exploded day and night, and took a heavy toll of life, as many as fifty officers and men being killed and wounded on one occasion by a mine which exploded under our front line.

Raids for identification purposes on both sides were common. Like most other front line soldiers I consider that these raids were far too frequent, and that the information gained did not justify the loss of life. It was generally only the best men who were sent on them and, in consequence, these were always "going west."

During the period just covered, I heard on the 29th of January 1916, on coming down from the line, that my youngest brother Harold had been killed in H.M.S. *Viking* which was in the Dover Patrol and to which he had not been long appointed. The ship had been hit by a mine.

I had been on leave a fortnight before and had seen him in London. His last words to me as we parted were: "Well, goodbye, Lionel. I suppose I shall see you again if I'm not killed by one of those bloody mines."

Like so many others in the war, he had no doubt a foreknowledge of his fate. My mother and father had gone to Dover to see him that week-end. As they waited for him in the hotel dining-room, a telegram was brought in announcing that he had been killed. The shock to them both expecting to see him in a few minutes and then hearing of his death, was terrible, and neither of them ever recovered from it. I had two days' leave to go to his funeral at Freshwater, our village in the Isle of Wight, but had no time to send home word that I was coming. As I walked into the house at Farringford I met my mother half-way up the stairs, and thinking it was my ghost she cried out: "My God, have you gone too, Lionel!" and fainted in my arms.

Harold was a high-spirited fellow, full of jest and humour, and immensely able. So much did he impress his contemporaries in the Navy by his brilliance and ability that many of them have told me that but for his death in the war, he must have risen right to the top of his profession, an opinion with which all the senior officers under whom he served concurred.

On 30th April I was mentioned in despatches by Sir Douglas Haig, who had recently inspected our Brigade and had expressed his admiration of their behaviour and smart appearance. The Brigade shortly afterwards entrained for Calais to refit after their strenuous time in the line, and the command of it was now given to Brig.-General the Hon. Leslie Butler, D.S.O., who had been commanding a battalion of Irish Guards. General Butler was a most capable, fearless and gallant soldier, and very popular with all ranks.

The first week of June 1916 the Brigade was again in the line under General Butler. Almost immediately the Germans made a strong offensive against the Canadian positions on Observatory Ridge to the right of our Divisional Sector, and despite a gallant resistance drove them from Hill 62 and the precincts of Sanctuary Wood with very heavy losses. Our Headquarters were then in the Ramparts near the Menin Gate, and General Butler sent me up the Menin Road to find out the situation. Most of the Canadians, after their desperate struggle, had been relieved the night before. A few, however, had been left behind, and amongst them a Corporal and four men whom I happened to pass on the Menin Road, making their way back utterly spent, drooping with fatigue, and all covered in mud and blood.

Just as I met them the battle started again.

At the sound of the sudden uproar all five stopped dead in their tracks, their backs straightened and they turned about, the lust of fighting in their faces.

"Come on, boys," said the Corporal. "We can't miss this fun." And back into the battle they went. If ever five men deserved to get through and win decorations, these five men did. But who knows their fate?

In July 1916 we moved from Ypres to the Somme. Not much to be thankful for, one would think, in the light of after-events, but in war any change generally seems a good one. We had all become heartily sick of the accursed Salient. So many good fellows had "gone west" there, especially in our last abortive gas attack in support of the Canadians, that such of us as remained were overjoyed to be moving South. The Brigade took up a position opposite Serre. This had been manned by the 1st Battalion Rifle Brigade just prior to our arrival, and the front line had been blown in on the eve of an attack by them. As soon as we arrived, General Butler and I had to crawl round these trenches to see if they could be reconditioned. Never in my life had I been through anything like this. Ugh! Dead faces were looking up at one everywhere out of the mud, while the smell was too overpowering and awful for words. Not long after this I saw that famous actor of pre-war days, Basil Hallam, killed. His captive balloon had been shot loose about three miles behind our lines, and was drifting over them. I saw something which looked like a sack falling from it. This was the body of Hallam who jumped whether with or without a parachute, I don't know. At any rate he was killed. Only two days before, Humphrey de Trafford and I had been into Amiens to dine with him at the famous Café Gobert. Hallam was in riotous spirits. A piano and an accompanist were produced, and he sang to us some of his old songs. "You're here and I'm here," "Gilbert the Filbert," and others which many of us still remember. Strangely enough the last song that he sang when the party broke up to allow us all to get back to our billets was "Good-bye, girls, I'm through."

We had some excellent partridge-shooting in the Hebuterne Sector behind our support lines, but when one or two fellows got hit, this form of sport was stopped.

In the middle of August we were relieved by the Guards Division, and after a short rest moved up in support again. From our new position we had our first full sight of the devastation of the

Somme. Away to the East one saw the village of Fricourt now reduced to heaps of bricks and rubble. To the left of Fricourt were the ruins of Contalmaison, and right on the skyline ahead of us the skeleton of Mametz Wood. We soon heard that we were destined to attack the village of Guillemont, a village half a mile East of Trones Wood. This position was very strong and had already repulsed five separate divisions. Its capture was, however, essential to the Commander-in-Chief's plans, and captured it had to be at all costs. Despite the tremendous task before them the men were in very good spirits and when, though with severe casualties, they repulsed a German forestalling attack on 23rd August, their confidence rose higher still. Meanwhile for one cause or another the attack on Guillemont was postponed three or four times although the work of artillery preparation went on. To myself, as I watched, the whole German front line appeared to be continually blown up: the air simply quivered and the din was terrible. The unburied corpses of English, German and French soldiers were lying thick all over the countryside with the carcasses of dead horses and mules, while the stink was almost unendurable and all water in the area became undrinkable. In the midst of these various delays the weather set in wet, and the ground became nearly impassable for an attack. Nevertheless the Germans made another big assault, accompanied by a terrific bombardment with gas-shells and high-explosive, on our 59th and 61st Infantry Brigades, who had dreadful casualties but succeeded in repulsing the enemy. I remember meeting Captain P. P. Curtis, M.C., Brigade-Major of the 59th Brigade, and discussing with him the prospects of the Guillemont attack, now fixed for the 3rd September.

"Listen to the men laughing and joking, Lionel," said he. "One can hardly believe in men being so light-hearted with such an awful ordeal in front of them."

"One can believe one thing, anyhow," I answered. "That we shall take Guillemont. No troops in the world could stand up against men like ours."

On the grey dawn of Sunday, 3rd September, from 6 a.m. onwards our bombardment became tremendous, intense fire being concentrated on ground N.E. of the village of Guillemont. At 12 noon (zero hour) with grim faces our splendid fellows went over the parapet. The great attack had begun. The Germans fought with wonderful gallantry and no mercy was given on either side. By half-past twelve our troops had gained their first objective, and by 1 p.m., after a desperate battle amongst the ruins of Guillemont, the whole village had passed into our hands, thus removing an obstacle that had held up the whole of the right wing of the British Army for six weeks. The casualties on both sides were fearful and innumerable deeds of valour were done. My cricketing friend and also my commanding officer at a later stage of the war, Lt.-Col. L. H. W. Troughton, did magnificently and captured a machine-gun single-handed, for which splendid feat he received the Legion of Honour. A great many V.C.'s were earned that third day of September 1916, but not everyone who earned one, as Troughton undoubtedly did, could get one. I myself was again lucky to escape with a slight wound which did not prevent me remaining at duty. The newspapers, however, reported me killed, and I was obliged to telegraph home to deny the statement.

I now went back to the 12th Battalion Rifle Brigade, as second in command to the late Col. Ham Riley, as the loss in regimental officers during the recent battles had been very great.

The Guards by one of their most famous attacks had just taken Guinchy, a few hundred yards beyond Guillemont, and we relieved them after this magnificent enterprise. I remember seeing Sir Ian Colquhoun of the Scots Guards. In his hand was a pick-handle covered in hair and blood with which he had killed twenty Germans.

Shortly after this, our division was engaged with thirteen other divisions in the attack on the villages of Lesboeuf, Morval, and Combles, and during it I was wounded and returned to England.

MY THIRD WOUND: THE WAR ENDS

As I lay in hospital recovering from my wound, the war eddied and volleyed up and down the fields of France. Old friends had gone—scores and scores of them. New friends had been made and had gone too. Human life ceased to count in this earth-shaking colossal struggle. It might be one's own turn at any moment.

Nevertheless when my mother died that winter, I suffered an acute sense of loss that I could hardly realize. She had been to me all that a mother could be, my truest friend, my dearest companion, and the bond between us had been very close. She died, indeed, a martyr to duty. The sudden shock of my brother Harold's death had lowered her vitality, but she would take no rest, working night and day in her Afton Down Hospital which she and my father ran under the War Office. She caught a chill which developed into pneumonia, and the end came in a day or two.

I went down to her funeral at Freshwater, and found my father greatly altered. His footsteps had grown heavy, his back was bent, and he had changed from a middle-aged into an elderly man. His sorrows and troubles had hit him hard.

A week after my mother's death the following verses with their brief and touching introduction appeared in *Country Life*.

They were written by an old friend of the family, F. W. Bourdillon.

AUDREY TENNYSON

Obiit. Dec. 7. "Lady Tennyson as Audrey Boyle was the most lovely creature. But ah! how many years ago."

(*Extract from a private letter*.)

Alas and Alas! What word to be said
For beauty dying and gladness dead
   And a world left grey?
Every year the flowers arise,
Pass in a pageant before our eyes
   And die, yet they
Come again with the same sweet face
Each again in the same dear place,
But ah! her beauty and ah! her grace
   That is dead to-day!
Earth shall not see it again, nor tears
Wash out remembrance of her bright years
   That a man might say
"Though she is dead, there shall be her peers"
   Ah nay! Ah nay!

As soon as I was passed fit for duty, I went to Aldershot to attend the senior officers' course under General Kentish. I was there some weeks and played in two or three cricket matches, many fine players being stationed in Aldershot at that time, notably Harry Makepeace, the Lancashire and England cricketer, Colonel Teddy Wynward of Hampshire and England, the Hon. Harry Mulholland, an ex-captain of the Cambridge Eleven, and many others.

Colonel Hon. Wilfred Egerton was then commandant at the Farnborough Flying School, and he and his wife had a house in the neighbourhood at which they were kind enough to ask me to stay during the period of my course. I owe them a great debt of gratitude for their kindness and splendid hospitality, doubly appreciated when one knew that soon one must return to the filthy discomforts of the war. I passed out of the senior officers' school "fit to command a battalion" and set off *en route* for France again about the middle of June. Incidentally while crossing the Channel the ship behind ours was blown up. On the way to the front, whilst waiting to be detailed to a battalion, I spent a week at Boulogne, where I lost a lot of money at cards to an officer in the A.S.C. I was eventually posted to the 10th Battalion of the Rifle Brigade, 59th Brigade, as second in command to Lt.-Col. L. H. W. Troughton, M.C., who has already been mentioned in these pages. "Troutie" (as everyone knows him) reminds me that he could not help smiling when his quartermaster brought him a wire from me saying "Send two limbers, pack horse, and charger to railhead for me and my kit." However, they came, as our Brigade was then at rest at Pernais, just back from the line where they had had a gruelling time. I have never liked "travelling light," and so, though the amount of kit I arrived with may, in fact, have aroused a certain amount of astonishment, I was quickly forgiven by my commanding officer as well as by everyone else, when they found that it included, amongst other things, a case of champagne. We lived like fighting-cocks in these rest billets, with white table-cloths and proper glasses, the best champagne, port, brandy and whisky, and Corona Corona cigars! I do, in fact, remember what grand dinner parties we used to give. However, if such high living might conceivably have had any ill-effects on us as soldiers, these were nullified by the Brigade Order that the C.O., 2nd in Command, and all other officers and men had to run each morning at 6 a.m. Whilst we were at Pernais some Divisional sports were held. At these our battalion won five first prizes. I was very successful myself individually, winning the prize for the best turnout on "Troutie's" mare "Susie," also the hundred yards and the quarter-mile.

Besides this, during the three weeks of our stay here, there was a lot of cricket played. We had a strong side in my battalion; our Colonel, Troughton, later captain of the Kent Eleven, was, of course, a member of it, and it also included Captain S. J. Pegler, D.S.O., who had played for the Transvaal and South Africa, and several other good cricketers. In fact the battalion was never beaten, although we took on the division. Shortly afterwards when at Proven, we played a match against the Guards. The cricket pitch on this occasion was rather peculiar. To make it playable at all, we stuffed sand into the cracks and holes in the field, and covered the sand with canvas. Before the Guards' side went in, as they had won the toss, we suggested to them that the wicket was "a bit of a flier." As a matter of fact the exact contrary was the case, and off the canvas the ball wouldn't rise more than six inches. Our opponents were out for some ridiculous score, most of them clean bowled "with their heads well in the air." "Troutie" and I then made some runs, and between us we hit nearly our entire stock of balls into a filthy pond in the middle of the ground. Without reckoning the slight inconveniences just described, and barring the entire absence of ladies, it was like a country-house match before the war, a band playing, the Divisional and Brigade Staffs looking on, and lots to eat and drink.

The Brigade now went back into Lord Cavan's noted XIV Corps as part of the reserve to the 38th Welsh Division in an attack they were delivering against Pilckem Ridge on 31st July. My battalion spent their time carrying up to the front line materials for an assault, and a very unpleasant time it was, as we used to get bombed by aeroplanes eight or nine times nightly. I remember that on one occasion a man with whom I was talking was killed within five yards of me by an unexploded anti-aircraft shell. The shell went right through his body into the ground. On 30th July we moved forward to an area called Carden Farm, and the next day the battle started. This battle, which went on for two months and was to become known officially as the 3rd Battle of Ypres, at the time was usually called the Battle of Passchendaele. It was probably the foulest, grimmest, and most costly battle with the most problematical results ever fought in the history of war. It has been described so often in books, and everyone has such an acquaintance with the conditions under which it was fought, that I personally do not propose to attempt to describe it again, but will confine myself to the operations of our own Division.

One of the earliest incidents in the battle which was not without its ironical side, was the gassing of our Divisional Commander, Major-General Matheson, whilst up in the line. Only the day before, General Matheson had issued an order to the Division that cases of gas-poisoning were due to lack of discipline through not putting gas helmets on quick enough, and that any man, therefore, who got gassed must be severely dealt with. Having got gassed himself in defiance of his own order General Matheson had to go to hospital, and Major-General Douglas Smith then resumed command of the 20th Division and was given the task of capturing the town of Langemark.

Between our objective and ourselves lay a stream of water known as the Steenbeek. The 38th and Guards Divisions had established positions along the eastern bank after hard fighting on the opening day of the battle, but now it remained to cross the stream. On 11th August, the 10th K.R.R.C. attacked and got to the other side, but were driven back with great loss. Three days later six companies comprising the 10th R.B. (my battalion) and half the 11th R.B., all under command of Lt.-Col. L. H. W. Troughton, M.C., were ordered to deliver an attack against a concrete "pill-box," nicknamed "Au bon gîte," which completely commanded any attack from our front. At four o'clock (zero hour) our divisional artillery put down a barrage, and under cover of this and after some grim fighting, we got within fifty yards of our objective. The Germans then delivered a strong counter-attack, and by nightfall what remained of my battalion and the 11th R.B. were back on the eastern bank of the Steenbeek. During the day's fighting the South African cricketer, Sydney Pegler, who was in my battalion, did magnificently and gained the D.S.O. Our losses had been very heavy—eleven officers killed, four wounded, and two hundred casualties amongst the men. Two days later, units of the 60th and 61st Brigades captured "Au bon gîte" and its garrison, and then went on to take Langemark with four hundred prisoners, several guns, and two dozen machine-guns. Our Brigade then went into reserve in the area round Proven for about three weeks, and spent the time in re-fitting and training for another offensive. This was on a section of trench called Eagle Trench about a thousand yards east of Langemark. After two days' fighting and very heavy losses, my battalion managed to capture it in cooperation with the 12th K.R.R.C. Ninety-four German prisoners were taken, with ten machine-guns.

This was our last operation in the Ypres Sector. On 1st October our Brigade entrained for Bapaume, the 20th Division having been transferred from the 5th Army to the 3rd Army commanded by Gen. Hon. Sir Julian Byng (afterwards Lord Byng).

At 4 a.m. on 2nd October the Brigade detrained at Le Transloy and remained in that district for about a week. We were now in the 3rd Corps, and for the next few weeks we had a quite pleasant and uneventful time with Battalion Headquarters in a quarry to the south of Gouzeaucourt. The attack on Cambrai was in course of preparation, but the Germans were quite unsuspecting. This was almost the first occasion during the war when the tactical asset of "surprise" was employed by the Higher Command, a hitherto quiet sector of the front being chosen over which to launch a big attack by "tanks." Everything was done behind our lines to lull the enemy into a state of security, and all war material, munitions, and barbed wire were brought up, in vast quantities, by night. On the day of the battle which started at 6.20 a.m., our Brigade, the 59th, was in reserve to the 60th and 61st Brigades of the 20th Division in the neighbourhood of Gouzeaucourt. Our leading Brigades were preceded by tanks and with little difficulty they took their objectives, and at 11.30 a.m. my battalion moved up to the firing line and on to the villages of Marcoing and Masnières. The Germans defended the main bridge in Masnières stoutly but we eventually secured it, and entering the village received an enthusiastic welcome from the inhabitants, who were sent back to the rear. The battle which had begun in a blaze of glory and had been celebrated in London by the ringing of the church bells, now began to go the way of all battles on the Western Front. The German resistance stiffened, and our battalion could only consolidate their positions and hold on as best they could.

Hearing the noise of increased machine-gun fire on the part of the enemy, I, who had been left behind with the Transport as second-in-command, went up to the front line to find out from "Troutie" if I could be of any assistance. He was cool and cheerful as usual, but he told me the German resistance was stiffening, and that he thought before long there would be a counterattack made by them. On my way back I was wounded for the third time, and was immediately evacuated to England, where I was sent to Lady Carnarvon's hospital in Bryanston Square.

Troughton's diagnosis of the situation was correct. On 30th November the Germans, advancing in a mist, captured himself and his headquarters, while our adjutant, Capt. Henderson, M.C., a splendid soldier, was killed. Captain Pegler then assumed command of the battalion which consisted of fewer than thirty officers and men.

Lady Carnarvon's hospital, to which I was now taken, was with Lady Ridley's in Carlton House Terrace, to which I had gone on the occasion of my previous wound at the end of 1916, the best in London. I was very lucky to go to these two hospitals, and to be able to recover under such care and supervision. No attention was too much trouble, the nursing was wonderful, and the food given us exquisitely cooked and served. Lady Carnarvon's devotion to the cause of the sick and suffering did not cease with the end of hostilities in 1918. She now owns her well-known nursing-home at 7 Portland Place. I wonder how much gratitude and affection she has won in the course of her life—much more than falls to the lot of most people, I am sure!

After recovering from my wound, and leaving the hospital in Bryanston Square, to which I have attempted in a few words to pay my small tribute of admiration, I was given six months light duty, and was for two months attached to Headquarters, London District, and then sent as one of the chief instructors to the Army Machine-gun School at Grantham. My duties there comprised giving eight or ten lectures a week, and preparing schemes for officers in which the tactical use of machine-guns was the chief consideration. During my time as an instructor, hundreds of officers passed through my hands.

A few months previous to the date of my appointment, an event occurred which greatly influenced my life. This was my marriage to Clarissa, only daughter of Lord Glenconner. She was and still is one of the most beautiful women of the day.

Clare and I took Barrowby Manor near Grantham, and had house-parties most week-ends. The war was still going on, now in its fourth year, and to persons unacquainted with the secret history of events, there seemed now no particular reason why it should ever stop. There was, in fact, every probability that we should be at war for the rest of our lives, and that these lives would not be very long ones. It was a reckless time, in which one not only gambled with one's very existence, but also in every other way possible. At Barrowby, during the week-end, we sometimes played cards far into the night. To do my wife justice, she did not very much care for the gambling proclivities of myself and my friends, but we had gambled in the line—in woods whilst we waited in support, and in billets while we rested in reserve—and shell-fire and aeroplane bombs on more than one occasion had broken up our games. The reckless hazards of the war had produced in some of us a reckless spirit that needed the stimulus of high play to keep us going.

At Barrowby, I also hired a small shoot of about two thousand acres. I believe that my friends and myself, in our determination to get our money's worth, shot practically every living thing on the place.

I must now come to another event which also greatly influenced me. The great German offensive campaign of 1918 began shortly after my marriage, and whilst we were up at Grantham. My brother Aubrey had been invalided home from Salonika and was holding a staff job in the Southern Command, but just before the German advance began he was sent out to France again. One day whilst the battle was raging, I had a sudden awful feeling, the nature of which I cannot hope or attempt to explain, that my brother had been killed. A day or two afterwards, this was confirmed by the casualty lists, but it was some time later before we had full details. He was killed in command of C Company of the 9th Battalion Rifle Brigade, near Fleury Le Martel. His Colonel, the Hon. Noel Bligh, stated that his death was instantaneous, and due to a machine-gun bullet as he was crossing the open to get in touch with a battalion on his right that had given way. Colonel Bligh said that Aubrey's men believed in him absolutely, and that he was splendid, cool, and absolutely fearless in action. His sergeant, G. E. Chaplin, wrote that he was greatly loved by his Company, and was one of the finest and bravest officers ever seen, and that if anyone had ever earned the V.C. he had done so. To tell simply the bare truth, there was never anyone, rich or poor, old or young, who did not love my brother. He was the most popular fellow known to me both at Eton and later—a character absolutely straight and honourable without an enemy in the world. To me, his loss was the most terrible shock.

Both my brothers had now been killed and I, myself, had been three times wounded. The authorities, I think, had decided that my family had done enough. At any rate, they made no move to send me back to France, although I was due to return there just as the war came to an end. That summer I played a lot of cricket for the Machine-gun Corps, making several large scores of over a hundred. There are two principal incidents, however, of that cricket season which stick in my mind. The first is a record hit which I made on the School ground, playing against Rugby School. This particular hit over some large elm trees dividing the cricket ground from the football ground still remains a record, I believe, at least I have never heard that it has been beaten. The other incident which I vividly remember is that of my first meeting with A. P. F. Chapman, then a schoolboy at Uppingham. A good many years afterwards when in 1928–1929 Percy Chapman was the captain of the victorious M.C.C. team in Australia, the editor of a certain well-known daily newspaper asked me if I thought I could celebrate Percy's triumph in verse for an adequate remuneration.

I have always been of the opinion that one doesn't know what one can do till one tries. So though I had never till that moment indulged in the art for which my name is famous, I replied that, on account of my admiration and affection for Chapman and also because of my need for a little ready cash, I would certainly try to compose a stanza or two in his honour.

A day or two afterwards, I handed these verses to the editor's representative.

Now here's a health from o'er the sea,
　　A word of greeting o'er the foam,
In England's hour of victory,
　　To those who bring the Ashes home.
Sydney, Melbourne, and Brisbane know
　　What England knows who sent them forth,
How gallantly, come weal or woe,
　　They play the greatest game on earth.

Their names a mighty book would fill
　　And furnish many a powerful rhyme,
Our lordly Hobbs' classic skill
　　Mellowed but not subdued by time,
Our giant captain's cheerful grin,
　　The grin that masks a leader's guile,
Duckworth whose hands hold fast as sin,
　　Geary who bowls you with a smile.

Stubborn Sutcliffe's Yorkshire bat,
　　Broad and big as a great barn door,
Hendren quick on his feet as a cat,
　　Hammond's slash for an offside four,
Larwood's swift and terrible ball,
　　The fasts of Tate with their lift and fire,
The courage of Jardine cool and tall,
　　The craft of White which cannot tire.

Their great achievements and their praise
　　Henceforth shall furnish history's page,
How for the space of seven long days,
　　In one stern fight they did engage:
And how, defying even fate,
　　They fought and turned the game again,
Therefore from those who watch and wait,
　　A health to Chapman and his men!

"Fine, Lionel!" said the editor's representative, an old friend, after reading these verses through. "They'll do just right. What do you want for them?"

"For poetry," said I, "I couldn't think of asking less than a hundred pounds, cash on delivery."

"A hundred pounds!" exclaimed my friend. "A hundred pounds!! My dear Lionel, that's more than your respected grandfather ever got; more than Mr. Rudyard Kipling gets; and incidentally twenty times as much as the poet Milton got for writing the whole of 'Paradise Lost.'"

"That may be so," said I, "but none of them ever captained England at cricket, and when did one captain of an England Eleven ever before write a poem in honour of another captain of an England Eleven? My dear fellow, these verses are unique in English literature."

"Well, Lionel," said my friend, "I'll just go in to the boss and see what he says."

On his returning, I was informed that £50, cash on delivery, was the most the newspaper could "spring" for my verses, which, having an exalted opinion of poetry in general (as is only right considering my ancestry) and no mean opinion of my own verses, I indignantly refused.

Alas! No higher bid came, so I now present my only poem to the public—free, gratis, and for nothing!

CHAPTER XV

LIFE AFTER THE WAR: I CAPTAIN ENGLAND AT CRICKET

ALTHOUGH a soldier by profession and now the Hon. Colonel of the 51st Territorial Brigade Anti-Aircraft Gunners, I frankly disapprove of war if it can be avoided, and regard it as justifiable only if no other possible way of settling disputes can be found.

Four years of muddle, blood, discomfort, carnage, inconceivable expenditure of lives and money, and in consequence the whole world upside down with what seems to me a very remote prospect of standing on its feet again!

Of course, after the peace in 1918, I, together with all other individuals and communities which it affected, now supposed it was time to settle down. Those four years, however, which had elapsed since the Declaration of War had made vast changes in my surroundings and in myself.

I was now a married man, and the two following years saw the birth of my two sons, Harold and Mark. My two brothers had been killed; my own mother was dead; and my father, now greatly aged, had grown into a kind of hermit who never much cared to see anybody, and insisted on keeping everything at Farringford untouched that reminded him of the wife and sons he had lost. He had now been quietly married again to Mrs. Hichens, one of the friends of his boyhood.

My stepmother was a member of the Prinsep family; she had known me all my life, and was always extremely good and kind to me. Nevertheless Farringford was no longer the old home that it had been before the war. It was full of ghosts.

I therefore went there less and less, but on the other hand my wife and I went about a good deal, not only dining out or dancing most nights in London, but staying in country houses for shooting-parties and hunting.

Amongst well-known people we visited constantly in the years immediately succeeding the war, were Lord and Lady Lovat. Lord Lovat, whose recent sudden death was a great blow to a host of friends, was, when clad in Highland dress as the chieftain of the clan Fraser, the most magnificent figure I ever saw. Looking at him thus attired and with his foot on his native heath, all the legends and romance of Highland history seemed to me embodied in his gallant and stately presence. Another Scottish friend who lived in Perthshire and was very hospitable to us was Major Murray-Graham, the most courteous of men. My wife and I often stayed with Lord and Lady Ancaster, not only at Grimsthorpe Castle, their place in Lincolnshire near Peterborough, but also at Drummond Castle in Perthshire, close to Gleneagles. It was here that I got my first stag, a thirteen-pointer weighing about twenty stone. I remember a fellow-guest of mine at Drummond Castle who had been out stalking coming back very late for dinner.

"Well," asked Lord Ancaster, "have you had a good day?"

"Wonderful! Wonderful!" was the reply. "I killed four stags and wounded six."

His Lordship's reply is unprintable.

Clare and I also sometimes stayed at Glen, my father-in-law Lord Glenconner's house in Peeblesshire. I was very fond of my father-in-law. He had a most sympathetic nature and simply adored his family.

We frequently dined with my wife's uncle and aunt, Lord and Lady Oxford and Asquith, and more than once stayed at their house, The Wharf, Sutton Courtenay, where they had very interesting and amusing parties, of which bridge was a prominent feature. At this game, which was apt to be very expensive at the points which were played in the reckless decade after the war, as I have found to my cost, Lady Oxford was too impulsive and Lord Oxford not sufficiently concentrated to excel. He was a very pleasant and amiable companion, quite devoid of any personal vanity and fond of meeting young and gay people. With Aunt Margot one had always to be distinctly on the *qui vive*. She invariably said exactly what came into her head whatever the time or the circumstances. The contrast between the two, as Lord Oxford was the very embodiment of Yorkshire canniness and reticence, was very peculiar.

Other friends whom I continued to see belonged to the gambling set in London.

I have always been a gambler by nature. It is in my blood, and I have often been in the mood when I could bet on two flies climbing up a wall. Perhaps had the war not broken out when it did, I might have marked and digested the lesson received on the racecourse which I have described in an earlier chapter, and which was a pretty sure sign of what is actually the case, that sooner or later the gambler must pay forfeit. The war, however, as I have written previously, was not exactly a circumstance to encourage the growth of moral precepts or to instil the maxim of "safety first." The other old motto, "A short life and a merry one" seemed far more appropriate, and it was the one to which the majority of my friends and acquaintances paid most heed. So the gambling fever in my veins was not so much allayed by the four years ordeal through which I had passed as considerably intensified. It had, in fact, become a confirmed habit of which nothing but bitter experience could break me.

For a time, of course, all went well, and I purchased a black-and-white Rolls-Royce car in which I drove in state to several race meetings. Alas! the black-and-white Rolls only lasted three weeks, and then the turn of the tide came. About this time also I lost £7000 in one evening at a gambling party. This blow I might have recovered from had I been paid all the gambling debts owed me at various times, but this was far from being the case. On one occasion, for instance, I won over £10,000 from an individual who shall be nameless. He said he would pay me if I wished, but for the sake of his relations must subsequently throw himself over Westminster Bridge. To save him from an untimely grave in the river I had to let him off the debt.

My affairs from this date began to be much embarrassed, and at the same time my wife and I, finding our flat at 3 Buckingham Gate too expensive, moved to 88 Elm Park Gardens. I had left the Regular Army about eighteen months after the war as a Major, and at the age of thirty-one. I had been mentioned twice in Despatches but, though recommended two or three times for a decoration, for some reason never got one, while many hundreds who never saw a shot fired did. I spent some time at the Depot at Winchester, and from there captained Hampshire at cricket. Now my battalion was ordered to Baghdad, and being a married man with a family I did not feel inclined, especially as the county were anxious for my regular services, to make such changes in my life as a transference to the Far East involved. I therefore sent in my papers in 1920 and became captain of the Hampshire Eleven from 1919 onwards.

As captain, I have always been treated royally by the Chairman, Sir Russell Bencraft and by the various members of the Hampshire Committee. Sir Russell has, indeed, been a pillar of Hampshire cricket for many years; he is an old captain of the County team, and its interests mean much to him. Although now, unfortunately, in somewhat indifferent health, he never fails to watch every home match and to encourage those who have any cricket in them.

My account of Hampshire County cricket during the years of my captaincy must necessarily be brief; let me say, however, that the team has always supported me loyally, and that on the whole we have not done so badly in the Championships. Our principal lack has been in bowling, although we possessed two of the finest bowlers in England, Kennedy and Newman, who have each bowled heaven knows how many hundreds of overs since the war. Jack Newman, in fact, strained his heart and had to retire a year or two ago, but the indomitable Alec Kennedy still goes on bowling as well as ever. We had also two very fine young amateur bowlers during this period, Peter Utley and Giles Baring, but we lost them both. Utley, forfeiting what must have been a distinguished career in the Flying Corps as well as on the cricket field, became a monk; and Baring was crippled in a horrible motor accident. It has been hard to fill their places, though Stewart Boyes has done splendid work for us for many years. Philip Mead was one of the world's greatest batsmen, and is still a great force in County cricket, though no longer in his first youth. His feats for Hampshire really deserve a book to themselves. George Brown was, in his prime, first-class in every department of the game, bowling, batting, fielding and wicket-keeping. I think such versatility must be unique in the annals of cricket. He is a bit rugged in character, and devoted to fishing and shooting, at which he is just as good as he is at cricket. Walter Livsey, once one of the best wicket-keepers in the country, was for many years, until he broke down in health, my personal servant. Many of our young players promise excellently, and in a year or two I think the County side will be very strong indeed.

A. Bowell, W. Livsey, G. Brown, A. Kennedy, Y. Newman, W. Smith,

P. Mead, C. P. Brutton, L. H. Tennyson, P. Lawrie, W. Shirley

[Image credit:] *Albert Wilkes & Son*

[Image credit:] *Albert Wilkes & Son*

Cricket in England during the years after the war was, as all students of the game remember, in a poor way. In 1919, from a wish to speed up the game, an attempt was made to introduce two-day instead of three-day matches in County cricket. This proved a dismal failure and most unattractive to the public. Perhaps the low standard of skill shown by the players after the four-year gap in serious contests, also contributed to the poor gates and lack of enthusiasm among the spectators during that season. Or perhaps again, as in every other department of life, it was impossible or too early to return to the pre-war atmosphere. The visit of the Australian Imperial Force Team to our country in 1919 first showed how marked the decline in our cricket skill had become after the war years. I played against the Australians two or three times in elevens supposed to represent the full talent of the home country then available, but as there was no official England side on any occasion, these matches have not been included in the series of Tests. The Australians were a good team, the majority of them recently discovered and very promising young players: it was in this respect that our own sides were most markedly deficient. When two years afterwards the Australians came over again, the situation had not altered. The promising young bloods in the Australian team had now grown into most formidable and matured cricketers, while there were still no youngsters in this country who appeared definitely to have reached Test Match rank, or to possess the combination of nerve and skill requisite for International contests. I remember one amateur who played for England being so nervous that he could hardly hold his bat, while his knees were literally knocking together. I endeavoured to put some heart into him by a few timely words when I joined him at the wicket, but it was useless; his nerve was gone, and the first straight ball was enough for him. In this instance all the requisite skill and science were there, but the player in question had not the particular temperament necessary for the biggest cricket. In other instances the temperament may have been good enough, but the skill was missing. So the English selectors, Harry Foster of Worcestershire, John Daniell of Somerset, and Reggie Spooner of Lancashire, had not a very easy or enviable task. This they carried out to the best of their ability by warning a numerous band of cricketers to be present on the various Test Match grounds in case their services were needed; and on one occasion the English captain, my old friend John Douglas, confronted with fourteen aspirants for the honour and glory of playing for England and faced at the last moment with the necessity of leaving three of them out, exclaimed in despair: "What's this damnable side of picnickers they've given me?"

This state of affairs preyed on Johnny's mind. He was always apt to get a bit worried when things were going wrong and, through excess of desire to put them right again, was wont to try to do too much himself.

Two other factors which militated strongly against the English sides in these contests were, firstly that the great Jack Hobbs, then in his prime, was unable to play; and secondly that, with the exception of the almost equally great Frank Woolley, the rest of the team had wholly forgotten how to play fast bowling. The so-called "two-eyed stance" had taken the place of the old left-shoulder-forward and left-foot-down-the-wicket style taught to my contemporaries and myself at Eton when every County team included at least one really fast bowler. Against that famous pair, Gregory and Macdonald, whose names will ever be remembered in cricket annals, such methods were hopeless. These two great Australians created a regular panic amongst the English batsmen. Some players even went so far as to declare that they were dangerous, and that it was almost a crime to be asked to play against them. The honour of playing for England seemed to these somewhat spiritless exponents of the finest game in the world an honour that might, in the circumstances, be far too dearly bought.

That Gregory and Macdonald were a "tough proposition" to face, it would be foolish on my part to deny. Macdonald, in fact, with the exception of our own Sydney Barnes, I consider to have been the finest bowler I have ever seen. His swift and graceful run, his beautifully easy action, his speed off the pitch, his power of turning the ball both ways when bowling his fastest, his subtle changes of pace, made him the ideal fast bowler of the imagination. Gregory, though not so great a master of his art, was almost equally formidable on wickets to his liking. Six feet four inches or more tall and extremely powerful, he hurled the ball down, after a long bounding run resembling that of the kangaroo in his native country, from a great height and with an action that seemed all composed of legs and arms, and could make it fly round one's head and shoulders in a very disconcerting way.

From their play against the Counties to start with, and then from the result of the first Test Match at Nottingham, it soon became evident that England, unless new blood was discovered, must fare disastrously against a side which included (besides the pair I have just named) such great players as their captain, the giant Warwick Armstrong, the brainy Arthur Mailey, on his day finest of all googly bowlers I have met, and that magnificently daring batsman Charlie Macartney, the famous "Governor-General."

What some people might imagine to be the greatest day of my life was now rapidly approaching, although quite unsuspected by me. On the eve of the second Test Match at Lord's, I was sitting with some friends in the Embassy Club in Bond Street, smoking my second cigar. To my amazement, towards one o'clock in the morning, just as I was thinking about going off to bed, a telephone message reached me from the selectors, that at the last moment I had been chosen to play for England and must be at Lord's next day in time for the opening of the game.

I replied that I was deeply grateful for the honour conferred upon me, but that if the selectors had informed me of their intentions a bit earlier, I should have gone to bed at a timelier hour and knocked off a cigar or two.

What had happened was this. Commander C. B. Fry, the famous All-England player of former days, then playing for Hampshire under my captaincy, had, on his own responsibility and counting on his tremendous prestige, travelled up from Southampton to interview the selectors and to impress upon them the fact that, in his opinion, I was the most likely bat available at that moment to knock fast bowlers off their length. As a matter of fact, I have always thoroughly enjoyed fast bowling, though much more vulnerable against the slow stuff. On one occasion, Richmond, the Nottinghamshire googly artist, said to me in the heat of an argument, "Well, sir, all I can say is that I'd like to take you about in my cricket-bag to bowl at." Thus implying he could get me out whenever he liked.

However, exceedingly clever as Arthur Mailey was, on this occasion it was the fast bowling that appeared to be the chief menace to England, and only the day before the second Test Match I had scored 131 not out against Jim Tyldesley, the Lancashire fast bowler, following on a score of 101 against Yorkshire a short time before. So C. B. Fry's earnest words impressed the trio whose duty it was to choose England's representatives, and my great chance had come.

Fate had the laugh of me, however, when I went out to bat next day before an audience of 34,000 people. All our men had failed again, except Frank Woolley and John Douglas. Could I now take a spectacular advantage of my chance? Retrieve the situation, and at the same time indulge my natural taste for a crack at the fast bowling?

Sad to say, all I did was to have a smack at Arthur Mailey too soon in my innings, and to return to the pavilion with only 5 runs to my credit.

There had not been wanting a considerable amount of criticism at my last minute selection, and as I mounted the pavilion steps the three grim faces of the selectors seemed to indicate their appreciation of the fact that they had been "bounced" into an error of judgment by Commander Fry's enthusiasm.

"Never mind," said I to them with a wave of the hand, trying to dissipate the general gloom and their obvious dissatisfaction with myself, "next time I'll get over 50 for sure."

My temperament, as I have frequently remarked in the course of these memoirs, is optimistic and, whatever the attendant drawbacks, that is surely the spirit in a crisis. Perhaps if more members of our side had been similarly endowed by nature, we might have made a better fight of it. England, of course, was hopelessly beaten, the Australians getting well ahead of us on the first innings and again getting us out for a very moderate score. Frank Woolley with 95 and 93 did marvels. What of myself? The optimistic spirit triumphed again and, in my second innings I scored 74 not out, hitting the fast bowlers for 10 fours in the course of it, and showing that they were only human after all if one dealt with them in the right way. I was, however, black and blue all over when I returned to the Pavilion with the bruises caused by their express deliveries.

John Douglas had now captained England in seven successive defeats in Test Matches, and following the great Napoleon's maxim that it is no use appointing an unlucky general, it was decided to find another leader. It was suggested to C. B. Fry that he should emerge from his semi-retirement, but that great player was now doubtful of his fielding powers under the strain of Test Cricket. This time, failing the acquiescence of Fry, the three selectors, after my display in the second innings and the sanguine mood I had shown after failure in the first, were no longer doubtful. If depression had settled down like a blanket on the minds of most players, my cheerfulness seemed the proper antidote and the best chance of charming the fates. So amidst a general chorus of approval in the Press, I went up to Leeds to the Headingley cricket ground as England's captain in the Third and perhaps deciding Test of the series, we having already handsomely lost the other two.

The weather was lovely, the wicket fast and true. All seemed set for a grand match, and our chances of winning quite fair, seeing that Hobbs and Hearne were now both able to play, even though Phil Mead had to cry off at the last moment owing to injury. Could my light-heartedness manage to change England's fortunes which had hitherto gone awry under the leadership of the dour John Douglas, now, like a true sportsman, playing for England under my captaincy?

Alas! The game had not been going an hour when the first of our misfortunes happened—one that befell me personally. I was fielding at silly point to the bowling of Jack White, the famous Somersetshire left-hander. Charlie Macartney hit the ball hard at me, and, in fielding it, I split my left hand so badly in the web between thumb and forefinger that I was obliged to leave the field and have three stitches put in it. So here was Johnny Douglas back for a time in his old position as captain! Then, in the course of the game, came a second and more terrible blow. Jack Hobbs was suddenly stricken with appendicitis, and removed to hospital without playing a ball. A little later as a climax of misfortune, Douglas heard that his wife was seriously ill with the same complaint, thus adding to his already great anxieties.

The Australians, owing principally to a brilliant century by Macartney, scored over 400, and then on our side the usual panic (or, as it is now the fashion to call it, "inferiority complex") set in. Our batsmen pottered and wavered and got themselves out in mere passivity of mind, no one except Douglas, who was in one of his most magnificently stubborn fighting moods, showing any real power or will to withstand the Australian attack. He, like a lion, fought on, though his colleagues one after another departed and the game became more and more hopeless. Up in the pavilion I watched the rout, my injured hand in bandages, and as one and all (even myself) imagined out of the game for good. My readers can perhaps imagine my feelings at thus being quite useless at such a crisis of England's fate. Then, as our wickets kept on falling, the idea came to me suddenly that perhaps I could bat after all. I have always been abnormally strong in the right forearm, fingers and wrist; could I wield a bat right-handed for a bit and get at least a few runs for our side that day? I went to my cricket-bag and took out the lightest bat there, and made one-handed a few tentative strokes. Yes, it might be possible. I could use the bat in this unorthodox way fairly well, it seemed to me. Before the innings ended, I would go out to do my best. When on the fall of the eighth wicket, I was seen coming out of the pavilion there arose all round the ground from the spectators, who were, of course, every one of them conversant with my misfortune, such a tempest of cheers and applause that it was enough to nerve any man to glorious deeds. All my doubts vanished on my way out "to the middle." Then taking "guard" and gripping my bat firmly with the right hand alone, I prepared to face Australia's fast bowlers.

Cricket history in which (so the newspapers declared at the time) my innings at Headingley will always find a place as long as the great game is played, records that I made 63 runs in not much over the hour, hitting ten fours and sending the ball to all parts of the field. The ovation I received on returning to the pavilion was wonderful. Crippled as I was, this innings of mine, compared with the efforts of those who had preceded me at the wicket, astonished and thrilled the spectators. Perhaps it was luck, but then my right forearm and wrist are really exceptionally strong, and batting one-handed was not so very difficult for me. I went out to field in Australia's second innings, and was even fortunate enough to make a one-handed catch.

Cricket is only a game, though it is one to which I have devoted a large part of my life. Nevertheless where international contests are involved, for good or ill this same game becomes something more than a game. Tens of thousands of spectators are present, their eyes and minds fixed on every ball bowled and their mood identified with that of the players in the field. Success or failure elates or depresses them accordingly, and after the long series of defeats England had sustained from Australia, the feeling that something was wrong with the "old country" if she must always thus be the "underdog" was very prevalent, nay, almost universal.

(HON. L. H. TENNYSON AND WARWICK ARMSTRONG) ENGLAND *v.*
AUSTRALIA, MANCHESTER, 1921

[Image credit:] *Central News*

"THE INDESTRUCTIBLE BATSMAN: OR, THE SKIPPER COEUR-DE-LION."

CARTOON BY E. T. REED, IN THE *Bystander*, JULY 13, 1921. *By permission.*

[The cartoon reads as follows.]

1: UNDER NORMAL CONDITIONS THE HON. LIONEL TENNYSON IS A FAIRLY HEFTY INDIVIDUAL, WITH NO EXAGGERATED RESPECT FOR THE BOWLING, BUT <u>WHEN</u> <u>IT</u> <u>COMES</u> <u>TO</u> <u>THIS</u> — (SEE #2)

2: SOME PEOPLE MIGHT BE A TRIFLE DISCONCERTED AND PUT OFF THEIR GAME BY <u>THIS</u> AMOUNT OF DISABLEMENT — BUT NO-O-O!! — BLESS YOU. —

3: <u>THAT</u> SORT OF THING DOESN'T WORRY TENNYSON HE

4: JUST GOES ON HITTING BOUNDARIES. —

5: UNTIL HE'S GIVEN OUT "<u>TORSO</u>-<u>BEFORE</u>." THE IRREDUCIBLE <u>MINIMUM</u>!

THE AUTHOR BATTING ONE-HANDED, TEST MATCH, ENGLAND *v.* AUSTRALIA, LEEDS, 1921

GREGORY — CARTER — TENNYSON — MAILEY

[Image credit:] *Sport & General*

From the time, however, of this one-handed innings of mine there crept, I believe, into the general consciousness the idea that England could, sooner or later, come up the right side again. The fourth and fifth Test Matches, in which I was also captain, were drawn, it is true, but, if anything, we had the better of the game in both, and never again did the Australians show over us that crushing superiority which made people think that our performances at cricket were the outward symptom of a universal physical and psychological decline.

The day when I played one-handed against Gregory, Macdonald and Arthur Mailey (incidentally I hit the latter for six in the second innings when I also played one-handed and scored 36) was perhaps the greatest day in my life; and I like to think that during it I did a little to restore our country's waning prestige.

If, indeed, I was lucky enough to create cricket history by this one-handed innings at Leeds, I was also unlucky enough in the Fourth Test Match at Manchester to make more history by an illegal declaration. The first day of the match had been a blank one through rain, and on the Monday I declared England's innings closed at ten minutes to six, having been advised by the three England selectors, also by three old England captains, Maclaren, Warner and Douglas, to do so, none of them knowing the rules any better than myself. Actually I was not entitled to declare that day unless a hundred minutes remained for play. Warwick Armstrong who was captain of the Australian side did not know the rules either, and it was only Carter the Australian wicket-keeper who was acquainted with them. Having all of us retired to the pavilion and consulted the laws of cricket, the mistake was rectified, and England continued her innings, Armstrong bowling the first over. This was another breach of the laws, as he had bowled the last over before the declaration, and so had bowled two consecutive overs.

This was my greatest year. I finished top of the England Test Match averages with an average of just over 57, having succeeded by the way in getting 51 in the last and final Test Match at the Oval. I also captained the Gentlemen v. Players at Lord's and at the Oval.

HUNTING AT MELTON MOWBRAY

MELTON MOWBRAY is to hunting men and women what Lord's cricket ground is to cricketers. The name of this small town in the heart of agricultural England is known all over the world. From all the five continents come eager sportsmen to this paradise of foxhunters. Millionaires from vast America, rich squatters from Australia, and European noblemen anxious to have a taste of the cream of English sport, all pour with their horses and grooms into this minute little town with its old-fashioned streets and aspect of another century.

Nothing much alters round Melton, even over the course of years, except the sportsmen and sportswomen who come and go. The big grass fields remain the same; so do the historic covers from which innumerable runs famous in hunting annals have taken place. Rarely does grass become plough. No wire desecrates the long succession of fences which cross the big pastures. Who there has heard any stories of irate farmers, gun in hand, turning the hunt off their land? There are places more beautiful, but to a foxhunter the view from Ranksborough Gorse is the finest view in Europe, and it has never been essentially changed for a great many years.

Of course money is the reason for all this. The Shires are really a vast pleasure ground preserved for the rich sportsmen of all nations. With so many wealthy people coming there, the funds at the disposal of such famous packs as the Cottesmore, the Quorn, and the Belvoir, are large enough to enable them to eliminate all the difficulties with which provincial hunts have to contend.

Funny things, as all sportsmen know, can indeed happen in countries where fox-hunting is not the prime consideration.

In this connection, and if a slight digression is pardonable, I am going to relate a somewhat peculiar episode of which I myself happened to be an eyewitness. It occurred a few years after the war while I was staying for a shoot with a gentleman with whom my acquaintance was of the slightest—in fact my visit to his house was only at the last moment, and at the instance of a mutual friend, who had enticed me thither, principally by tales of what a wonderful shoot we should have.

Our host had made, I believe, a large fortune during the war, though what the particular field of his activities was I have either forgotten or never knew. The chief point was that the money was there, and that he had acquired a large country house and estate in one of the Home Counties, and was now also busily endeavouring to acquire some, at any rate, of the traditions of an English country gentleman.

After his strenuous business life, shooting had become his principal hobby, though, as the sequel shows, he had not yet been able to extend the same wholehearted patronage to the local Hunt.

Certainly, too, there was nothing to complain of about his hospitality, and when the party were assembled next morning in the covers (most of them ex-business men like our host) the only fear was that some of us might have done ourselves too well over-night to bring much down. Unluckily there were not as many birds as our host hoped, and, as I had guessed, a lot of missing. Added to this, some of the dogs were not well under control, and were at times disconcertingly in evidence in the covers. Our host by lunch-time was, in consequence, somewhat out of temper. To this unhappy state of mind an unfortunate witticism of my own, which I'm afraid he must have overheard, that "there seemed to be more dogs about than birds," may perhaps have contributed.

Before the first beat after lunch, he sent for his head keeper and told him that if sport in the afternoon was not better he would know the reason why.

"I'm sorry, Sir Isaac," said the man, considerably agitated. "As I wrote to you, the 'ounds ran through 'ere three days ago, and it's my belief, Sir Isaac, that they've been and scared the birds away."

"To hell with the hounds," roared our host. "What business have they in my covers when that bloody fool of a Master knew as well as I did we were shooting to-day?"

We, the guests, murmured our sympathy, at the same time saying that, despite the *contretemps*, we had had a marvellous morning.

Hardly had we taken up our stands again, than clear on the breeze came the notes of a hunting-horn.

"Good Lord—the hounds," thought I, dismayed at their proximity so doubly unfortunate after the scene at luncheon. What my host thought or *said*, as he was at the other end of the line, I don't know. Suddenly, however, I heard him bellowing in a positively frenzied voice:

"Shoot him! Shoot him!"

And slipping along the line a big dog-fox was seen. Scared by the advancing beaters, he doubled back in front of our host who loosed off both barrels at him and killed him stone dead. There on the green turf was the corpse of "Charles James," when an instant or two afterwards the huntsman and first whip and ten or twelve couple of hounds suddenly made their appearance in our midst, followed shortly afterwards by the Master and the field. For some time, needless to say, the air was positively blue, but Sir Isaac decidedly had the last word by saying that if the hunt didn't clear off his land he'd shoot the whole lot. Our shoot ended for the day, and whatever his City friends did, I returned to London as quickly as possible.

Writing one's memoirs is a form of confession, and here let me state right away that I could never really afford to hunt in the Shires, though, all my life, obsessed with a great desire to do so. I felt that nobody who had not had such an experience could possibly really know fox-hunting. As, therefore, my wife and I had a great many friends staying at Melton and hunting from there in the winter of 1921; and as she was as keen on hunting as myself, we decided to blow the expense and to have about half a dozen horses at this historic hunting town. We then set to work to acquire this moderate-sized stud, and were very fortunate in our dealings. Two horses we purchased from a horse-dealer named Harold Field at Chichester, and these turned out trumps, one being my wife's favourite hunter. The others we bought from Harry Beeby the well-known horse-dealer at Melton, who did us extraordinarily well, and from Bert Drage of Northampton with whom our dealings were equally successful. So I say again, as regards our horses, we were very lucky, as we could not afford to pay big prices for them. Later I bought a couple of horses off Major Charlie Clarke, my old Eton contemporary, and on one of these I won my money-making race against Colonel Gordon Colman, of which more later on.

Craven Lodge (now so well known as a resort for the smart hunting world) had then just been opened, and we were practically the first people to take up our abode there. It was run by Major-General John Vaughan, the well-known cavalry-man, and his wife, who was the mother of Captain Mike Wardell, another cavalry officer, a great friend of mine and a very fine horseman, who also with his wife Hilda assisted in the management. Craven Lodge is spacious and comfortable. It is divided up into several flats for married couples, and there are bachelor rooms as well. The cuisine and cellar are first-class, and there is stabling for about a hundred horses, besides a squash court which His Royal Highness the Prince of Wales, who frequently stayed at Craven Lodge during our time, used every day, playing regularly morning and evening, however long a day's hunting he had had. He is the most energetic man in the world and perfectly indefatigable. It is really amazing how much physical exercise he takes considering the vast amount of mental work he has to do. At the moment I am writing of, he was never so happy as when on a horse. Considering there were several others better mounted than he, it was astonishing how bravely and successfully he went, and emphatically held his own with anybody up there. His Royal Highness is known to be one of the pluckiest sportsmen going; in fact, I don't suppose he has any notion of fear at all. His presence at Melton drew immense crowds to the meets. Thousands of people on bicycles and on foot, and hundreds of cars thronged all the roads to see the heir to the English throne come out hunting in his modest and unassuming way. He was easily the most popular man up there, and joined in all our amusements with the utmost good nature and enjoyment. His two A.D.C.'s, Capt. Hon. Bruce Ogilvy and Major "Fruity" Metcalfe were both good fellows and excellent company, "Fruity" being a first-class horseman and manager of His Royal Highness' stud.

Admiral Lord Beatty was another famous figure in the Shires, having a house in the Quorn country. Despite his enormous prestige, he made himself pleasant to everybody, and often gave very jolly parties at his house. I went to more than one, and stayed till the early hours of the morning. A true Irishman, he was thoroughly at home on a horse and, of course, splendidly mounted. He came out nearly every day during the season. He certainly has the most impressive appearance; his face is full of power and character.

The Melton hunting set were probably the smartest in the world and the hardest thrusters across country, as well as keeping it up to all hours at night. They must have been pretty tough, otherwise their nerve would surely have gone in a season or two, but there they were, winter after winter, always much the same crowd and all on friendly or even intimate terms with one another, but with a not very ready welcome for strangers. In fact, we became a clique. Whether in their evening-frocks or in their hunting clothes, these perfectly turned-out Dianas struck the mere man with unqualified admiration, and how magnificently some of them rode and what splendid horses they had! First of them all I must always put The Hon. Mrs. Freddie Cripps (then Duchess of Westminster). She was magnificently mounted, and had perfect hands, a perfect seat, an unerring eye for a country and absolutely dauntless courage. Her sister, Mrs. Keld Fenwick (now Mrs. Colin Buist) was very little behind her, and certainly never meant to be outridden by her. To see these two sisters coming at a fence together hell for leather, and each determined not to yield an inch to the other, was something to be remembered.

During the seasons we hunted up at Melton the Master of the Cottesmore was Captain James Baird, who married Audley Porter Porter. She did not hunt, but always drove with her husband to the Meet in a dogcart, whatever the distance. James was small and wiry in figure. On occasion he became rather irritable with his field, when he did not spare his language. However, these storms quickly passed.

It was a proud moment of my life when he gave me the Cottesmore button. I personally liked the Cottesmore country the best, it being, I think, the finest galloping country in the Midlands, while the fences are of moderate size and mostly stake-and-bound. Let me now say a few words about some of the best-known members of the Cottesmore Hunt.

Taking the ladies first—one of the finest horsewomen up there was Miss Lexie Wilson, sister of that well-known amateur rider, "Boy" Wilson. No fence was too big to stop her, and she knew the country thoroughly, having hunted up there all her life. So, whoever kept ahead of her during a run was doing well. Mrs. Jim Montagu (now Lady Kimberley) was another of the celebrated women riders. She and her husband, Jim Montagu, who used to be at Eton with me, lived at Cold Overton in the heart of the Cottesmore country. Lady Ancaster also came out occasionally. Major Jack Harrison who, with Lord Rosebery, is supposed to be the finest heavy-weight horseman in England, however, hunted principally with the Belvoir and the Quorn. He and his wife, Margery, had one of the nicest houses in Melton and entertained largely. The Adonis of Oakham, Hugh Molyneux (now Lord Sefton) frequently came out with the Cottesmore. He was always faultlessly turned out, and followed everywhere by admiring female eyes. He has survived many a battery of ardent glances, and so far no woman has been able to lead him to the altar. Another splendid figure, but with his side whiskers and stock more in the fashion of an eighteenth-century ancestor, was the Marquis of Londonderry. He has the most polished manners in the world, and was rather shocked at me once for appearing at a debate in the House of Lords with a cricketing tie on and brown shoes! He is probably on all occasions and in all circumstances the best-dressed man in England. Other well-known characters were the Hon. Lancelot Lowther and Lord Ivor Churchill, the latter of whom, besides being a good man to hounds, is an excellent judge of pictures.

Another pack we used to hunt with was the Quorn, of which Major Algy Burnaby and Major E. Paget were joint Masters. Major Burnaby I consider to have been the finest Master of Hounds in England at this time. He possessed a great personality, and consequently had complete control of his field. It was not often that he found it necessary to reprimand anyone, but at such times offenders might be perfectly certain they were in the wrong, as he was not one of those Masters who let fly on all trivial occasions. Captain and Mrs. Wardell often hunted with the Quorn. Mike Wardell was one of the boldest horsemen in Leicestershire, and did quite a lot of steeplechasing as well as hunting. He had terribly bad luck in losing an eye when jumping a fence. A bramble hit him in the face, and a thorn pierced his eye and destroyed its sight. He has now given up hunting, and is on the *Evening Standard* and a very important man in the newspaper world. The Misses Betty and Zandra Crawford went very well with the Quorn, and were in great demand at all the dances. One of the members of this Hunt, and possibly the raciest character in Leicestershire, was Major Charlie Carlos Clarke. There is nothing he would not put his leg across, and hardly any event that he would not dare to commemorate in verse. He is a great raconteur with a very pretty wit of his own, which must be heard to be appreciated, because neither his stories nor his verses are ever likely to be on sale at a bookstall, nor are his efforts to secure a private circulation for them always appreciated by the victims.

On one occasion some years ago I, myself, was the subject of one of his ballads, in which with considerable licence he described my pedigree, my personal habits, and my probable future. However, I bear him no ill will, though I do not intend to quote this particular ballad in these memoirs. A highly interesting character often to be seen out with the premier packs of which I have been writing, was the ill-fated Belgian financier, Loewenstein, known in the Shires as "Low." It will be remembered that he lost his life in mysterious circumstances by a fall from his private aeroplane, while it was crossing the Channel; whether this was an act of private revenge on the part of some enemy, an accident, or a case of suicide was never cleared up, in spite of the many rumours abroad at the time. Loewenstein was clean-shaven and Semitic in appearance, and had a very beautiful wife. He had a house at Thorpe Satchville furnished and stocked regardless of expense, and the finest stud of hunters conceivable. Several people round Melton took shares in his Companies, and on one occasion a gentleman thinking he had lost his money threatened Loewenstein with a hunting-crop unless he repaid him at par the money invested, which the financier did. A few days later the shares increased in value over 100 per cent, and our friend afterwards felt he had acted in rather a precipitate manner, especially as he not unnaturally ceased to be a friend of Loewenstein's.

The Marquess and Marchioness of Blandford had a house at Lowesby and came out hunting regularly. Blandford is very fond of practical jokes, a form of humour which does not appeal to everyone, though this taste of his has waned considerably with the approach of middle age. He is now one of the biggest chicken farmers in England, and takes a great personal interest in the welfare of his poultry. When I stayed with him this year, I was lost in admiration at the dexterous manner in which he forcibly fed his hens. He has a considerable natural talent for painting, and has lately cultivated it quite seriously. On one occasion, when requested by his wife to entertain a guest for whom he had a considerable aversion, he drew and painted the most appalling caricature of this individual with his name in large letters at the foot of the canvas, and put it on an easel in the hall, so that the first thing the guest saw on arriving was this hideous and life-like travesty of his own appearance. This method of relieving himself of an unwelcome visitor was highly effective, as the man he disliked so much left the next morning. Major Charlie Clarke is now Lord Blandford's agent. With such marked talents on either side, it is really surprising that they do not write poems about and caricature each other all day long.

During my time in the Shires, Major Tommy Bouch was Master of the Belvoir and hunted hounds himself. Opinions about his skill in this direction were somewhat divided, but I personally thought him a very fine huntsman, and I believe that after he gave up the Hounds most of his critics discovered that they wanted him back again. Tommy Bouch has a great many sides to his character and, judged by conventional standards, is decidedly weird. He is an ardent Liberal, and once stood for Parliament in the Isle of Wight. His speeches, however, were somewhat too eccentric for the taste of his audiences, and he never actually contested the election, retiring a few weeks before polling-day in favour of another candidate. He writes serious poetry, which he sometimes sends as Christmas gifts to his friends, and is without doubt a poor bridge player. Although he loses so heavily at bridge, he has won considerable sums on the Continent at baccarat, which he plays with consummate nerve. He was a marvellous host and had a wonderful cellar.

Two other well-known people who hunted up there were Lady Ursula Grosvenor and Miss Monica Sheriffe. Few packs could have had two more amusing girls following them. Lady Ursula was the better horsewoman, in fact one of the best in England, and thought of practically nothing else except horses, hounds and hunting. She afterwards married Filmer Sankey, a fine amateur steeplechase-rider, now Master of the South Notts. Miss Monica Sheriffe is still on the unattached list, and he will be a lucky man who gets her. Monica's sister, who married the Hon. Toby Greenall, was killed out hunting not many years ago, and Toby's brother Gilbert was also killed in a motor-accident in Windsor Great Park. I had only been talking to him in Buck's Club about an hour before. A tragic fate seems to have pursued this family. Both the Greenall brothers went magnificently, and were fine horsemen. I always consider Toby as a future Master of the Belvoir.

Colonel George Paynter, an old friend of mine in the Brigade, whom I have before mentioned, was Field Master of the Belvoir and a splendid one too. He had great prestige both as a local landlord, a gallant soldier, and perhaps the most determined horseman of modern times. He still rode in steeplechases at a fairly advanced age, and was a great example to modern youth.

Colonel C. S. Whitburn and "Tiddles" his wife, owned the biggest house, Warwick Lodge, at Melton. He is the kindest hearted, most generous friend in the world, and nobody knows the amount of good turns he has done. His wife and he were very popular in the Shires.

A good many Americans hunted up here at this time. They were all well mounted and went bravely. Among them I might mention the Ambrose Clarkes, the Converses, and the Strawbridges. "Brose" Clarke was easily the best rider of the American contingent, and his wife won the 1933 Grand National with her horse Kellesboro' Jack (D. Williams up).

Every coterie has a comic character, and the man who played this part at Melton was Captain Tommy Graves. He was a bit of a buffoon, and enjoyed doing things to raise a laugh. His entry once to a fancy dress ball at Craven Lodge, got up as a "Carrot," brought the house down, but his attempts to dance later in the evening like this interesting vegetable were the cause of somewhat acid criticism on the part of some of the ladies present.

From Melton I used sometimes to go and stay with Lord Dalmeny (now Earl of Rosebery) at his lovely house, Mentmore, in the Whaddon Chase country. Lord Dalmeny being very hospitable, as well as Master of the Whaddon and the most celebrated heavy-weight in England, used to lend me some of his finest horses to ride. I have had many a good hunt with the Whaddon Chase, their huntsman Boddington being one of the best in the country. On Sundays we used to go round the well-known Mentmore Stud. The following famous stallions have stood there in their time—Ladas, Sir Visto, and Cicero, all winners of the Derby, and Neil Gow, winner of the 2000 Guineas.

The horses I had at Melton were not as good as some belonging to other people. Where other hunting men would pay £500 to £600 for their mounts, the top price I ever paid was £200, and as by this time I rode nearly sixteen stone, it was obvious that I could not expect to keep in the first flight during a fast run. My first year in the Shires I had about twenty-five falls, four in one day off a horse I was trying and subsequently didn't buy, but was lucky enough to break no bones during that season. My best horse was a black called "Sepoy," aged eight and standing about seventeen hands. Harold Field of Chichester sold him to me. He was a splendid jumper, but when raced in point-to-points never liked open ditches with a rail in front, and used to refuse, so consequently I never won anything with him. I afterwards sold this horse to Mr. Harry Beeby of Melton, who also, I believe, was unable to cure him of this propensity.

My favourite was a bay called "Prince," an aged horse bought off Major Charlie Clarke for £120, after I had tossed him whether I would give him £100 or £120 for it. It was on this horse that I rode my race against Colonel Gordon Colman at the Belvoir Point-to-Point. The match arose in this way. One night after dinner at Craven Lodge where we were staying, and while the port was circulating briskly, I said to Colman, who rode about the same weight as I did: "Let's have a match at the Point-to-Point next month, my horse Prince against your famous grey."

"All right," said Colman. "£50 a side."

Colman's grey was well known in Leicestershire for its jumping powers, and I believe he had paid £700 for it. The match therefore looked greatly in his favour. Money began to be wagered on the result at once, and most of those at dinner that night had a bet. During the intervening weeks also I found plenty of people willing to lay me odds, as much as 10 to 1 being laid against my chances by two friends of mine, Humphrey de Trafford and Arthur Bendir. I took every bet I could get, and by the day of the race stood to win £700 or more. Our match was the last event of the programme, Major Bouch having consented to have an extra race in addition to the usual six. My horse being admirably trained by Major Charlie Clarke, it looked as if I had a good chance, as the going was heavy and I thought that Colman would probably lie back, expecting my mount and myself to fall, whereas I meant to take that risk and get as far ahead as I could in the first mile, and trust to him not being able to catch me again. I jumped the first fence just ahead of him, but my horse hit it like a ton of bricks and I landed up between his ears, just managing, however, to scramble back into the saddle again. Colman was by this time well ahead, but by cracking on the pace I caught him up at the fourth fence, which we jumped alongside each other. After we cleared it, Colman said to me:

"Do you want to break your bloody neck? Let's stick together for a bit."

"No," said I. "You won't see my hindquarters for dust."

And I went on at the same pace as before. For the rest of the way my horse made not a semblance of a mistake and I won by over a quarter of a mile, gaining a very good reception from the spectators, many of whom had backed me. Colman took his defeat in a sportsmanlike manner, but he can hardly have expected to be beaten, especially by such a great distance. As a matter of fact, I had taken the precaution before the race of walking round the course with that famous rider, the late "Tubby" Bennett, who two days afterwards won the Grand National on Sergeant Murphy, and he suggested to me where to jump each fence and at what pace I could take them with reasonable safety.

Winning this money was very useful to me, as by this time, it being the end of the hunting season, I was very broke.

It is a pity hunting is such an expensive game. I have always been passionately fond of it, ever since first riding to hounds as a small boy on a leading-rein, but have never had enough money really to do it properly. It has always been by shifts and devices, involving in the end a certain amount of financial embarrassment, that I have managed to obtain my days in the saddle. I cannot, however, honestly pretend to regret any extravagance in this direction. My memories of the Shires will always be thrilling and happy ones, and although eight years have now passed since I galloped from Turner's Gorse to Prior's Coppice, from Tamboro' Hill to the Coplow, or through Botany Bay to Baggrave, I hope that my hunting career may not have definitely ended. The feel of a good horse under one and a good stretch of galloping country ahead is one of the greatest sensations in life, and it is only with the packs of which I have been writing and a few others perhaps in England, that a perfect combination of the two can be achieved. My hunting at Melton came to an end, partly, although I did it on a fairly moderate scale, because of the expense involved, and partly because, in the ensuing seasons, I was asked, first by the late Mr. Solly Joel, to captain his cricket side in South Africa in the winter 1924–1925, and then to go with the M.C.C. side to the West Indies in the winter of 1925–1926.

CHAPTER XVII

THE late Lord Harris was never exactly what one might call a friend of mine. For nearly half a century he had occupied every position of importance in the councils of the M.C.C., and consequently what he said there was absolute law. To my mind, it was a pity that there was nobody to stand up to him and that towards the end of his life, as must frequently happen in the case of an autocrat, his judgments were sometimes mistaken. In my own case, I believe, had I been more friendly with him, and had he liked me more, I might have captained both a side to Australia and to South Africa; and on my form shown as England's captain during the Australian visit to England of 1921, of which I have already given some slight account, few will deny that I had a good claim for this position. Lord Harris, however, saw fit to disagree (for reasons unnecessary to repeat here) with the choice of myself, and I therefore lost the chance of captaining an M.C.C. side in Australia, which had been the ambition of my life ever since my boyhood in that country. Mr. Arthur Gilligan's team sailed to Australia in the autumn of 1924, and there is no doubt he took with him the pick of the cricketers in England for the particular job in hand, though other players of great skill and renown remained behind.

At this time the late Mr. Solly Joel, who had begun in his middle life to take a great interest in cricket (amongst other things having an annual cricket match at his place at Maiden Erleigh near Reading every Sunday after Ascot, in which I captained one side and my friend and partner in business, Mr. P. G. H. Fender of Surrey, the other) had an inspiration. On this particular Sunday in the summer of 1924, when the South African touring side were down at his place for the day playing against a side captained by me, they expressed a wish that a really strong team of cricketers might come out to South Africa that winter. Our host then said that he would send one if the South African Board of Control agreed, and would also contribute most of the out-of-pocket expenses himself. Solly had always been a very good friend to me, and promptly asked me if I would skipper this side for him, which I agreed and was very delighted to do. Solly Joel was, if one may say a word about him before passing on to the cricket tour which he sponsored, a most magnificent host in his own home, and never so happy as when entertaining his friends.

He had a real, genuine love of hospitality, and it gladdened his heart to see people enjoying themselves. The Sunday before Ascot week was known as "Solly's Sunday" at Maiden Erleigh. A huge marquee was erected in the beautiful grounds, and two hundred or more of his men friends sat down to a sumptuous luncheon at which food, champagne and cigars were all of the very best conceivable. Besides the floral decorations, the table was laden with the gold cups which his horses had won at Ascot and other meetings; and after all his guests had eaten and drunk their fill, speeches were made, and Solly's health proposed, and all good luck wished him for the races taking place during the ensuing week. The late Lord Dewar, generally held to be about the cleverest after-dinner speaker in England, was a friend of his and usually came to these midday banquets. It did one good to see Solly laughing at Dewar's witty sallies.

The Sunday after Ascot, on which the cricket match to which I have already alluded took place, was known as "Mrs. Solly's Sunday." Hosts of her lady friends and their husbands watched the cricket which was of a light-hearted nature, no batsman being allowed to bat for more than a quarter of an hour and four innings being completed in the day's play. There was a bottle of champagne in ice under every tree, and more of it flowed at luncheon and tea. There never were a more amiable or jollier host and hostess than Mr. and Mrs. Solly.

To return, however, to the course of my story. Before many weeks passed a cable came from the South African Board of Control saying that they would appreciate a team in South Africa that winter, and Archie Maclaren, the famous old England cricket captain, who accompanied us to South Africa as our manager, Solly Joel, and myself, selected the side as follows:

1. Major Hon. L. H. Tennyson (Hampshire), Captain.
2. J. C. W. M'Bryan (Somerset), Vice-captain.
3. Captain T. O. Jameson (Hampshire).
4. C. S. Marriott (Kent).
5. A. H. Gilligan (Sussex).
6. Capt. F. W. H. Nicholas (Essex).
7. Lieut. E. H. D. Bartley (Royal Navy).
8. P. Holmes (Yorkshire).
9. E. Tyldesley (Lancashire).
10. A. C. Russell (Essex).
11. E. H. Bowley (Sussex).
12. A. Kennedy (Hampshire).
13. G. Geary (Leicestershire).
14. C. Parker (Gloucestershire).
15. W. E. Astill (Leicestershire).

Many judges thought this side little inferior to the one on the way to Australia under Mr. Arthur Gilligan's captaincy. Our great weakness, however, was lack of a really fast bowler. This could not well be helped, as fast bowling during the few years after the war had temporarily ceased to exist.

Before leaving England the Lord Mayor of London, Colonel Sir Louis Newton, gave the South African team and ourselves a dinner at the Mansion House, many well-known cricketers being present, while Mr. Solly Joel also entertained us at the Savoy Hotel. As captain of the team I had to speak at both dinners, and was not a little gratified at having made a speech (once during my life, at any rate!) at the Mansion House. On both occasions I was very optimistic as to the prospects of our tour.

Mid-October saw the side collected on the station platform at Waterloo *en route* for Southampton and the Cape. Solly Joel, owing to the illness of his wife, was not there, though he had hoped to see us off. His two sons Stanhope and Dudley were, however, accompanying us on the trip. A bevy of ladies were also present to say good-bye. Amongst them were Lady de Trafford, Lady Blandford, Lady Ancaster, Mrs. Rudolph de Trafford and Mrs. Gilbert Russell. Besides the ladies we left behind, there were a number coming out with us, namely, my own wife, Mrs. Jameson, Mrs. Nicholas, Mrs. Maclaren, Mrs. Marriott, and my cousin, Mrs. Birkbeck.

Solly, so that his side should not feel lonely, had generously promised to pay the passages of the wives as well as of the husbands. It was indeed a kind gesture, but candour compels me to admit that feminine squabbles and rivalries, due largely to a too partial interest in the fortunes of their menfolk on the part of the wives, occupied rather a larger share of the skipper's attention than was desirable! Pacifying indignant women became such a common occurrence with me, that by the end of the tour I really acquired quite a paternal manner.

However, that October morning at Waterloo Station these things were hidden from my eyes; and when Mrs. W. A. Gilligan (mother of Arthur, Harold and Frank) handed bunches of white heather all round, we felt that nothing could mar the serenity of our comradeship.

On board the *Edinburgh Castle*, commanded by Commander H. Strong, R.N.R., we had very good fun, and did our best to liven up the ship. Captain Nicholas was a really wonderful pianist, and so as not to waste his abilities, Harold Gilligan, who played the water whistle and the saxophone, and myself who handled the cymbals and drums, joined together with him to make a band to which everyone danced nightly on board. This band afterwards performed with considerable success at impromptu dances during our tour, and even appeared twice on the stage in Johannesburg. During one of these evenings on board, when the attraction of our band had proved so great that not only all the passengers but most of the ship's officers were dancing, a well-known novelist became rather nervous.

Going up to the chief officer he enquired: "Will you kindly tell me who is up on the bridge? All the ship's officers appear to be dancing down here."

The chief officer was a bit of a wag. Looking the novelist up and down and presumably sizing him up, he answered: "Why do you want to know?"

The novelist replied: "I am anxious about the way this ship is being run, and I don't believe there is anybody on the bridge at all."

"Oh, that's all right," replied the chief officer, "you see it's like this. Our Chef on board has passed all his navigation tests, and when the other officers are dancing or engaged in any other hobby, and the Chef is not really wanted in the galley, he goes up on the bridge and takes a watch."

At this the novelist was perfectly furious and said he would report the matter to headquarters. Whether he did so or not I don't know. It is needless to remark that there was, of course, an officer on the bridge the whole time, there being a supernumerary officer on board who was dancing.

Besides these usual evening dances there were one or two fancy dress balls on board. During one of these I created somewhat of a sensation. Dressed as a fairy, complete with wings and gauze skirt, but unfortunately without silver shoes, for which a pair of cricket boots had to do duty, my fifteen stone avoirdupois was lowered down by two sailors during dinner directly over the captain's table. Swinging as gracefully as I could in this position, I recited the following verse:

Hail, captain! I'm your fairy queen,
  A lovelier fairy never yet was seen.
I am a little spirit from the sea,
  So fill your glasses now and drink to me.

Time and place are, of course, the essence of a joke: and if this bit of light-hearted buffoonery does not appear as funny in print as it did on the occasion it took place, I can only assure my readers that it caused a great deal of merriment at the time, and that there are still a good many people who have not forgotten it.

The team all arrived fit and well at Cape Town, having kept themselves in good condition on board ship with games and sports.

The ladies of the party were also well in body but not quite so well in hand, and I had had already to exert a certain amount of diplomacy in dealing with them. However, the sight of Table Mountain with its flat top outlined against the brilliant blue of the morning sky, its gigantic rocky sides, and the white houses of Cape Town spread gleaming at its base (a spectacle most of our party had never seen before) put them all in a good temper again before they went ashore.

We had a great reception on landing, and were afterwards entertained to lunch by the Mayor of Cape Town. At this luncheon I met my old friend Lieut.-Colonel Vollie van der Byl, President of the Western Province Cricket Association. I had not seen him since my trip to South Africa before the war. There were also many other old friends of mine present. Our team was immediately christened the "Jolly Souls," a name which stuck to us throughout the trip. That day, on arrival, I also met a new friend, Mr. Algy Frames, who was to be our South African manager throughout the tour. A most capable manager too he proved, and the burden of all the work fell upon his shoulders, Mr. A. C. Maclaren (supposed to be our English manager) proving somewhat indolent and lugubrious, especially when sometimes given a sleeping berth over the wheels of a train. However, to make up for this, I believe his cricket articles in the South African Press were much appreciated. There was an innovation on this tour in our first match at Newlands of which I, personally, heartily approved. We played there against a selected Fifteen of the Colleges and Schools of Cape Town. I was very glad that the boys should have some first-hand experience of the giants of the game. Charlie Parker of Gloucestershire certainly proved a giant in the bowling line with his left-arm spinners, taking six wickets for one run in the first innings, and doing the hat trick. I had the ball mounted for Charlie and gave it to him as a memento. One of the boys playing, and caught and bowled by Parker for nothing, was W. L. Creese, now a member of the Hampshire team, and a very hard-hitting batsman, who has greatly improved this year with experience, and has made several fine scores.

After playing the Western Province, a match which ended in a draw, we had three days in the train across the veldt to Maritzburg. At the time these vast rolling plains covered with stunted bushes and from which here and there lofty mountain ranges rise, were all burnt up by the sun. The dust on this journey consequently was frightful, and being unable to shut the windows owing to the heat we were absolutely smothered in it from head to foot. Despite the distance to be covered we arrived punctually to the minute and had our usual hearty welcome from the City authorities and other notables. The match here against Natal was drawn. A most interesting experience was a visit to the wonderful Howick Falls about fourteen miles away. They are 365 feet in height, and fall into a great chasm over some rocky cliffs.

From here we went to Durban and stayed at the Royal Hotel. The staff were all Zulus, than whom there are no more trustworthy servants in the world. Mr. Walter Greenacre, then President of the Natal Cricket Association, whose son afterwards joined the Guards Brigade and has been A.D.C. to the Prince of Wales, told me that when he went away from home he always left two Zulu servants in charge of his house, and that he had never lost anything. There is a first-class golf club and course at Durban, where our players had every incentive to keep on the fairway, because we had been told before starting our round that the rough was full of black and green "mambas." These snakes are supposed to go as fast as a galloping horse, and to be the only ones that will make an unprovoked attack on man. Charlie Parker, who might have won an Open Championship at golf in England if he hadn't taken to slow bowling, and with whom I used to play a lot on our tour, was especially nervous of these terrifying reptiles.

The match here at Durban against Natal was again drawn. The English side were out first innings for 154 (Percy Holmes being top scorer with 62), and for 296 for nine wickets (declared) second innings, Jack M'Bryan scoring a brilliant 120. Natal replied with 116 first innings (Herbie Taylor scoring 49), and with 172 for four wickets, second innings. Archie Maclaren writing in the Press after this match, said that Taylor was a model for any young batsman, and that the youthful South African players should watch him as much as possible and form their style on his. A young bowler called D. P. Conyngham did well enough in this match to secure a place for South Africa in the First Test Match.

On 26th and 27th November we played against Pretoria and District at Pretoria, and in my speech at the Mayoral dinner given us at Polley's Hotel I congratulated Pretoria on having made ten more runs than any local side had scored against the M.C.C. on any previous visits.

The Governor-General, the Earl of Athlone and his wife, Princess Alice, were then in residence at Government House. As is well known, they were the most popular couple that ever represented the Crown in the South African Dominion.

We played Griqualand West next at Kimberley with heavy scoring on both sides. Ernest Tyldesley made a brilliant 174 for us, whilst L. E. Tapscott 102, W. V. Ling 91 and 75, and C. M'Kay 111 not out did very well for the opposing Eleven.

Whilst in that town we went over the diamond mines. Everyone has heard tales of the precautions taken by the De Beers' Company to prevent natives employed in the mines, or other unauthorized persons, secreting diamonds somewhere about their persons and taking them away. I should have supposed that the captain of Mr. Solly Joel's team above suspicion, but not a bit of it! Struck with admiration for a particularly brilliant specimen which had just been sifted out, I picked it up to examine it closer. Immediately there came a peremptory order to put it down again at once, and not to touch any more diamonds on pain of being ejected from the place.

For fourteen years there had been no English cricket team in Rhodesia, but this time it had been decided that we should go to Bulawayo. Naturally the Rhodesians were delighted to see us, and got up a dance at the Grand Hotel where we were staying, which was a great success. The Governor of Rhodesia, Sir John Chancellor, K.C.M.G., D.S.O., kindly telegraphed to me wishing us a pleasant stay and regretting that business prevented him from watching the match. I replied by wire thanking him, and saying that "we would take away with us the memory of a game played on the frontiers of the Empire in the spirit in which it would have been played at Lord's." We won the game by eight wickets, Ted Bowley getting 131 for us, and George Geary bowling magnificently. This was our first win of the tour. Mr. A. G. Hay, President of the Cricket Union of Rhodesia and (as far as I remember) of almost everything else in the town, was never weary of helping us to enjoy ourselves, being very popular with us all. Amongst other things, he arranged for us to go and see Cecil Rhodes' grave in the Matoppo Hills. Next to Rhodes' is that of Dr. Jameson, and over these two graves there sits day and night a native keeping guard. Cecil Rhodes considered the view from here the finest in the world: I agree with him. His nephew, Frank Rhodes, is a great friend of mine, and travelled with the last cricket side I captained in Jamaica, where he was the life and soul of the party.

We now had a week off cricket, and went up by train to the Victoria Falls. The native name of these falls, which were discovered by Dr. Livingstone in November 1855, is "Mose-oa-Tunya," which means "the smoke which sounds." This is very appropriate, as the huge column of spray has been seen twenty-eight miles from the falls, and the roar heard sixteen miles away. The falls are a mile and a quarter broad, and the drop is four hundred feet. When the sun is shining, a perpetual rainbow hangs over the vast chasm into which the waters are hurled. The noise of this huge cataract is simply astounding, and the rush of water incredible unless one has seen it. Whilst staying in the hotel up here we had to take ten grains of quinine every night, as in that hot, steamy atmosphere malaria is very prevalent. We saw several hippos in the river just above the falls, and many enormous crocodiles lying out sunning themselves.

Stanhope Joel, Nicholas and myself were given leave by the Governor of Northern Rhodesia, with whom we had lunched at Livingstone, to do some big-game shooting on the Zambesi. So, sallying forth one morning at 2 a.m. and being rowed two or three miles up the river by natives, we landed on the opposite shore to Livingstone. Here we plunged at once into thick grass, and my friends suggested that, having polo-boots on, I should go first to make a track for them, which I consented to do.

Monkeys gibbered in all the trees, and we saw several large snakes squirming off into the undergrowth. There were only two rifles in the party, and these were carried by Nicholas and myself, Stanhope Joel arming himself with a shot-gun. For some time we only saw the tracks of big game such as hippo, and various kinds of deer. At last we spotted large numbers of the latter in the distance, but owing, perhaps, to our being inexperienced hunters could not get near them. Finally as we reached the brow of a hill, we came upon a numerous troop of baboons. They were feeding in some grass amidst rocks with their sentries out, as is their custom. The sentries gave the alarm, and the baboons began scampering off in a body. Nicholas and I let fly a round each, but failed to hit anything. This, though annoying at the time, may have been lucky for us, because, as we were told on returning, if a baboon is wounded he cries out like a child, and all his friends and relations come back and tear the aggressor to pieces. This would have been a melancholy end for the captain of the "Jolly Souls" cricket team! We hunted on land for about three hours without any success, but on returning to the boat and taking to the river again, we killed two crocodiles but could not recover their bodies from the water into which they sank. By the way, before we embarked, Stanhope Joel nearly had a right and left because, unloading his gun, he pressed the trigger inadvertently and the charge went off between the heads of Nicholas and myself.

Another day, Alec Kennedy and I went out fishing for tiger fish and were quite successful. Our boatman had half a dozen pet monkeys which he kept near his boat-shed chained up to stakes. He was very disconsolate when we returned that morning to find nothing but the stakes and chains left. A crocodile had eaten the lot!

After these delightful days on the Zambesi, we returned to Johannesburg, where we played the Transvaal and won by eight wickets on the Wanderers' ground, Kennedy taking six wickets for 46 runs in the first innings, and Ernest Tyldesley making another brilliant century. In the Transvaal's second innings, M. Y. Susskind scored 88 and H. G. Dean 118.

Tuesday 23rd December, the date of the first Test Match, was now fast approaching, and Messrs Frank Grey, F. B. Perring and Frank Reid were chosen as the three South African selectors. Their first bold stroke was to appoint V. H. Neser as captain of South Africa in place of Herbie Taylor. Neser had just kept wicket brilliantly for the Transvaal against us, and had also batted well. Taylor with his brilliant record as a batsman still continued, of course, a member of the side. The South Africans were selected as follows:

1. V. H. Neser (Transvaal), Captain.
2. M. Y. Susskind (Transvaal).
3. H. G. Deane (Transvaal).
4. E. P. Nupen (Transvaal).
5. A. Hall (Transvaal).
6. H. W. Taylor (Natal).
7. A. D. Nourse (Natal).
8. W. Billing (Natal).
9. D. Conyngham (Natal).
10. W. V. Ling (Griqualand West).
11. R. H. Catterall (Rhodesia).
12. L. E. Tapscott (Griqualand West).
    Umpires : Messrs Laver and Verheyen.

During the few days before the Test Match we played against the East Rand at Benoni where Ted Bowley scored 152, but this two-day match ended in a draw as usual.

From Johannesburg we visited the Robinson Deep gold mine, and there saw a war dance by natives clad in multi-striped football jerseys, horse-tail switches, and war paint. As somewhat of an expert in dancing myself, I could not help being fairly astonished at the time and rhythm kept by these scores of native boys bounding and capering. I even expressed a wish to train the members of my team to perform a similar sort of dance on their return to England. They, however, while admitting it would cause a sensation, declined to be instructed!

The English side for the first Test Match was:

1. Hon. L. H. Tennyson (Captain).
2. J. C. W. M'Bryan.
3. T. O. Jameson.
4. C. S. Marriott.
5. E. D. Bartley.
6. A. C. Russell.
7. A. Kennedy.
8. C. Parker.
9. E. Tyldesley.
10. G. Geary.
11. E. H. Bowley.

We won the toss; and having gone in to bat before the Governor-General and Princess Alice and a large crowd, we were all out for 198, Ted Bowley and myself getting top scores with

57 apiece. "Buster" Nupen was in great form for South Africa, taking five wickets for 54 runs. Neser and Nourse got 80 and 71 respectively out of a total of 295 for South Africa. In our second innings we collapsed for 149, Nupen again taking five wickets. Bowley and Tyldesley both scored 50 odd, but all the rest failed.

South Africa thus won the first Test by nine wickets, Nupen's bowling on matting being far more dangerous than it had been on the varied turf wickets of England, where he was a failure.

Just prior to the Test Match, our amateurs had been elected members of the Rand Club, where on 19th December we were entertained at the Jockey Club dinner. The Rand Club has the largest bar in the world. After two or three cocktails it looks about a quarter of a mile round, and a megaphone seems necessary to invite a fellow at the other end to have a drink.

The South Africans, as well they might be, were very much pleased with their victory in the first Test over such a powerful side as ours, and made consequently only two changes in their team for the Second Test Match at Durban, C. M. François of Griqualand West and R. Duff of the Transvaal coming in for W. V. Ling and W. Billing.

"Father" Marriott was not well and Jameson had not come off in the first Test, so on our side W. E. Astill who was coaching at Cape Town and Percy Holmes who had had "flu" took their places. I was fortunate again in tossing, and we made 285. Bowley was once more in tremendous form, getting 118. According to an invariable custom on the Durban ground, he planted a tree to commemorate this century, as is always done by anyone making a hundred in a Test Match there. The rest of the side batted rather ignominiously, in fact I myself had second top score with 34. Nupen again took five wickets for 65, bowling with great skill and proving himself undoubtedly far the best bowler in South Africa. Catterall and Deane fielded magnificently in the deep.

For South Africa, Herbie Taylor batted with all his old brilliance and, relieved of the cares of captaincy, made 112 out of 211. Charlie Parker had hurt his leg and was ineffective, but Billy Astill, for whose timely help that day I said a prayer of thankfulness, bowled till he almost dropped, taking five wickets for 82, while George Geary had four for 35. Nupen again bowled marvellously well in our second innings, taking seven wickets for 46 and helping to get us out for 174, for 81 of which Percy Holmes was responsible. This left South Africa 249 runs to win. However we dismissed them for 200, the English side thus winning by 48 runs, Kennedy taking five for 51 and Geary four for 85.

We were now one all.

While the team went to play the Northern Districts at Ladysmith and the Northern Free State at Bethlehem, both of which matches were drawn, my wife and Mrs. Jameson went to stay with Sir Abe Bailey on his farm, where they had a wonderful time.

15th January 1925 brought us to the Third Test Match at Cape Town. The same English side was selected as in the Second Test, but there were numerous changes in the South African team.

At this moment I had to face a furious lady, the wife of one of our players who had not been chosen. After a somewhat stormy interview, in which most of the thunder and lightning came from her side, she said that she and her husband wished to return to England, so I promptly sent them their tickets. They, however, thought better of the matter and remained. I have alluded to this just to show that the life of a captain of a touring side is not all "beer and skittles."

We fairly routed South Africa, who won the toss, getting them out for 113 owing mostly to Geary who took six for 37, and ourselves replied with 224, Tyldesley making 50 and Russell 54. Hall bowled well for South Africa, taking six wickets. Our opponents again failed in their second innings, getting only 150, and we won with great ease by ten wickets. One of the umpires was strongly criticized by the Press and by the spectators for some of his decisions, but the South African captain, Neser, and myself were quite satisfied and announced that fact in the newspapers.

My wife and Mrs. Jameson were again off on visits while the team went to play against the Country Districts at Worcester. The most remarkable thing about this little town is the number of donkeys there. I had never seen so many in all my life, great teams of them drawing wagons and hauling timber over the veldt. I was told they could be bought for sixpence a head.

We won our match here, and after it was over were invited to a picnic at Brandvlei Hot Springs where the water comes out of the ground boiling. On our way to the Springs, we received many presents of the most delicious fruit from farmers in the neighbourhood.

From Worcester we went on to play the South Western Districts at Mossel Bay. This is a glorious place with wonderful bathing from the Santos Beach and with another bathing pool behind a barrier of rocks which keep the sharks away. The cricket ground is situated within a few yards of the seashore. Our opponents' captain, H. N. Vincent, most pluckily played with an artificial leg, having lost the one given him by nature in a motor accident. In a long experience of cricket I have known only one other player to do the same, namely Captain "Bunny" Tattersall, D.S.O. who might easily have kept wicket for England but for losing his leg in the war.

Here we went out fishing for sharks and caught quite a lot of moderate-sized ones, killing them with a hammer when pulled into the boat. Most of the team were very seasick, and would not very much have minded if a shark *had* snapped a limb or two off them.

January 28th and 29th saw us playing the Eastern Province at Grahamstown. The students and schoolboys were all away on holiday at the time, which was a pity, as with their presence we should have had a larger and more enthusiastic crowd.

Our next match was against the Border at East London, where my old friend and a former cricket international, Gerry Hartigan, captained the opposing side. After a few very pleasant days in this neighbourhood, spent bathing and golfing when not engaged at cricket, we left for Johannesburg for the Fourth Test Match, due to start on 6th February, where we found crowds of people staying in the anticipation of a keen struggle.

We ourselves put up at the Carlton Hotel, and had a couple of days good practice. The only change made in our side was Jameson for Astill, Marriott being curiously enough a failure on matting wickets; the South Africans, however, had the strongest team put in the field so far. Besides the usual eight, T. Siedle of Natal, one of the finds of the present tour, W. V. Ling and D. Y. Meintjes (Transvaal) came into their side.

Winning the toss once more, we were all out for 239, Russell making 80 and Jameson 53 not out. Nupen and Hall each took three wickets.

South Africa were all out for 193, Susskind being top scorer with 55. Geary bowled extremely well, taking four wickets. He was a wonderful bowler on matting and really seemed to have mastered Taylor. On the Sunday I did my record golf-round in South Africa, a 74 over the Johannesburg Golf Course.

In our second innings Holmes, Bowley, MacBryan, Geary and myself were all given out l.b.w., about which decisions there was considerable dissatisfaction on our side, which was dismissed for 164, leaving South Africa 211 to win. Nupen again bowled well, taking five wickets for 51.

It rained all the next day, so the game ended in a draw. I was asked to agree to play an extra day, but as the Test Matches were fixed for four days, I did not think that such a concession would be in the interests of cricket and refused.

February 13, 14 and 16 we spent at Bloemfontein, playing the Orange Free State, Jameson making 133 for our side, and S. Coen 103 for them, but the match was drawn. One of the umpires was the Mayor, Councillor John Reid, the only time I have seen such an exalted civic dignitary in this position.

This brought us to the final contest of the tour, the fifth Test at Port Elizabeth, on February 20, 21, 23 and 24. This was the fiftieth Test Match of that wonderful South African veteran Dave Nourse, and the spectators testified their appreciation of his long and striking services by handsomely supporting a collection raised for him on the ground.

Bartley, our wicket-keeper, was in great form in the South African first innings (they having won the toss) and caught four catches. Their total was 183, of which Siedle made 52; Geary again bowled splendidly and took five for 63. Then came our poorest performance of the trip, and before the onslaught of Nupen and Hall we were all out for 94.

In their second innings South Africa got exactly 200. We had a bit of bad fortune, because Catterall, who made 86, was caught off his hand by Geary at second slip when he had only scored 8, and, on appeal, was given in. Before going in to bat, he had been promised a gold watch and chain and a substantial cheque, if he scored over fifty, so his luck was in.

On the evening of the third day we were in a very strong position, having scored 219 for four wickets of the 290 runs required for victory, Tyldesley being not out 72 and Jameson not out 32. The next morning, therefore, which dawned fine and sunny, we came to the ground full of confidence that we should win the rubber with a triumph in this last match, seeing that we had six wickets left and only 71 runs to make. Of course all sorts of accidents and unexpected happenings can occur in cricket, it is part of the charm of the game, but really none of us could have anticipated what was going to take place that day. The attitude of the local umpire seemed decidedly weird, and a series of decisions followed which I can only describe as unorthodox. Tyldesley, Kennedy, and Geary were given out l.b.w. and I, myself, was adjudged caught at the wicket though the ball came in reality off my pads and not off my bat. South Africa, therefore, won by 21 runs, and the series of unofficial Tests ended in a draw with two wins for each side.

I have given the details of this cricketing tour somewhat fully, partly because I think they may interest a good many of my South African friends, and partly because I want to indicate what an immense amount of travelling over vast stretches of country it involved. A mathematician in our party reckoned, indeed, that by the time the last game had been played, we should have travelled over eight thousand miles in the Dominion alone.

Full as my description has been, I have been unable to do justice to the clubs, private hosts and hostesses, public bodies and all others who made our days and evenings so happy and enjoyable. I am sure that our visit did good; and the Press were generous enough to ask me about any opinions I might have formed or criticisms I had to make. I could only respond to such good sportsmanship by speaking frankly, and I said that in my opinion South African cricket had deteriorated somewhat since my last visit before the war, but that there were hopes for the future in many good young players.

It may be said that I have criticized rather strongly some of the umpiring on the tour. If I have done so, it has been with the sole intention of improving what seems to me a possible defect. In South Africa there are not the same opportunities for the training and bringing forward of umpires as at home; but were the coaches that come out from England every year to combine with their instruction in other departments of the game some definite teaching, out of their greater experience, to those who have claims to the important position of umpire in South Africa, I personally think that cricket out there would benefit greatly.

CHAPTER XVIII

WEST INDIES AND JAMAICA

IT was in December 1925, on board the s.s. *Inanda* of a line of steamers belonging to a friend of mine, Major Jack Harrison, that I had the roughest voyage I ever remember. It was most unpleasant at the time, but is now something to look back upon as an adventure. We started from the West India docks in London in a thick fog, and had crawled about two miles down the river when we had to stop. Whilst anchored there, we were nearly cut in two by a huge liner, which missed us by inches. We remained at anchor all night, and took the opportunity of having boat drill, as the crew were all Indians fresh from Calcutta and knew nothing about the ship.

Two days out from home it started to blow, and our little craft of about 4000 tons began to roll and pitch in a really frightening way. Crossing the Atlantic it blew harder and harder till off the Azores we had, what the Captain, A. B. Nicholas, one of the finest sailors that ever went to sea, described as the worst gale he had been in during his fifty years' experience. We were obliged to heave-to for half the night, and to throw out a deep-sea anchor. By early morning the weather had moderated a little, and we were able to proceed on our journey, but at 6.30 a.m. the ship gave such a roll that we thought she was never coming back again, and several of the lady passengers rushed out of their cabins with handbags packed, thinking we should have to take to the boats.

[Back row:]

L. G. CRAWLEY   G. COLLINS
(*Essex*)   (*Kent*)

[Middle row:]

F. WATSON   C. F. ROOT   W. R. HAMMOND
(*Lancashire*)   (*Worcester*)   (*Gloucestershire*)

E. J. SMITH   W. E. ASTILL   R. KILNER   P. HOLMES
(*Warwickshire*) (*Leicestershire*) (*Yorkshire*)   (*Yorkshire*)

[Front row (seated):]

T. H. CARLTON-LEVICK   H. L. DALES
(*Manager*)   (*Middlesex*)

HON. L. H. TENNYSON   HON. F. S. CALTHORPE
(*Hampshire*)   (*Warwickshire*)

T. O. JAMESON   C. T. BENNETT
(*Hampshire*)   (*Middlesex*)

[Image credit:] *Cleary & Elliott*

CAPT. T. O. JAMESON, HON. F. S. G. CALTHORPE, AND LORD TENNYSON: JAMAICA, 1926

The occasion of this voyage was the despatch by the M.C.C. of a touring cricket side under the captaincy of the Hon. F. S. G. Calthorpe to several of the West Indian Islands. The tour was to last for three months, and was described by Lord Harris, at a luncheon given us by the West India Club in London prior to our departure, as the best side that had ever visited the West Indies. The team was composed as follows:

1. Hon. F. S. G. Calthorpe (Warwickshire) Captain.
2. Hon. L. H. Tennyson (Hampshire).
3. T. O. Jameson (Hampshire).
4. H. L. Dales (Middlesex).
5. L. G. Crawley (Essex).
6. C. T. Bennett (Camb. Univ.).
7. E. J. Smith (Warwickshire).
8. F. Root (Worcestershire).
9. P. Holmes (Yorkshire).
10. R. Kilner (Yorkshire).
11. W. E. Astill (Leicestershire).
12. F. Watson (Lancashire).
13. W. Hammond (Gloucestershire).
14. G. Collins (Kent).
   Manager: Capt. T. H. Carlton-Levick, C.B.E.

Our party was accompanied by Mr. and Mrs. W. V. Wakefield of Chelmsford, Essex, friends of Freddy Calthorpe's, and by his wife, Dorothy Calthorpe. In addition to ourselves there were on board the following well-known people going as Parliamentary delegates: Viscount Peel, G.B.E.; Lord Queenborough; Commander C. Bellairs, M.P.; Rt. Hon. F. O. Roberts, M.P.; and Mr. A. E. Jacob, M.P.

I played a lot of bridge on the way out with Lord Queenborough, Wakefield, and Tommy Jameson, and for once in a way came out a substantial winner. It was a considerable time (in fact before the war) since a cricketing side from England had visited any of the West Indian Islands; so none of us quite knew what sort of opposition we had to face. As I have said, the M.C.C. had been on the safe side, and had selected an extremely powerful team. Incidentally it was on this tour that Wally Hammond first indicated without a doubt that he was going to be one of the world's master batsmen and greatest all-rounders. The games between this M.C.C. side and the All-West Indian Teams all resulted in better matches than we had anticipated. Well as the West Indians did in the three Test Matches of this tour, it is astonishing to myself who have played against them in Jamaica afterwards in four out of the last seven years, what extraordinary progress they have made in all departments of the game. I am now convinced that under conditions that are familiar to them and in their own country, it is no use preparing to meet them with a side short of full England strength; and that they are the third best side now playing in International Cricket. Before long they may easily prove to be the best. It has been one of the most genuinely proud recollections of my life, that by taking three sides to Jamaica myself and by going with two others, I may have been somewhat instrumental in sponsoring this barely credible advance in West Indian cricket. The whole population of these beautiful and romantic islands is cricket mad. The stands, on the day of every match, are packed to capacity, and every tree which overlooks the ground is festooned with enthusiastic supporters of cricket. All the heads of these sable spectators are turned in one direction and at the same angle, and are perfectly motionless as they watch the play in a fixity of concentration. Suddenly the ball speeds from the bat across the field and then all these heads move together as one, and a flash of white seems to cross these innumerable faces. It is their eyeballs rolling as they grin and shout their delight at a fine stroke. Should it perhaps be made by one of the opposing side the applause is just as great as in the case of one of their own players, and I really cannot express in words how much I appreciate all their enthusiasm and affection. I believe that a considerable number of little black babies in Jamaica have been called after members of my side who have particularly distinguished themselves on the cricket field. God knows how many little black "Lionels" there are running about this Island, as I have been the leader of most of these cricket ventures. I hope, however, that travellers to Jamaica in future years will not labour under any misconceptions on this account. To show that it is merely enthusiasm for cricket that is responsible for using English cricketers' names so frequently at baptism, I set down the following witty lines. They were inspired by a conversation with Plum Warner, himself born in the West Indies, and sent to the Press signed "Clarence Macfadden."

"Look here, Lionel," said Mr. Warner before
Mr. Tennyson started from home on the tour;
"If you go and make too many hundreds out there
Any native-born babies will certainly bear
Your full name, I am sure, for at least a decade."
And so poor Mr. Tennyson's greatly afraid,
For he is *such* a very particular man.
He just trembled on learning the risk that he ran.
If he came here again, as we hope he may do,
Well . . . extremely embarrassing, gentlemen, you
Will quite see that he thinks it would certainly be
To land here with small "Tennysons" swarming the quay
But we know the proclivities, leanings and arts
Of the simple Tenn . . . *denizens*, sir, of these parts:
So pray let us assure you, we'll all understand!
If you collar the bowling, why, don't stay your hand,
For we promise our motto shall be for the nonce:
"*Honi soit*," Monsieur Tennyson, "*qui mal y pense*."

Having given a short description of some at any rate of the spectators one gets in cricket matches in the West Indian Islands, let me now turn back to my first experience of them under Freddy Calthorpe's captaincy. We landed first at Barbadoes, staying at the Pomeroy Hotel, and played there one match against the Colts, two matches against the full strength of the Island, and one Test Match against the West Indies. We made 597 for eight declared in this first Test Match, Hammond getting 238 not out. The West Indians in the first innings made 147 and in the second 21 for six, rain stopping play. The great West Indian batsman, George Challenor, was playing for them and made 63. Their captain was Major A. G. B. Austin, who retired from first-class cricket at the end of that season. He and I never hit it off at all, and mutually disliked each other.

Barbadoes is not as picturesque as the other Islands, being less mountainous and largely given over to cultivation. A pleasant drive across the Island was to the Crane Hotel, where anything like a *souper à deux* immediately became the common property of the whole place, and ran the risk of being magnified into a scandal the next morning. The bathing, as in all the other Islands, was wonderful, but we probably ran some risk in bathing off the pier, as sharks simply swarmed farther out at sea.

We left Barbadoes on 17th January 1926 in the coastal steamer *Belize*, and arrived at the Port of Spain, Trinidad, the following day. There are several little islands at the entrance to the Port of Spain, and on one of these we saw working in the grilling heat a gang of life-convicts from the Island of Trinidad. Another of them is the Island of Gasparee, on which there is an hotel where bathing and week-end parties frequently take place, and where there are wonderful stalactite caves. The scenery in Trinidad is simply marvellous. The interior of the Island is decidedly mountainous, and one has the most wonderful views over precipices, ravines and forests of palms out towards the blue of the tropical ocean. Amongst interesting places to visit are the pitch lakes which look, by the way, exactly what they are, and which fill up again at once as soon as any pitch is taken out of them. Whilst in Trinidad, our team band, composed of Astill, Hammond, Collins and myself, played amongst other functions at a ball given by His Excellency the Governor and Lady Byatt. We played for several hours, not even stopping during the supper interval, but on going to get a glass of champagne to reward our exertions found that the other guests had finished it all! There were also some amateur theatricals given by the residents in the town during our stay. H. D. Swan, a member of the M.C.C. Committee, who had joined us as an unofficial member of the party, never left the stage for a single instant, so great was his desire to act. Our headquarters were at the Queen's Park Hotel, and I made great friends with Wilfred and Peggy Alston, who had a house near by and gave some good parties.

There was a slight earthquake during our visit, but no damage was done except that a few chimney-pots tumbled down. We played two matches against Trinidad, and also the Second Test Match there, which we won by five wickets. The great Constantine was playing against us, and when he was bowling at the end of the match, his deliveries were flying so high that Jameson and I, who were in together, had to play overhead tennis shots at them, since they were nearly out of reach. I made the winning hit, getting 21 not out.

We took a French ship from Trinidad to Georgetown, Demerara in British Guiana. It was a filthy little vessel, the cabins being indescribably dirty and full of cockroaches, and the food uneatable. The climate of Demerara was the worst we experienced. Malaria is bad there owing to the heat, the mosquitoes and the low level of the land.

Besides two matches against Demerara, we played in Georgetown the Third Test Match. The West Indian side made 462, Browne, the best all-rounder then in the West Indies, making a splendid 102 not out after being hit on the head and knocked out by a bouncer from me. Our own scores were 264 in the first innings, and 243 for eight wickets in the second. Astill and I helped to save the game, each getting over 50 when rain stopped play. I stayed in Demerara with Colonel "Woolly" Woolmer, who attempted to defeat the dry nature of the climate by a handsome allowance of whiskies and sodas, of which he always had a couple for breakfast. By the close of day he was not always wise in what he said. When we dined together at Government House, Her Excellency happened to remark to me that she had two boys at Eton.

"And I," bellowed Colonel "Woolly" Woolmer from the other end of the table, "have seven bastards in Georgetown."

This reminds me of another story of Charlie M'Gahey, the old England and Essex cricketer, when dining at Government House in Australia. The Governor of Victoria's wife asked him: "Do you hunt at all in England, Mr. M'Gahey?"

He replied: "Yes, I am passionately fond of hunting. I do a lot round Leicester Square at nights!"

From Demerara we went first to Port Lemon in Costa Rica on board the Elders & Fyffe ship *Cavina*, and then made a journey of about eight hours by train to San José, the capital. It seemed a very dangerous railway track with horrifying curves and insecure-looking bridges. As a matter of fact, a day or two afterwards there was a disastrous accident in which numbers of people were killed. In Costa Rica there were the loveliest girls I had ever seen. We had an excellent opportunity of taking stock of them, as there was only one train a day and these girls used to crowd the station platforms to watch it go by. From here we went to Colon, stopping there a few hours and inspecting the famous Gatun Lock on the eastern side of the Panama Canal. We saw two ships going through it.

From Colon, our ship took the M.C.C. team to Kingston, Jamaica, where we received a rapturous welcome on arriving in the harbour. Going to Jamaica is for me like going home. I have such scores and scores of friends there, while every corner of the Island is familiar to me, having been there with cricketing sides five times since the war. It is not, therefore, out of any want of interest for the doings of Jamaicans whom I regard one and all as my friends, and who I earnestly hope reciprocate my sentiments, that my visits have to be described in a somewhat curtailed and general manner. Reasons of space are the only ones which make it necessary for me to devote fewer pages than I should like to the chronicle of my doings in the loveliest of islands.

Let me first say that, whereas their cricket representatives now form the bulk of a West Indian International team, on the occasion of my first visit under Freddy Calthorpe I do not think they had one player who fought against us in the Tests. Their captain for the first match was Charlie Morrison, who was succeeded in the following games by G. R. K. Nunes, a very fine batsman and first-class wicket-keeper, who had learnt some of his cricket, at any rate, at Dulwich College. Karl Nunes is a great personal friend of mine, and a man who has done a tremendous lot for Jamaican and West Indian cricket, having captained their first International side in England. At that time, consequently, a great responsibility rested on his shoulders; and not a little of their popularity with the English crowds is due to his wise precept and example. He is a steward of the Jamaican Jockey Club and a racehorse owner. His wife is a tremendous cricket fan and hardly ever misses a match. She is a very charming person, and most kind and hospitable to all teams which visit the Island.

Our matches in Jamaica the year of my first visit were remarkable for some high scoring, Holmes making 244 and Astill 156 in one game! The cricket pitches there are superlatively good, even better than they are in Australia, and this, perhaps, is one of the reasons why the Jamaicans are 50 per cent more formidable at home than they are abroad. On the occasion of this tour, I first became acquainted with some very fine players, of whom I was to see a good deal more in the ensuing years. Amongst these were E. A. Rae, a genial giant, a very fine fieldsman and hard-hitting bat; J. K. Holt, a clever bowler of slow or medium off-spinners and sound batsman; and T. C. Scott, one of the best leg-break bowlers I have played against, and with whom none of the sides with which I have been associated has ever been exactly at home. Another very fine cricketer whom I then met for the first time was F. R. Martin. He is a most capable all-rounder, a slow left-hand bowler and a batsman with a magnificent defence. C. M. Morales also impressed me a good deal, and has always done well against us.

By the way, no one can really have understood the poetry of motion, unless he had seen the two Misses Morales diving at Montego Bay. Far aloft on a board, scores of feet above the sea, stand the two sisters. Their perfectly formed limbs and figures make them look like goddesses. Then one after the other, with arms outstretched in the swallow-dive and descending in a faultless arc, they plunge far out into the water. By way of contrast, let me relate an exploit of a member of one of my sides, Trevor Arnott, who captained Glamorganshire a few years ago. There is at Bournemouth near Kingston, a very fine open-air swimming-bath with a dance-floor attached, to which we often went to swim or dance after dinner. One night, Arnott was challenged to make the high dive into this bath from a tower about forty feet high. Feeling, for some reason or another, unusually courageous that evening he decided to attempt the feat, but apparently scorned to make any change in his costume, which was that of ordinary evening attire. Clad therefore in a dinner-jacket and white waistcoat he descended feet first into the water. As he weighed about seventeen stone, the splash he made was quite out of the ordinary. Arnott was a very powerful hitter. I remember that in one unofficial Test Match in Jamaica in 1927 he hit six sixes in an innings of about 50.

I have said that cricket in Jamaica has improved in an extraordinary way since I first visited the Island in 1926. Much of this improvement is due to the enthusiasm and sound teaching of "Punter" Humphries, the old Kent cricketer, who was a coach in Jamaica for many years after retiring from first-class cricket himself. Other well-known professionals such as Jack O'Connor of Essex and Astill have carried on his good work.

The Jamaicans have also, no doubt, profited greatly from seeing so many of our leading English players in their own Island. That this came about, is due to the efforts of the genial Sir William Morrison, President of the Cricket Board of Control, and of Major G. S. Cox, late of the West Indian Regiment. In the years, 1927, 1928 and 1932 they arranged with myself and in 1929 with Sir Julian Cahn to take sides out to Jamaica. Here are the names of some of those who have been members of these teams: Ernest Tyldesley, Phil Mead, Jack O'Connor, P. G. H. Fender, G. T. S. Stevens, M. S. Nichols, Andrew Sandham, G. D. Kemp-Welch, C. F. Walters, the Rev. F. H. Gillingham, the late "Dodge" Whysall and poor Roy Kilner. What a charming fellow

Roy Kilner was! He was the life and soul of our party when I went on tour with him.

Up till the year of my last visit, 1932, there had not been much to choose between the elevens of invaders and defenders, but that year Jamaican cricket proved so strong that it was the unanimous opinion of the members of my side that nothing, as I have already written, short of All-England strength would be sufficient to cope with them in their own country. One, indeed, had appeared who I think has claims to be considered the best batsman in the world, at least as formidable, even, as Sutcliffe, Hammond, or Don Bradman. I refer to George Headley.

During the period of my visits to Jamaica, the Governor for the most part of the time has been Sir Reginald Stubbs, now Governor of Cyprus. So much esteemed was he in the Island that he was asked to remain for another term of office at a largely increased salary voted by the Legislative Council, which proposal, however, he was unable to accept. He has been very hospitable to the various teams, has made many speeches in their honour, and has been most faithful in attendance at cricket matches in Kingston.

The Colonial Secretary was Sir Arthur Jelf, C.M.G., a very good after-dinner speaker. This is a useful gift anywhere, but more so in Jamaica than in most places, as the inhabitants have one and all a passion for oratory. It is quite common for speeches to be made even after dinners in private houses. The level of such efforts from constant practice is therefore pretty high. I remember Jelf telling a story at a club banquet which much amused me. "One day in ancient Rome," said he, "there was a Christian waiting in the arena to be devoured by a lion. The lion came bounding in, but after a few words from the Christian went out again with its tail between its legs. Having thus miraculously escaped death he was sent for and asked by the Emperor what he had said to frighten the lion so. 'I only told him,' said he, 'he would have to make a speech after dinner.'"

If Jelf wished to disarm criticism by this flight of fancy, in his case, at any rate, it was not necessary.

Which shall I now write about first—after alluding in necessarily brief terms to the two most important men in the Island, the Governor and the Colonial Secretary—the marvellous beauty of the Jamaican scenery, or the friends I have made there in the course of my numerous trips? On the whole I think it best to ask my readers to imagine themselves members of one of my cricket teams, and therefore visiting in turn the principal places and beauty spots in the island and there being introduced by me to various people, who will all do their best to make life pleasant for them and, in fact, see to it that they have the time of their lives.

A new arrival in Kingston will be struck, as his ship berths alongside the wharf, with the gay colours in which the native population are attired. He will see every type of African blood amongst them: a little later he will realize that they are all intensely loyal to the Empire, and tremendously proud of being British citizens.

On the wharf in the last few years you would certainly have come across Mr. Sam Burke, a polo player of distinction and a very fine horseman, who once acted as manager for our side. Mr. Burke would not be long in asking you what was your public school, and on your replying, would inform you that he himself was an old Harrovian, possessing a large stock of anecdotes about that famous Harrovian master "old Teddy Butler." If you had time to hear them, and possibly before Mr. Burke had got quite to the end of them (assuming that you were a patient listener), Inspector Owen Wright, head of the police in Kingston, might have strolled up, and tactfully enquired whether you were thirsty and thus inveigled you towards the nearest bar.

Kingston as a town is largely modern, as about a quarter of a century ago it was destroyed by an earthquake and then by fire, and most of the existing houses have been built since that time, except in one quarter of the town. A fine building is that of the Jamaica Club, of which touring cricket sides have always been made honorary members, and where a dinner in their honour has invariably been given with the most lavish hospitality. Another club immensely popular with my teams is the Liguanea Club, some three miles out of Kingston. Here are tennis-courts, a golf-course, a dancing-floor, a bar, and wide verandas to sit under whilst enjoying an iced drink and the conversation of some lovely companion of the opposite sex, of which there are great numbers in Jamaica. There are few pleasanter experiences than a dinner in the open air on some warm tropical night at the Liguanea Club, and Mr. Kindersley, the secretary, will do everything in his power to make you happy. Here you will probably meet, amongst other people, Mr. Harold Alexander, Solicitor and Clerk of the Legislative Council. He will ask you how you are enjoying yourself, show the greatest interest in your welfare, and before he says "good night" arrange for you to dine with him at the very earliest opportunity.

In the Club you would probably see a most attractive and animated lady sitting and chatting amidst a ring of male friends. Possibly, if you admired female beauty, you would ask to be introduced, and then learn that the lady's name was Carmen Pringle, and that she was in the habit of giving the most wonderful picnics on the shore at Dunn's River, not far from her husband's plantation, where the bathing is absolutely safe, the ubiquitous sharks being kept away by a barrier reef. If you made yourself pleasant, she would not be long in inviting you to one of these, and in introducing you to her husband, Ken Pringle, the most hospitable of men.

You might then possibly meet Mr. Lake. He would most certainly ask if you were a golfer; and, in the event of your being one, ask you to have a game with him at Constant Springs, the golf-course up at the foot of the mountains. After playing there, you would surely agree that it is amongst the most picturesque courses in the world, and that the water recently laid on to every green must be a vast improvement, as, too, are all the other alterations made since I first knew the course seven years ago. I think, also, you would have a word of praise for your caddie, a little curly-headed black imp about four and a half feet high, as keen as mustard, always grinning with pleasure, and, assuming that you sometimes strayed off the course, a wonder at finding your ball. My sides have always played a team match against a team of Jamaican golfers collected by Mr. H. A. Lake, and very good matches they have been. I think, however, that the Jamaicans, on their own course, have generally been a bit too good for us, even though there have been some first-class golfers amongst us.

On the way out to Constant Springs (where, by the way, there are two first-class hotels, the Constant Springs Hotel and the Manor House Hotel) you would pass in your car through the district where the Jamaican business men live. Their houses are very picturesque and built mostly of wood, since the earthquake proved that this type would be much safer in the event of another similar catastrophe. These houses all have lovely gardens, and are partially concealed from the road by beautiful flowering trees and shrubs.

Talking of cars reminds me of the fact that the Jamaican taxi-drivers are amongst the most furious in the world, and are generally in charge of pretty high-speed motors. As the local population invariably slope and moon about the streets in the most casual manner, it seems an absolute miracle to me that hundreds of little black children and their mammas are not slaughtered annually. The foot passengers and the taxi-drivers, however, manage somehow to avoid each other, though one's journeys through the streets of Kingston are rendered fairly lively with narrow shaves, hootings and shouts. On one occasion, I remember, when Sir Reginald Stubbs, G.C.M.G., was entertaining the team at Government House, which is about seven miles out of Kingston, I was, I regret to say, late as usual, and we had only ten minutes in which to make the journey. We got there in time, though it was dark by then and the roads are narrow, but poor Ernest Tyldesley, who was one of my companions and was suffering from a dislocated shoulder owing to a bad motor-accident a few days previously, still remembers that drive, I believe, with awe. He never said a word of protest at the time—a fine example of pluck and discipline.

Reference to Ernest Tyldesley's unfortunate accident, which kept him out of cricket for some time in England, and also may have spoilt his chance of breaking the record for the highest aggregate in Jamaican cricket matches, so splendidly was he playing at the time, leads me to the name of Dr. Robertson, the well-known doctor at Kingston. It has been his practice to attend *all* members of English touring teams *free of charge.* It would hardly be possible to return thanks adequately for such generosity.

Having reverted to the subject of cricket, and before leaving Kingston with my readers, I must mention with admiration and gratitude Mr. Michael de Cordova, editor of *The Gleaner*, the most famous daily newspaper in Jamaica. In my opinion, which is possibly worth something as I have played cricket nearly all over the world, there are the best reports on the game in this newspaper that I have ever read. Once a week a pink sheet appears in *The Gleaner*, and when this happens members of touring sides have an opportunity of learning what personal impressions they may have made. Let me say that these personalities, though lively, are always kindly and in good taste, and often illustrated by admirable sketches, photographs and verses. G. St. C. Scotter is the very able sports reporter of *The Gleaner*.

Well, my team must be moving on soon, but before doing so, we must thank Mr. Evelyn of the South Camp Road Hotel, where some of us always stay, for the wonderful care he has taken of us and for the way in which he has somehow managed to anticipate our every want.

I, myself, have nearly always stayed at the Myrtle Bank Hotel, of which my friend, Mr. Hook, is Manager. What more wonderful restaurant in the world is there than the open-air one at the Myrtle Bank, where the palm trees are lit with electric light and the tables are set in leafy arbours, and at the bottom of the garden the innumerable tropical stars shine down upon the gently lapping waters of the bay?

Our Test Matches are always played at Kingston, but we play the counties of Cornwall and Middlesex on their beautiful grounds at Montego Bay and Port Maria respectively. We have also twice played at Port Antonio.

If we go by car, the way to Montego Bay takes us right through the centre of the Island, past plantations of coconut and palm, and later amongst the luxuriant growth of tropical trees and ferns fringing the road, with humming-birds and gorgeous butterflies flitting to and fro.

The Doctors' Cave Hotel at Montego Bay is perched right above the sea, and from one's bed in the morning one can watch the fish swimming about in the blue, transparent water. Here is some of the most wonderful bathing in the world and, if inclined, one can stop in the water for two or three hours or, in fact, the whole day, without getting chilly. The sunsets over the vast stretch of ocean are the finest I have ever seen. Good friends of mine at Montego Bay are Mr. and Mrs. F. M. Kerr Jarrett, Mr. and Mrs. Jack Ross, Mr. Altie de Cordova, Mr. Clifford de Lisser, and Mr. Edmund Hart. Near Montego Bay is Shettlewood, Montpelier, the home of Mr. J. W. Edwards. He has a famous herd of Indian pedigree cattle, and his house is approached by an avenue of palms. Their trunks smooth and round as pillars, and some thirty feet high, are a sight not easily forgotten.

The road from Kingston past Morant Bay to Port Antonio on the north side of the island is wonderfully beautiful, leading, as it does, between the bush on one hand and the palm-fringed shores of the perfectly blue tropical sea on the other, while in the distance the Blue Mountains, the highest peak of which is over 7000 feet, soar up against the cloudless sky. The harbour in which Port Antonio is situated is exquisitely lovely, and the Titch-field Hotel, surrounded by palms, stands on an eminence above it. Mr. P. Carder was the presiding genius here, inextinguishable in enthusiasm and energy, with a welcome for all which made the welkin ring, and a ringing laugh calculated to cheer up even a cricketer who had made six "blobs" running. The ground we play on is called "Carder's Park" in his honour.

The view of Port Maria on the curving bay with deep blue sea in front and green hills behind, as one looks down upon it from the mountain road, is one of the loveliest I have ever seen—in fact absolutely magical in its beauty. Important and delightful people here are Mr. and Mrs. C. L. Clemetson, Mr. and Mrs. A. D. Goffe, Mr. and Mrs. Ken Robinson, and Mr. and Mrs. Roy John-son. Not far away is "Nonsuch," the residence of Mr. and Mrs. Ronald Macdonald, who have most hospitably entertained mem-bers of my teams and whose son, Mr. Herbert Macdonald, was at one time secretary of Sabina Park Cricket Ground in Kingston. Another kind host in the neighbourhood has been Mr. R. P. Sim-monds, who owns a big banana plantation. His Honour the Cus-tos of St. Mary, Mr. A. C. Westmorland, has always been a keen supporter of our matches at Palmer's Park, the cricket ground at Port Maria. We have invariably been made honorary members of St. Mary's Country Cricket Club, and on Sundays have played a match against the members on their beautiful golf course at Robins' Bay. It is on this links that there is the famous Waterloo Hole, at which one hits (or tries to hit) one's ball across an arm of the sea.

May I end this chapter on the West Indies once more on a personal note?

It was against their 1928 team in this country, whilst playing for Hampshire at Southampton, that I made my highest score in first-class cricket, my partner for most of my innings being Jack Newman. He scored 112 while I myself got 217.

It was, on the other hand, after one of my visits to Jamaica that I played what was, I think, the most unfortunate innings of my career. Peter Eckersley, the Lancashire captain, and I went over to stay for some fishing at Nassau in the Bahamas. They had never had any first-class cricket there, and so a match was got up in honour of Peter and myself, the local cricketers no doubt expecting us each to make huge scores. Having been given first innings to amuse the spectators, we came out to bat together and Peter took first over. He scratched about terribly and was eventually bowled for five. Then came my turn to face a gigantic negro who now had the ball. Down it came at considerable speed, and making contact with the earth rose at such a remarkable angle that, hitting me on the hand, it broke one of my fingers. After receiving medical attention and not wishing to disappoint the crowd who had gathered in considerable numbers to see Peter and myself play, I faced the negro once more. Down came his second delivery. This one I also missed completely. After striking the pitch, it reared up and hit me on the forehead just above the eye, and "the subsequent proceedings interested me no more." I was helped off the ground and had three stitches put in my eyebrow which remained black and blue for weeks.

One more reminiscence of Jamaica, and then, although I would willingly have made it longer, this chapter must come to an end.

This incident concerns the only century (although more than once in the eighties and nineties) that I have managed to make against all Jamaican Teams in the West Indies. I was playing on the occasion in question at Sabina Park for Sir Julian Cahn's team, and at the very moment I obtained my hundredth run the donkey who pulls the roller on that ground gave birth to a foal. This animal (good luck and long life to it!)—to commemorate the occasion—was promptly christened "Lionella."

———————

Good Heavens! I had nearly forgotten Reggie Matcham. Everybody in Jamaica knows him. Reggie is an unofficial member of any team from England which visits the Island. He is a huge, fat, black man about six feet high with a voice like a bull, and a gigantic golf umbrella presented to him by myself and striped with the M.C.C. colours, which he always carries. He follows us from cricket ground to cricket ground, is on friendly terms with all the members of the team, and invariably acts as our baggage man, being the owner of a very commodious truck. However great the tumult of applause at a fine stroke, or however deep the hush at the crisis of a match, the brazen voice of Reggie can be heard bellowing impartial encouragement from the ring side. He knows every point of the game, and his interest in the cricket is so great that he is practically twelfth man on both sides.

CHAPTER XIX

AMERICA! A land of boundless hospitality and the rarest contrasts!

I have visited many different countries, but never have I been more interested or enjoyed myself more than in the United States. There is nothing quite comparable anywhere else to the life and atmosphere of the great American Continent, or to the point of view of its inhabitants, with their quick and penetrative minds that seem to understand what you are saying almost before you have said it.

It was in 1928 that I first went to the States after the conclusion of a cricket tour in Jamaica. My companion was Peter Eckersley, captain of the Lancashire Cricket Eleven. From Kingston in Jamaica we sailed in an American "cruise-ship" to the Island of Nassau in the Bahamas and, as I have already stated in the previous chapter, played cricket there with disastrous physical results to myself. In spite of these disabilities I had managed at Nassau to get in a week's very good fishing with Peter, and amongst other things had caught a shark of about 100 lb. weight, which, however, had been more than half devoured by other sharks by the time we landed it. From Nassau we crossed to Miami.

Miami Beach fairly astounded me. I had never seen skyscrapers before; or private houses built on islands artificially fashioned from the mud of the harbour; or such wonderful waterways, also artificially constructed, down which speed-boats with their cargoes of beautiful women and their male escorts rushed hither and thither like great water-beetles; or such palatial yachts of every description lying at anchor. As our "cruise-ship" steamed in, there was lying in the foreground on the beach a large three-masted schooner lately driven ashore by a hurricane, and nearer at hand a big motor-boat, its engines stilled and under arrest by the Revenue Officers. It seemed quite fitting that a stranger to the United States like myself should thus early in my visit make acquaintance with some actual and indubitable proof of the operation of that most extraordinary law of Prohibition.

The motor-boat (as we were later informed) was full of contraband liquor, and I confess that this immediate demonstration of the power and vigilance of American Revenue Officers considerably startled me. I began to wonder whether I should have to "go dry" for the first time in my life, and what were the pains and penalties for drinking a modest whisky and soda, if detected. However I need not have worried. There is, according to all available evidence, no nonsense about the Prohibition Officers, nor are they perhaps amenable to bribes; nevertheless somebody had managed to get as much alcoholic drink into Miami as any reasonable man could desire, and even more!

Miami, I discovered, was the world's greatest paradox, for while the drinking of anything more potent than iced water was officially forbidden, the people there actually drank more than I had ever dreamed human throats capable of swallowing. All the time they drank they kept telling the stranger what a vast improvement in the morals, manners, character and capacity for work of the American population the Prohibition Laws had brought about. Frequently even one saw the very Revenue Officers in control of the arrested launch (by the by it was soon joined by several other companions in misfortune) having "a quick one on the quiet." It might perhaps be thought that a recent arrival in the town who did not know his way about would have had some difficulty in circumventing the Law, but I can only say that so far as I personally was concerned, I found myself perfectly free to lead the life of the average man. I had what I wanted when I pleased, and in the homes that I visited, for all the inconvenience that Prohibition could entail, one might have been at a series of country-house parties in England.

On the surface Miami is one of the world's chief pleasure-grounds, although I suppose, if the truth were told, it is a place like all others where there are sorrows, tragedies and heartbreaks. Outwardly, however, life there had the appearance of being one long rollicking picnic, where money existed only to be spent, and the means of pleasure and expenditure were on a gigantic scale. Not a soul ever appeared to think of the morrow, or to have a single care in the world. At that time there was indeed so much money in the States that economy had gone quite out of fashion, and to an English visitor *recklessness* seemed hardly a strong enough word to describe the apparently complete indifference of the inhabitants of Miami to anything else except enjoyment.

The next year I went to Palm Beach, home of American millionairedom, on the same Florida coast as Miami. The houses of the millionaires, such as those of Joe Widener, Harold S. Vanderbilt and others, are truly splendid, with private swimming baths, patios, tennis courts, gorgeous gardens, and pergolas rioting with roses. The air is inconceivably brisk, and a minimum of sleep is required. Parties went on all night though the guests had been vigorously swimming or playing golf or galloping after the polo ball all day long. There were two famous Golf Clubs, the "Seminole" and the "Gulf Stream" at a short motor drive's distance from Palm Beach, and the "Everglades Club" in Palm Beach itself. Before a member can be elected to the two former clubs, he must pay many thousands of dollars. As at Miami, it is remarkable how one loses all sense of money values, and after a short stay in Palm Beach even 20,000 dollar subscriptions seemed a mere bagatelle, especially if one went to the house of Mr. Charlie Munn (who by the way introduced dog-racing into this country). Whether Mr. Charlie Munn or his brother Gurney ever read "The Arabian Nights" I do not profess to know, but certainly their places were the last word in all that is beautiful and luxurious. At Palm Beach it was impossible to be dull. The climate was so beautiful, the people so kind and hospitable and everything was so comfortable. Amongst those who were good enough to give me some of the pleasantest hours of my life was Mrs. Irving Chase, at whose house, "El Palmer," I twice stayed. Her house was right on the sea and I was allowed to come and go there as I liked, her one desire being that I should enjoy myself. Her daughters, Elisabeth and Dorothy, often went riding and golfing with me.

Other hostesses who entertained me were Mrs. Stotesbury, Mrs. Atwater Kent, at whose lovely house in Philadelphia I afterwards went to stay, Mrs. Edward Hutton, and Mrs. Wiley Reynolds, with whom I also stayed. Captain Bob Wilson, brother of Sir Matthew Wilson ("Scatters"), also often asked me to his house, and introduced me to the game of backgammon. His wife is an American and a great beauty. I used to play golf with him, Ed. Hutton, Frank Shaughnessy, Wiley Reynolds and one or two other friends for pretty considerable stakes. Wiley Reynolds, who is head of the Reynolds Spring Company at Jackson, Michigan, had a private car on the railroad in which he and his staff travelled luxuriously.

On most nights during my stay at Palm Beach, I went to dance either at the "Everglades," the "Embassy," or the "Colony" Clubs, to what I am quite decided was the best dance music I have ever heard in any part of the world. Almost invariably dancing was rounded off in the early hours by a visit to Colonel Bradley's Club, where we supped. Colonel Bradley was a rich man and a racehorse owner. He started this Club for the festively inclined visitors and undoubtedly it was a great boon and a tremendous success. In addition to thus benefiting the rich, he was most generous in charitable contributions and was well known in America as a philanthropist.

One of my great amusements at Palm Beach was fishing for Tarpon and Sale fish, but I was never lucky enough to catch a fish of any considerable size except on one occasion an 85 lb. Amber Jack.

The following year after a second visit to Palm Beach I went to Chicago.

As even those least conversant with American affairs may imagine, a visit to this truly magnificent city on the shores of Lake Michigan (which, by the way, according to our ideas is more an inland sea than a lake) had a certain stimulating thrill about it. Chicago, as I expect everyone knows, is the original home of gangsters, "bumping off," "taking for a ride" and machine-gun battles in the streets. The city, in fact, lived up to its reputation as far as I was concerned, for on the very day of my arrival two policemen were shot dead. In Chicago I quickly made many friends, but it was not owing to my fear of gangsters that I only spent a few days there. This was due to the fact that I was invited to pass most of my time at Lake Forest, about thirty miles away. There were a certain number of English people living at Lake Forest who had formed what is a sufficiently rare thing in America, namely, a cricket club. Of this club they had the great courtesy to make me Honorary President. Here I met various members of the Swift family who own the big Stock Yards in Chicago, where something like ten thousand head of cattle are slaughtered daily. From Lake Forest I went to another smaller town in the neighbourhood which, for reasons that can be appreciated, shall be nameless as during my stay in it I had a really rather extraordinary adventure though through no fault of my own. I had first met the beautiful lady I am going to write about at Palm Beach where she was on a visit, and there I often went out and danced with her. Having heard that I was staying in the neighbourhood of her home, she invited me to come and see her. Her husband, I must mention, was a business man in Chicago and away at his office practically all and every day.

218

My last morning in the neighbourhood at 10.30 a.m. this gentleman, who had stayed at home instead of going to business as usual, suddenly made his appearance as I had come to make my adieux, and without the slightest warning pointed a huge automatic revolver at my head.

"Get out of here," he bellowed. "What the hell do you mean by playing around with my wife?"

His face was purple, his eyes were red with rage, (or, as I afterwards discovered, excess of alcohol had possibly something to do with it) and his finger trembled on the trigger, as the muzzle of the automatic waved up and down about four yards from my head.

The lady shrieked and fainted, and I, after a second or two of stupefaction, exclaimed:

"What the hell do you mean?"

"I've heard all about your doings in Palm Beach," yelled the infuriated man, paying no heed to his insensible wife. "Your last hour has come. I'm going to shoot you dead."

"Don't be so damned ridiculous," was the best answer I could think of.

"I am," hissed he, "so prepare to meet your God!"

"Well then," replied I, opening my coat, and hoping really that the revolver was not loaded, "if you are determined to shoot, shoot here," and forthwith I pointed at my heart. "Make a clean job of it, and if I understand the Laws of your country it's the electric chair for you, my boy."

The madman was too far off for me to rush him, and I spoke thus as a bluff, while trying to look as cool as possible though I was really far from feeling so inwardly, since he seemed quite insane and capable of anything.

Then came a loud bang. The revolver, which had been travelling in a semi-circle in his wavering hand during the conversation just described, had gone off, and by an extraordinary piece of luck done no more damage than make a hole in the wall behind me.

The explosion seemed to sober my inebriated friend. For a moment he stared stupidly at the barrel, and then collapsed into a chair. This was the moment for action on my part.

In a second I was at him, wrenching the weapon from his fingers and standing over him with it.

After a heated argument he rang the bell for whisky and soda, subsequently despatching half a dozen "highballs" in about as many minutes. Meantime his wife had recovered from her swoon and was screaming and praying, so it was not much good trying to make formal adieux to either of them. Being due to play a round of golf, I left the house without any more words, thankful for such an extraordinary escape. Strangely enough I played afterwards the best round of my life!

This was an extremely unpleasant adventure. I discovered subsequently that the husband had had some business worries and had been drinking to drown care, and on the top of that had become insanely jealous, although his wife and I were really no more than excellent friends. I also heard later that this maniac's chauffeur was so terrified at the prospect of being shot at for taking a wrong turning that he sent in his resignation about an hour after I left the house. In fact he told me this himself, when later, with a peculiar sense of humour, writing to me for a character. This I sent him, and in gratitude for my escape at his late master's hands made it the finest testimonial ever received by an employee in America.

I have paid several visits to New York and know it almost as well as I know London or Paris. I once stopped several weeks there with Mr. Ralph B. Strassburger at 49 East 72nd Street. In his house I had one floor to myself and could come and go freely at all hours. Mr. Strassburger frequently had parties, and was never so happy as when he was conducting the band. He is the most generous and hospitable of men. One of his principal interests is horse-racing, and he has stud-farms in Philadelphia as well as in France, and a considerable number of horses in training. He has also a magnificent house in Paris in the Avenue de Tourville, and a lovely villa at Deauville covered in flowering creepers.

Another host of mine in New York was Mr. Percy R. Pyne, who is one of the few American members of White's Club in London. He has a house at Rosslyn, Long Island, and is madly keen on golf, being a performer of about the same class as myself. We have had some desperate battles on practically every golf course in Long Island, of which there are about forty within twenty minutes of his door. His place is one of the sights of Long Island for its lovely gardens, and he has a collection of sporting pictures, only equalled I believe by that of Lord Rosebery. He is President of the Brook Club, which is one of the most exclusive clubs in New York. This club takes its name from my grandfather's poem "The Brook," in which are the celebrated lines: "For men may come and men may go, but I go on for ever." The hidden meaning of this is that the club never closes night or day. To cope with this situation, there are three relays of servants.

When in New York, I usually stayed at the Ritz Hotel, which, although not one of the newest and most absolutely up-to-date hotels, is, I think, the most comfortable. There one meets all kinds of interesting people, and there I have been able to return some of the lavish hospitality received from my numerous New York friends. I'm afraid that the little I have been able to do is a very poor requital for the numerous kindnesses experienced, such, for instance, as my Honorary Membership of the Racquet and Tennis Club, a marvellous institution where everything of comfort and interest is installed.

I was not long meeting in New York several people who were anxious to show me all the sights, and during the time comprised in my various visits there and in spite of the fact that the city is about the same size as London, I think I must have been to see every object of interest in it.

I know New York in all its phases, by day and night, and were there space for it here, could write a pretty detailed description of the life of a New Yorker. As it is, a selection from my experiences must suffice, and some of the most interesting of these to me were my visits to the Home of American boxing at Madison Square.

From my earliest youth I have had a tremendous liking for boxing. I have seen contests in many parts of the world, but I have sat at no ringside possessing the atmosphere of that at Madison Square as it was pitched in the days of Tex Rickard. A most remarkable man was Rickard, quiet and of very few words, but though inclined to silence he could not disguise the fact that, as a fight promoter, he was one of the greatest gamblers of all times. He had been everything in turn: gold-digger, cow-puncher, professional gambler. My study of him made it difficult for me to reconcile him with the position he held at Madison Square. I could only imagine him astride a broncho, and as quick on the trigger as the sharp-shooters with whom he lived during his earlier youth. He made and lost many fortunes. Some of the greatest coups in boxing history were associated with his name and also some of the greatest "flops." He was a likeable man and in all his dealings as straight as a gun barrel. There was no non-sense about him and though he was not a talker, he won you over to him by the sheer force of his personality.

Madison Square was the home of the "Rooter." There is nothing in all the world comparable to a New York fight fan. He has a rasping tongue, and as I sat with him and his kind, I could not for the life of me understand how it was possible for this and that fighter to carry on under the floods of biting sarcasm from the onlookers. For one boxer to be invited "to knock the other's block off" was apparently just a little Bowery badinage, just as it is considered the proper thing at a baseball match in a stentorian yell to remind the striker that "he has a hole in his bat," or by way of variation that "he swings like a rusty gate." All the world is at Madison Square on Fight nights, and on my visits there I might almost say that I made the acquaintance of everybody from Jimmy Walker, then New York's mayor and one of the most entertaining men I encountered during my visits to the States, to the old used up and battered "pug." I can well believe how difficult it is for a stranger to adapt himself to Madison Square, but if a foreign fighter does capture the New Yorker he is indeed a hero to them. Poor Phil Scott! I recollect his being introduced from the ring; and how, on that occasion, he survived the very pointed reminders from the spectators of his former failures, I will never be able to understand. He was indeed, to employ the slang of Madison Square, *truly Roasted and Boiled.*" To the everlasting credit of Scott he didn't turn a hair.

In obedience to fashion, after a Fight night I did the rounds of the "Speakeasies." What an extraordinary woman I found Texas Guinan to be. She knew, so it seemed, everybody by name, and was indeed a queen of backchat.

A night in Harlem I would include among my imperishable memories. It is a world of its own, strange to the point of madness. The fury of it all, the glitter, the noise, the extraordinary coloured entertainers—it was all truly amazing. Everybody, it seemed, had a licence to do as they pleased. As for money, it was no more valuable than counters. Night life in New York must be seen and experienced to be believed.

The American Woman!

No account, however brief and inadequate, of the States could conclude without some reference to her. How proud of them their men are! The average American husband is the most indulgent of all husbands. It is his wife's presentation of herself in the world that matters to him most of all things. Whether this point of view is entirely beneficial to the female sex, a mere inhabitant of the old world must take the liberty of expressing some doubts.

CHAPTER XX

WELL—everything must come to an end, and so I have now reached the final chapter of this book.

On looking through the preceding pages it strikes me what a lot there is I have not written about. There is, for instance, no mention of White's or Buck's, of which two famous London Clubs I have been a member for very many years.

White's is, bar one, the oldest club in London, dating back in fact to the old coffee-houses of the eighteenth century which were the resort of the wits and beaux of the period. It has always been a very fashionable club, and its bow window looking on to St. James's Street is perhaps the most famous window in the West End. It has figured in many memoirs and novels. White's has always had a reputation for high, if not the wildest, gambling, even from its earliest days. When I was elected during the war, this reputation was still not undeserved, and I fear that, like the celebrated Mr. Charles James Fox of immortal memory, once a member of White's, I was not one of the least reckless.

Although White's has not followed the example of other clubs and admitted ladies (for which the gods be praised!) and there is no possibility of finding a couple of maiden ladies in the card-room, anything bordering on wild gambling is happily a thing of the past. It might be said that White's and Buck's are in a social sense the last of their kind in London, for in these two clubs everybody knows everybody and friendships are made in them that will endure for a lifetime. White's has a unique collection of prints of members that take one back to the eighteenth century, and two wonderful hall-porters in Reddie and Shepherd whose knowledge of men, things and the world generally is wide and profound.

Although the number of members has not actually increased, we have lately had to build a larger bar. This is not because we drink more, but because several (like myself, for instance) have got a little stouter with advancing years, and require a trifle more elbow-room. Doel and Fowler behind the bar are bankers as well as barmen; and many times, so it has seemed to me, they have, as if by magic, obliged with a truly welcome "fiver."

But to come to the more serious phases of my life! I succeeded to the title in 1928, becoming a somewhat impoverished Baron of the United Kingdom, with, of course, the right to sit and vote in the House of Lords, but, although a tolerably practised speaker at public dinners and on election platforms, my maiden speech has yet to be made in the Upper House!

Apart from playing cricket all the summer (I am now in my fourteenth season as captain of the Hampshire County Eleven, and the senior County Captain playing) I am a pretty busy man, being a partner in a wine business with Mr. P. G. H. Fender, the famous England and Surrey cricketer, and with Colonel Yetts.

I am also the Inspector commanding No. 1 Company of the Special Constables Flying Squad at Scotland Yard. Most of the men in my company have been recruited by myself, and had space permitted, some of our adventures in the General Strike in 1926 and later on would make interesting reading.

As Honorary Colonel of the 51st (London) Anti-Aircraft Brigade Royal Artillery (T.A.) I have in my Brigade Colonel Hunt, one of the cleverest officers in the Army, an expert in anti-aircraft gunnery, and a chief instructor at Woolwich; also Captain du Bern, our most efficient Adjutant. The senior Major, Gourlay by name, is my bank manager, not only an expert in gunnery but in overdrafts!

My activities likewise include a considerable amount of journalism.

I have had no lack of friends all my life. May I here mention a few whose names have not, I think, hitherto appeared in these pages.

To Lord Wimborne and his family I would express my sincere appreciation of their many kindnesses. Lord Wimborne has played in his time a distinguished part in politics, and occupied many important positions in the halcyon days of the Liberal Party. He was Viceroy of Ireland during the early years of the Great War, and was one of the few who emerged with credit from the enquiry into the causes of the Irish Rebellion of 1916. There is no greater sportsman. He it was some years ago who took out the last victorious British polo team to America. With Lady Wimborne he occasionally hunted at Melton, in the days when I was in the shires, from his house at Ashby St. Ledgers, where I frequently stay. Lady Wimborne is extremely attractive, beautifully dressed, and endlessly kind.

I have many times been entertained by Major and Mrs. Godfrey Mundy at Red Rice near Andover in Hampshire. Major Mundy is a very fine shot and his shoot is one of the best organized in England. One never gets a low bird there.

Sir Harold Bowden also frequently asks me to shoot at his place, Bestwood Lodge, Arnold, Notts. There are few better-known names in Industry than Sir Harold's. He is head of the great Raleigh bicycle firm which turn out about 7000 bicycles a week in the summer and 3500 in the winter. In his covers there is a famous stand called "Millers End."

Major and Mrs. James B. Walker, my near neighbours in the Isle of Wight, have the most delightful place near Yarmouth on the shores of the Solent, where they have asked me on many occasions. Mrs. Walker is reputed the best-dressed woman in the island, and she and I have been great friends since childhood.

I often stay with the generous and hospitable Mr. Arthur Bendir at his lovely place on the banks of the Thames, Medmenham Abbey. He has built there a covered tennis court and a swimming bath which, owing to an ingenious heating system, can be adjusted to the desired temperature at any time of the year. Long ago in the eighteenth century Medmenham Abbey was once the headquarters of the Hell-fire Club, frequented by the notorious Jack Wilkes and by other scandalous characters of that epoch. They toasted the Devil and indulged there in amusements and dissipations which created somewhat of a sensation even in those far from censorious times.

I have known the Duke of Sutherland since my schooldays at Eton, where he was my senior by a year or two. We have always kept up our friendship and I have stayed with him at Dunrobin Castle, where I had my first day's stalking and missed the only stag I shot at! His beautiful old Jacobean house, Sutton Place, near Guildford, is in striking contrast to his Scottish home; at each of these places there are world-famous gardens. The Duchess' father, the late Lord Lanesborough, was Second-in-Command of the 1st Battalion of the Coldstream Guards when I joined. She is slim and stately and looks a Duchess from the crown of her head to the soles of her feet. I went on a party to Switzerland with them in 1921, and Eileen Sutherland was also at Palm Beach three years ago when we several times went fishing together.

That great sporting character, the Earl of Westmorland, known far and wide as "Burghie," has long been one of my greatest friends. He started life in the Navy and still carries about with him a tang of salt sea air. He is a very breezy individual, and the most popular man amongst the younger sporting set, his interests and indomitable energies being divided amongst horse-racing, dog-racing, hunting, and football. He is a keen golfer, and he and I have brought off one or two rather startling coups together.

There was a day when we sat next to each other at the opening of Parliament and in our velvet and ermine were feeling decidedly uncomfortable. Without turning round he enquired:

"Well, keeping your end up in the old ship, what?"

To his horror I had given up my seat to a bishop, as he discovered on getting no answer to this remark.

Last, but not least, although he has always been known from his earliest years as "Shrimp," I must include amongst the circle of my close personal friends who have been so remarkably kind to me, Mr. H. D. G. Leveson-Gower, the old Winchester, Oxford, and Surrey Captain, the England cricket selector, and President of the Surrey County Cricket Club. "Shrimp" is an exceedingly humorous character, with an always unexpected turn of wit and "the soft answer which turneth away wrath." He is a great organizer of cricket festivals and tours. He has *made* the Annual Scarborough Cricket Festival, and often takes touring sides abroad. Last autumn I was a member of his Eleven which played at Gibraltar, and I have frequently played for him at Scarborough and on other occasions.

I should like to make mention of hundreds of other friends, but that is impossible. Space forbids. Nevertheless I treasure the memory of every one of them. We have had glorious times together, we have lived exciting days, and I am sure that they, like myself, have squeezed everything possible out of life. On my own part, I do confess that I have often bubbled over with the effervescence of youth, but now having reached the forties I hope I may pass as a model of industry and a prop of the British constitution. To the follies and the high adventures of my early days I have said farewell.

AFTERWORD TO THE PAPER EDITION

HOW I CAME TO CREATE THIS PAPER EDITION

I decided to create this paper edition when I was between contracting gigs. In these gigs, I create ebook editions from sources, that is, from the same computer files that were used to create the paper book. So, I thought that a good way to use my downtime was to learn something new by creating a paper edition of an older book for which no such sources exist.

I first came across *From Verse to Worse* while researching some family history. I got a copy by inter-library loan, and was delighted to discover what an interesting and entertaining book it was. So naturally it came to mind when trying to think of a book I might create during my downtime.

MY TENUOUS FAMILY CONNECTION

L. H. Tennyson was briefly married to my grandmother's stepbrother's widow, Carroll Elting Donner. This statement of our connection, though concise, merits some unpacking.

My connection to the Baron is through my step-great-grandfather, the metal magnate W. H. Donner. In his first marriage, W. H. Donner had a son, Joseph, who married Carroll Elting. After Joseph died, she was briefly married to the Baron. In his second marriage, W. H. Donner adopted a daughter, Katherine, who was my grandmother, K. N. R. Denckla.

THE COPYRIGHT

From Verse to Worse is protected by copyright until 2021: 70 years after the death of its author. A big part of this project was determining the copyright holders and contacting them to get permission to republish this book. Toward those goals, I was graciously helped by the following persons.

- Alan Tennyson
- David Tennyson
- Patrick John Leslie and other heirs of Mark Aubrey Tennyson

The book production process is usually secret. I will share my process here.

This edition was created by combining the results of OCR and manual retyping of the original. My hope is that the errors of these two processes are largely uncorrelated. If true, the combined process should have fewer errors than either of the two individual processes would have on its own, holding cost constant. In other words, my hope is that it is better to divide a fixed budget between OCR and typing rather than devote all of it to a somewhat higher-quality version of one process or the other.

To create the scans for OCR, I used a Bookeye 4 Basic planetary scanner. I had to do a non-destructive scan since I was using a library copy of the book. An unfortunate limitation of the copy I used is that all the photographic plates have been marked "UNIV. OF CALIFORNIA" with a perforating punch!

For the OCR itself, I used ABBYY FineReader.

For post-OCR processing, I used a variety of software from the Ubuntu distribution of the GNU/Linux operating system, including emacs, aspell, Inkscape, grep, Perl, PHP, and git. I wrote some small bespoke programs for this project, and adapted some others from previous projects. I ran Ubuntu under VirtualBox. I used Bitbucket as a central git repository and issue tracker.

I checked my underlying XHTML files using the W3C Validator Suite (now discontinued).

I produced the PDF using Prince XML.

For manual typing, I hired freelancers on Elance and oDesk for about $0.25 per 100 words. The book is about 77,000 words long, so this came to about $193. The quality of their work varied widely. One freelancer used OCR despite claiming to have manually typed the chapters assigned. This was easily detectable from the types of errors present. On the bright side, one freelancer's work was particularly high quality: Gordana Lukić, of Serbia.

DIFFERENCES FROM THE ORIGINAL

I have tried to tastefully choose which aspects of the original should be captured, from among those aspects that can be captured. I have tried to implement those choices with skill and grace.

Despite all this, I still regret what was lost in republication. I suppose I am susceptible to sentimentality for old paper books.

One way to mitigate the losses from the original is to document some of those losses. These losses will be discussed extensively in what follows. I will also discuss the more positive topics of what was retained, and even what I think was improved (corrections)!

INDEX SECTION DROPPED

Perhaps the most notable loss in this edition is the index section. The original includes three indices:

- General Index
- Cricket and Cricketers
- Great War

I chose to drop the index section to save time on the project.

PAGE NUMBERS

This page numbers of this edition do not match those of the original.

REFERENCES TO PAGE NUMBERS

Now, what about references to page numbers, as in an index, as opposed to the page numbers themselves? I didn't include such references in this edition. Most of these references didn't even have a chance to appear since I didn't include the index section. The original's only other page number references are in the table of contents and the table of illustrations. I didn't include those page number references.

BINDING, NUMBERING, AND PAPER

Most of the physical aspects of the original were lost, so I will document them here, out of respect not only for the object but also the anonymous Edinburgh workers who made it.

The original is bound in 18 signatures. The first signature is not marked. It is, implicitly, signature A. All 17 other signatures are marked with the capital letters B through S, skipping J.

It was sometimes the convention to skip J as a signature mark because it was not part of the classical Roman alphabet. Think of JULIUS written classically: IVLIVS! The book is not long enough for us to learn whether the letter U, too, would have been skipped.

All signatures except the last have 4 bifolios. The last signature has only 2 bifolios. So the book contains $17 \times 4 + 1 \times 2 = 70$ bifolios. These 70 bifolios yield 140 folios, or leaves, each having a recto or verso, yielding 280 pages. The last numbered page is 277.

The pages are counted according to these signatures. In particular, the plates, tipped in by gluing, are neither numbered nor counted in the numbering. In the table of illustrations, the page numbers given are for the pages that precede the plate in question.

The paper of the bifolios is laid or, more likely, the paper is wove but has a laid pattern imparted to it. I lack the expertise to tell the difference. The paper of the plates differs from that of the bifolios. I found no watermarks on either of the papers.

FONTS

The original uses a single font, except for the phrase "To the Memory of" on the dedication page. That phrase uses some variant of the blackletter font called Tudor Black. This font was identified for me by the generous experts on the Font ID forum of typophile.com. In this edition, I chose to capture neither this font excursion, nor the main font.

Like the original, this edition uses italic and small caps variants of its base font. Like the original, this edition uses italics for the common Latin words and abbreviations *v.*, *i.e.*, and *via*. This may strike some readers as quaint, belabored, or both.

COVER

The cover of the original is green cloth on cardboard. The front and back covers are plain. The spine has the labels "From Verse to Worse," "Lionel Lord Tennyson," and "Cassell." The labels are horizontal, in gold capitals. The font is intriguing but I have not identified it. To save time I have not included a scan of the spine, but I should have.

The cover of this edition will probably be viewed by some as an abomination of graphic design, but it was obtained at excellent value, since only my time was spent on it.

SECTION BREAKS

The original uses only vertical whitespace to indicate section breaks within chapters. This edition uses vertical whitespace for every paragraph break, so, I chose to re-represent section breaks with horizontal rules like the following.

This avoids ambiguity between section and paragraph breaks.

UNDOING BREAKS

Because the original used only whitespace for section breaks, it is impossible to tell whether certain page breaks were also thought of as section breaks. Where a page started with a new paragraph and a new topic, it was tempting to guess that a section break was intended and insert a horizontal rule in this edition, but I refrained from doing so.

This is similar to the problem of determining, in a poem, whether a page break is also a stanza break. This is only a problem in poems whose lines are not clearly grouped into stanzas by rhyme, meter, punctuation, or other formal convention or invention.

It is also similar to the problem of determining whether a hyphen at a line break is hard or soft. This can be a difficult problem, since whether to hyphenate two words or run them together is often a question of taste, and such tastes vary over time, place, author, and editor. For this edition, if I was lucky enough to find the same word not spanning lines, I used its spelling there as a way to decide on the hardness of the hyphen in the line-spanning case. In other cases, I was forced to guess. Sometimes I was able to use Google Ngrams and Google Books to get a sense of the hyphenation conventions of this book's time and place. In these cases at least my guess was a somewhat educated one.

These problems highlight a way in which re-setting a book is quite unlike typesetting a book for the first time. One of the main tasks of typesetting a book for the first time is breaking the text into lines and pages, but one of the main tasks of re-setting is undoing these breaks, in order to redo them elsewhere! Unfortunately, as we have seen, how to undo these breaks can be ambiguous.

LINE BREAKS

It is desirable for some bits of text to stick together. On the other hand, it is also desirable to provide as many line break opportunities as possible.

Keeping that tradeoff in mind, these are the line break decisions I've made for this edition.

In this edition I prevent line breaks in the following places.

- between initials in names like L. H. Tennyson
- in family names starting with de, du, van der, and von
- in names in group photo captions
- after St. (Saint)
- between the last two words or so of a long caption or chapter title

I prevent other line breaks, but only on an *ad hoc* basis, i.e. not as the result any rules. Some of these cases are as follows.

- in "I Zingari"
- between exclamation marks
- before a single letter, J, that ends a paragraph in this afterword

I permit line breaks in many cases where others might prevent them. Many of these cases involve a number that some people feel should stick together with a word, such as the following examples from the book.

234

- 85 lb.
- 365 feet
- 8.15 a.m.
- 50 per cent
- 7 Portland Place
- 111 not out
- 10 to 1
- George V
- July 13

CORRECTIONS IN GENERAL

Correction is tricky. The situation with text is similar to that in software, where what seems to be a bug may in fact be a feature, especially when considered from another point of view. The tradition of biblical scholarship gives us a principle worth considering:

lectio difficilior potior

This can be translated as "the more difficult reading is the stronger." Strict adherence to this principle interprets "stronger" as "preferable." Here is my interpretation, which uses, or perhaps abuses, the leeway afforded by translation: "the more difficult reading is more often correct than you might expect." This verges upon the saying, "truth is stranger than fiction."

Continuing biblically, consider this from Matthew 5:18:

Until heaven and earth disappear, not one *yod* or even one *tag* (serif) of God's law will disappear until its purpose is achieved.

If Jesus can be this orthographically humble, how much more so the lowly typesetter?

From the Talmud (Eruvin 13a):

He [Rabbi Yishmael] said to me [Rabbi Meir]: "My son, be careful with your [scribe] work, for it is the work of Heaven. Should you perhaps omit one letter or add one letter — it could result that you destroy the entire world."

While this book is hardly a sacred text, these traditions inform my care for words, which I consider to be a hallmark of civilized behavior, if not holiness. This care for words does not bar their correction. On the contrary, it implies a responsibility to correct, but only to correct responsibly. If possible, corrections should be documented, as I do in the sections that follow.

Though risky, corrections are one of those few areas where a new edition may improve upon its original. If one is lucky, one may fix more than one has broken. I hope all my corrections are correct, and I hope that they outnumber the errors I have undoubtedly introduced elsewhere.

DOTS REMOVED

In the original, "per cent" has a dot (period) after it in one of the two instances of that phrase. It is merely quaint, not wrong, to use a dot to note that "cent" is an abbreviation for the Latin *centum*. But, since it was done inconsistently, I felt I had the leeway to drop it. Though quaint, I felt it would be distracting to the modern reader.

In the original, some Roman numerals have dots after them but most do not. It is merely quaint, not wrong, to place a dot after a Roman numeral. It indicates that letters are being used to form a number not a word. Hebrew's *geresh* and *gershayim* are used similarly. But, as with the dotted "per cent," I felt that inconsistency left me with the leeway to move to the modern, dotless convention.

THE I ZINGARI DOT

In the original, "I Zingari" has a dot after the "I" in one of the four instances of that phrase. (Two instances are in the index section, so they do not appear in this edition). Perhaps this dot was added because the "I" was mistaken as a Roman numeral. Or, perhaps it was added because the "I" was thought to be an abbreviation of the Italian article "Gli" rather than the article "I" in its own right. Indeed "Gli" would be the standard Italian article to use there. But in that case, wouldn't an apostrophe be more appropriate, as follows?

'I Zingari

236

The origins of the use of "I" in "I Zingari" are shrouded in mystery. From the I Zingari website:

> Having availed himself of a substantial amount of claret, R. P. Long drifted off into a 'vinous slumber'. When the conversation eventually turned to a name for this fledgling [cricket] club, he deigned to murmur 'The Zingari, of course.'
>
> The next day, this became 'I Zingari', much to the continued confusion of defenders of the definite article and Italian purists.

The I Zingari Wikipedia page claims that the use of "I" rather than "Gli," though nonstandard, is dialectical. Whether this dialect is simply the one spoken by intoxicated English cricketers, it does not say.

I did find another example of the dotted "I Zingari": though there is no such dot in its title, see the essay "150 years of I Zingari: the vagrant gypsy life" by John Woodcock. It appeared in the 1995 Wisden Almanack and is archived on the ESPN "cricinfo" website.

Further research on this topic would be absurd, that is to say, right up my alley. Yet, I must press on. As with "per cent" and Roman numerals, I felt that inconsistency left me with the leeway to make my own choice. In this case it was not a choice of quaint *v.* modern. As far as I can tell it was a choice between a mysterious minority dotted convention and a majority dotless one. I chose to go dotless.

DOTS ADDED AND DOTS RETAINED

In the original, a few instances of "Mr" and "Mrs" are dotless, but the vast majority are dotted. I eliminated this inconsistency in favor of dots. I left the two instances of "Messrs" as they were printed: undotted.

Before leaving the scintillating topic of dots, I think it is worth mentioning one instance in which I preserved a quaint dot, despite its jarring look to the modern eye. In the original, "exams" is dotted, since the word is, or originated as, an abbreviation of "examinations." Similarly, "exam" is dotted in the index section, though that section is not included in this edition. Since there is no inconsistency to resolve, I felt I had no leeway to modernize, and retained the dotted form of "exams." I did mark it with a "sic" in square brackets, and made that "sic" link to this paragraph.

In trying to get a sense of the prevalence of the dotted form of "exam" and "exams," I ran across the following sentence from the story "The Last Term" in Rudyard Kipling's *Stalky & Co.*:

'An exam.'s an exam.,' etc., etc.

It fairly bristles with punctuation, does it not?

Though it uses an apostrophe rather than a dot, another word-shortening that, quaintly, is noted by punctuation in this book is as follows.

'planes

CORRECTIONS REGARDING HYPHENS

In searching for hyphenation inconsistencies I might have introduced while undoing line breaks, I discovered various hyphenation inconsistencies present in the original. I resolved the following inconsistencies in favor of the hyphenated rather than run-together form. (Links are to the instances that were run together.)

- fox-hunting
- heavy-weight
- life-like
- light-hearted and light-heartedness

In some of the cases above, the hyphenated form is in the majority. In other cases, where there is no majority, I favored the hyphenated form.

I will now briefly return to my handling of inconsistencies in hard-hyphenation. In contrast to the four words listed above, I opted for the run-together form of "setback." I cannot justify that choice other than to note that the hyphenated form only appeared in the index section. This is not that compelling a justification since in other situations I counted the index section as an equal partner to the main text in resolving inconsistencies in spelling.

I left the inconsistency of "Littlego" and "Little-go" alone since the hyphenated form only appears in a block quote. It may have been an explicit editorial decision to respect the choice of the author of the block quote, while making a different choice for the main text. This is a tricky area of editorial decision-making: what aspects, if any, of the main text's style should be imposed on quotes?

I added a hyphen to the one instance of "Carlton Levick" to match the one instance of "Carlton-Levick." Though this seems to be the arbitrary breaking of a tie, I find it more likely that a hyphen was accidentally dropped from a name than that it was accidentally added.

MISC. CORRECTIONS

I removed an apostrophe from "it's bow window."

MISC. CHANGES

The following are not corrections, in that they don't address issues that I think are errors. They are additions, deletions, or changes that I felt compelled to make for a variety of reasons, including my own preferences. A typesetter should usually suppress the urge to humor his own preferences, but in a few cases, I failed to do so.

I added row labels like "Back row," in square brackets, to the caption for one group photo. I thought this made the caption easier to decipher.

I added "Image credit," in square brackets, to image credits and moved them below all captions. In the original they are above all captions, tight up against the image, aligned to its right edge.

I added a few other things in square brackets, mostly in the front matter. Square brackets are not used in the original so anything in square brackets is my addition.

I "harmonized" the table of illustrations with the captions for the illustrations.

I did not replicate the original's generous (excessive?) spacing inside quotation marks.

I removed the dot leaders from both tables in the book. They are difficult to replicate in HTML and I didn't feel they were important.

I added em dashes to separate the names of four cricket players in a caption. In the original they are carefully spaced across the page, roughly following their locations in the picture. I found this is difficult to do and in this case would offer little reward.

QUOTATION MARKS

I turned one instance of nested double quotes into single quotes. In the following, "Little-go" is in double quotation marks in the original.

"Allow me . . . 'Little-Go,' . . ."

This instance of nested double quotes was caught by a program I wrote that checks for various forms of balanced punctuation, including double quotation marks, parentheses, and square brackets. These are easy checks to do, yet, to my knowledge, no popular software does them. As a result, one of the many crimes against literacy committed by new editions created using OCR is unbalanced punctuation stemming from OCR errors. Unless there is a bug in my program, there are no such errors in this edition. I am reminded of a famous remark by Donald Knuth, containing an inscrutable mix of hubris and humility:

Beware of bugs in the above code; I have only proved it correct, not tried it.

An imbalance of double quotation marks is allowed in order to capture the quaint style of block quoting used in this book. In a multi-paragraph block quote, all paragraphs except the last lack a right double quotation mark. Or, if you prefer, you can think of it as all paragraphs except the first having an excess left double quotation mark.

Curly braces are not used in this book, though they are candidates for such balance-checking. In languages such as Spanish, exclamation and question marks would be candidates as well! Single quotation marks are difficult to check, since the right-hand one is used as an apostrophe. And, as we shall see below, in this book the left-hand one is used where you might expect a superscript "c"! Such problems can be overcome by introducing a source representation of the book that respects such distinctions as right single quotation mark versus apostrophe. But this book makes sparing use of single quotation marks so it was easier to just check them by eye.

Though I did capture them in this edition, a few aspects of the original are still worth noting.

The left single quotation mark, or turned comma, is a familiar character, but it is used in what may be an unfamiliar way in this book. It is used where you might expect a superscript "c" in the following names:

- M'Bryan
- M'Gahey
- M'Kay
- M'Lean

It was tempting to replace these instances with a superscript "c," e.g. one of the following.

- McBryan (Unicode)
- McBryan (HTML sup)

But, for all I know, the use of turned comma was a conscious choice, not the result of typographic poverty. So I left them alone.

An aside: another case where turned comma and superscript "c" can be used somewhat interchangeably is in the transliteration of the Semitic letter *ayin*. I have seen this cause a lot of confusion. Fortunately Unicode now has a widely-supported code point devoted to this purpose, "modifier letter left half ring."

The book makes use of the ligatures for ae and oe in the following words:

- Cæsar
- mediæval
- bœuf
- manœuvres

241

In one place, ellipsis is used to indicate an omission. Since this seems like an inconsistency, I was tempted to substitute in my approximation of a two-em dash. But I resisted the temptation. It also seems like an inconsistency that in one of the two times this omission ellipsis is used, it is tight up against the K, whereas the other time, it is spaced away from it:

- K. . . . Old
- K . . . stammered

To me, the tight case seems to indicate K-period-ellipsis rather than what I believe is intended, K-ellipsis-period. There is one example of such spacing in the book. Whether this means that such spacing was allowed, or whether it was an accident, is hard to say. In all these cases, I resisted the temptation to change anything, for thus it was written (*sic erat scriptum*).

Ben Denckla
Los Angeles
20 January 2016
(adapted from the Afterword to the ebook dated 11 April 2015)

Lightning Source UK Ltd.
Milton Keynes UK
UKOW06f1824270416

273107UK00006B/120/P